D1603561

CARNIVAL COMEDY
and SACRED PLAY

CARNIVAL COMEDY and SACRED PLAY

The Renaissance Dramas of Giovan Maria Cecchi

Douglas Radcliff-Umstead

University of Missouri Press
Columbia, 1986

To Lula Louisa Ey with love

Copyright © 1986 by
The Curators of the University of Missouri
University of Missouri Press, Columbia, Missouri 65211
Printed and bound in the United States of America

Library of Congress Cataloging in Publication Data

Radcliff-Umstead, Douglas
  Carnival comedy and sacred play.

  Bibliography: p.
  Includes index.
  1. Cecchi, Giovanni Maria, 1518–1587—Criticism and interpre-
tation. I. Title.
PQ4617.C8Z86 1985   852'.4   85–999
ISBN 0–8262–0462–7

⊗™ This paper meets the minimum requirements of the American
National Standard for Permanence of Paper for Printed Library Ma-
terials, 239.48, 1984.

PREFACE

It is my aim in this book to provide a brief critical introduction to the dramatic works of Giovan Maria Cecchi for the English-reading public. Although Cecchi was a prolific writer in a variety of genres, it is his dramatic writings (both secular and religious) that count as his most important literary productions. Because Giovan Maria Cecchi's life reflected political, cultural, and religious events in sixteenth-century Tuscany, the opening chapter of this book explores historical developments under the Medicean Restoration and Catholic Reformation. An entire chapter examines some representative comedies of classical inspiration, since many of Cecchi's comedies derive from the ancient plays of Plautus and Terence, after first discussing the Italian Renaissance view of comedy as a genre. Comedies that express a modern ethic of love and nature but frequently adapt plot situations from novellas occupy another chapter. The next section includes an investigation of Cecchi's religious plays in their wide range from brief farces to bourgeois dramas and historical spectacles. The conclusion contains a study of Cecchi's attempt to reconcile the many traditions of theatrical practice influencing Italian Renaissance drama. This text's focus will concentrate on the two major aspects of the writer's work for the theater: carnival comedies and sacred plays.

After his death, Cecchi's works fell into critical neglect until the early nineteenth century when Italian philologists began to appreciate the lively Tuscan dialect of his comedies. Only recently have literary scholars in the English-reading world paid serious attention to Cecchi's theatrical writings. His secular comedies were the subject of a doctoral dissertation by Bruno Ferraro in 1975 for Flinders University of South Australia, on which occasion I served as an outside reader. Konrad Eisenbichler, then curator of the Centre for Reformation and Renaissance Studies at Victoria University, composed in 1981 a dissertation on Cecchi's sacred dramas for the

University of Toronto. I wish to express gratitude to Professor Eisenbichler for sharing his dissertation, the text of a public lecture on Cecchi's prologues, and his translation of Cecchi's best-known comedy *L'Assiuolo* as *The Horned Owl.* Throughout the text all translations are my own. Readers should consult the bibliography for the various editions of Cecchi's plays used for this study.

It has been to Lula Louisa Ey that I have turned while writing this book for the love and steadfast support to sustain me in bringing the project to completion.

Douglas Radcliff-Umstead
July 1985

CONTENTS

Preface, v

Chronology, ix

1. Introduction
   Cecchi's Life, Times, and Works, 1

2. Comedies of Ancient Inspiration, 36

3. Comedies of Modern Inspiration, 84

4. Dramas of Spiritual Inspiration, 127

5. Conclusion
   Cecchi's Reconciliation of Theatrical Traditions, 172

Notes, 178

Bibliography, 185

Index, 189

CHRONOLOGY

1518   Giovan Maria Cecchi born in Florence, Italy, to Ser Bartolo-
        meo Cecchi and Ginevra Sannini, March 14 or 15.
1527   Expulsion of Medici rulers and restoration of Florentine Re-
        public, May.
1530   Fall of Florentine Republic after ten months of siege by ar-
        mies of Emperor Charles V of Spain. Murder of Ser Barto-
        lomeo Cecchi. Return of the Medici to power.
1534   Death of Ginevra Sannini. Giovan Maria Cecchi becomes
        guardian of two younger brothers.
1537   Assassination of Duke Alessandro de' Medici, January. Young
        Cosimo de' Medici becomes head of state.
1540   Founding of Accademia degli Umidi that will become the
        Florentine Academy, most influential institution in the
        city's literary life, November 1.
1544   Giovan Maria Cecchi starts professional career as notary. He
        writes his first learned comedy, La Dote. The Company of
        San Bastiano de' Fanciulli accepts his dramas for perform-
        ances over the succeeding years of the decade.
1549   Sudden death of author's uncle Matteo Cecchi, January. Ar-
        rest, trial, conviction, and execution of Matteo's wife Pru-
        denza for poisoning her husband, April 10.
1550   Publication by the Giolito de' Ferrari Press in Venice of the
        Prose Comedies by the Florentine G. M. Cecchi.
1553–1554   Repeated arrests and convictions of Matteo Cecchi's son Piero
        for theft. Piero's final imprisonment in Florence's jail, the
        Stinche.
1553   Marriage of Giovan Maria Cecchi to Marietta Pagni. Three
        children, Baccio, Ginevra, and Niccolò, born of this
        marriage.
1559   Giovan Maria Cecchi writes La Morte Del Re Acab, the first
        of his sacred dramas. The author is entering a period of
        religious crisis, repenting his having led an unchristian life.
1562   Giovan Maria Cecchi chronicles Sommario de Magistrati di
        Firenze.
1563   Closing of the Council of Trent after eighteen years of irregu-
        lar sessions; beginning of the Tridentine era of the Catholic
        reformation in Italy.
1564   Semiretirement of Duke Cosimo in favor of his son Fran-
        cesco, regent for internal Tuscan affairs.
1567   Return of Archbishop Altoviti to Florence after a prolonged
        exile; start of intensive reform activities throughout Tus-
        cany, May.

1569   During an official visit to Tuscany, Archduke Karl of Austria
            attends a performance of Giovan Maria Cecchi's religious
            play *La Coronazione di Re Saul.* Pope proclaims Cosimo
            Grand Duke of Tuscany.

1574   Death of Cosimo. Francesco becomes Grand Duke.

1574–1579   Giovan Maria Cecchi resumes the writing of learned come-
            dies with *Le Cedole.*

1575   Francesco's wife Grand Duchess Joanna of Austria attends a
            performance of *La Morte Del Re Acab* by nuns at the con-
            vent of Santo Spirito.

1581   Giovan Maria Cecchi forms a partnership in the woolen
            industry.

1582   The author parodies the excessive formality of contemporary
            Florentine literary academies with his *Lezione o vero Ci-
            calamento di Maestro Bartolino.*

1585   Publication by the Giunti Press of Giovan Maria Cecchi's
            Verse Dramas.

1587   Death of Giovan Maria Cecchi at his country villa in Ganga-
            landi, October 28. That same year marks the death of Grand
            Duke Francesco.

1589   Performance of Giovan Maria Cecchi's sacred drama *L'Esal-
            tazione della Croce* as part of the festivities to celebrate the
            wedding of Grand Duke Ferdinando to Christine of
            Lorraine.

1
INTRODUCTION: CECCHI'S LIFE, TIMES, AND WORKS

The Medici Restoration

Giovan Maria Cecchi, the most prolific playwright of six-teenth-century Italy, lived during a period of political, cul-tural, and religious reformation in Medicean Florence. Cecchi spent almost his entire life and all his professional service as a notary and his artistic career as a dramatist under the rule of the Medici family in Tuscany. At the time of Cecchi's birth in 1518, Florence had been under renewed Medici domination since 1512, when the heirs of Lorenzo il Magnifico ended an exile of eighteen years. The only period when Cecchi did not live under the control of the Medici was during the brief return of republican government to Florence from 1527 until 1530. Among Cecchi's childhood experiences were the ten-month siege of Florence by the imperial army of Charles V of Spain and the fall of the Republic in August 1530. During his adult life Cecchi participated in the administrative institu-tions of the absolutist bureaucratic state that the Medici dukes created to impose stability and order throughout their Tuscan domain. In order to appreciate Cecchi's writings, es-pecially his dramas, one must become acquainted with the political and social environment of Medicean Florence.

Doubtless the ruler with whose reign Cecchi became most closely associated was Cosimo I, who came to power sud-denly in 1537 after the assassination of Duke Alessandro de' Medici. Cosimo succeeded in integrating the prevailing so-cial, economic, governmental, and ideological structures of the Tuscan state with its republican traditions of freedom and independence into a principate in which service to the court

1

took the place of constitutional liberties. While pretending to respect the various institutions of republican government, Cosimo actually designed an authoritarian regime that served completely the duke or his regent. During his reign, Cosimo sought to establish Tuscan independence of Spanish imperialist rule, to consolidate the control of Florence over all of Tuscany, to diminish the traditionally powerful role of the wealthy patriciate in Florentine government, and to exalt the Medici dynasty. As evidenced in several of Cecchi's comedies, the presence of Spanish soldiers on Tuscan soil proved a continuing source of humiliation and irritation until at last in 1543 the new duke secured the withdrawal of imperial garrisons. By marrying Eleonora of Toledo, daughter of the Spanish viceroy over the Kingdom of Naples, Cosimo identified himself as a loyal ally of Emperor Charles V and restored the dignity and pride of his Tuscan subjects.

Cosimo may rank as the first European ruler who was able to construct an elaborate state machinery into a centralized institution that furthered the aims of its monarch. To staff this complex bureaucracy the duke required the services of professionally trained experts such as judges, magistrates, notaries, ambassadors, and provincial governors. Giovan Maria Cecchi became one of a vast number of public servants recruited from the middle class to assist the state by holding official posts. Duke Cosimo firmly believed that efficient government required unquestioning and dedicated service by knowledgeable persons who would contribute their skills to the advantage of the monarchy. Perhaps the outstanding feature of Florentine society with which the new ruler had to contend was the exclusivity that divided classes against each other through the scorn of the patriciate, the attachment of the bourgeoisie to the economic advantages they had acquired through the medieval guild system, and the fierce independence of ecclesiastical units like the Dominican friars with their Savonarolan dream of a New Jerusalem. One has merely to look at the dramas of Cecchi for a portrait of Florentine society, restrained by the barriers of class and institutions. Against the continual threat of civil unrest and anarchy, Cosimo saw himself as the agent to restore order and public decorum.

While accepting the hierarchies that continued to divide

society, the Medici monarch endeavored to create a sense of civic security, equilibrium, and even cooperation among rival groups through his firm command over economic resources, education, public welfare, defense, and (especially significant for Tuscany) the region's cultural life. All authority derived from the sovereign. The foundation of the Medici's autocratic state was the large corps of functionaries (among them Cecchi) who applied their expertise to legal questions, the drawing of contracts, the registration of deeds, the assignment of dowries, and, particularly, the assessment and collection of taxes. Through rigid control over an acquiescent administrative force, the duke brought to a fragmented society an operational unity.[1]

Because a violent accident of history had elevated him to command over the Tuscan realm, Cosimo determined to crush all opposition to his reign. Under the Medici dynasty a citizen's first duty became absolute obedience to the sovereign. The duke enacted harsh laws against rebellious subjects with penalties of death, imprisonment, exile, or confiscation of property. An elaborate system of police supervision and spying emerged to keep the monarch informed about the activities and the opinions of his subjects. Every social group and setting had in its midst a spying *denunciatore* whose report might lead to confinement in the *secrete* (the political prison) or to banishment. Public assembly without official permission could be considered conspiracy, for which the punishment was death. Carrying or possessing arms became a crime. This ruthless suppression of dissent created a tense, suspicious atmosphere in which no one dared openly criticize the state, its officers, or, above all, the monarch. In the comedies of Cecchi, as in the writings of his contemporaries, there occur occasional caricatures of corrupt minor officials, usually when the setting is transferred to some safe location outside of Tuscany; but no author would openly censure the agents of the duke's regime. Cosimo's repressive rule inspired his subjects with a feeling of the futility of self-assertion in political and social affairs. The wise citizen cooperated with a government that claimed to have the best interest of the entire state as its goal in maintaining its autocratic administration for the public good.[2]

Recognizing that his regime was as much threatened from

without as from within, the duke set about to build a military force answerable to him alone that would protect the Tuscan domain from its enemies. Fortifications arose at key points along the frontiers and in internal areas easily vulnerable to revolt. Wishing to rival traditional maritime powers like Genoa and Venice, Cosimo ordered the construction of a fleet of war galleys. To defend the Tuscan coast from the menace of invasion by Turkish corsairs, the monarch had a naval base established on Elba and gave it the self-glorifying name of Cosmopoli. Constantly touring the various sections of his domain, the Medici duke remained alert to any danger menacing his supremacy over Tuscany. While many of Cosimo's defense expenditures were partly intended to enhance his reputation among Italian princes (since he agreed with Machiavelli's observation that fear alone inspired respect), the duke was prepared to strike swiftly and mercilessly against opponents. The Medici policy of territorial expansionism involved Florence in war from 1554 to 1559 with its perpetual competitor Siena. Victory in the Sienese conflict brought Cosimo undisputed control over Tuscany.

Since medieval times Florence had been a nation of shopkeepers. Florentine literature, from the novellas of Boccaccio through the plays of Cecchi, himself an entrepreneur, reflected the mercantile mentality of its citizens. But the disastrous banking practices of Medici rulers in the fifteenth century and the long period of wars and unstable government after 1494 had seriously disrupted the state's commercial life. Cosimo realized that his program of political reform had to include reversing the economic decline of the city's business world. Consequently, the duke instituted a series of protectionist measures to benefit the guilds in charge of manufacturing woolen and silk cloth, the industries that had long insured Florentine prosperity. Taking advantage of the new Tuscan alliance with Charles V of Spain, Cosimo secured a contract for the city's wool factories to supply the imperial army with its clothing. Through tax incentives and occasional state subsidies, the glass and ceramic industries began to revive. By rebuilding the port of Pisa and opening the new port of Livorno, Cosimo helped to create outlets for the multinational marketing of Florence's manufactured goods. The Florentines' international trade had always accompanied worldwide banking through the establishment of financial offices in foreign countries. Because the new regime pursued a policy of reconciliation toward many of the wealthy banking families that had gone into exile, the state eventually regained lost revenue from profits on international investments. Thanks to an efficiently operated government and peaceful conditions within the city, confidence in commercial enterprise brought about renewed prosperity. With the revival of industry and trade came an upsurge in population, as attested by the census that the Medici administration periodically conducted, from a low of less than fifty thousand inhabitants in 1540 to nearly eighty thousand in 1589. Economic well-being encouraged a sense of optimism for the present and the future.[3]

Cosimo's government also attempted to promote agriculture by having marshlands drained and by encouraging the planting of new crops from the Americas. But the economic system prevailing in rural areas tended to resist innovation. Frequently, the same citizens who were involved in industry, commerce, and banking also acquired farmland as a secure investment. The urban civilization of the Florentines involved development of a particular rural culture in which city and country evolved a relationship of mutual dependence. This interest of the bourgeoisie in the rural life of Tuscany alternated between the search for a bucolic refuge from the turmoil of the capital city and a highly realistic desire to diversify holdings through purchase of villas, vineyards, grazing and forest lands. Toward the end of Summer, in August and September, members of wealthy Florentine families would spend *villeggiatura,* vacationtime, at their country estates. Farmland provided well-to-do city-dwellers with a supply of wine, olive oil, eggs, milk, butter, flour, and meat for their larders. The arrangement that made possible this profitable situation for the urban investor, however, worked to the disadvantage of the peasantry whose labor was responsible for all the benefits. A system of sharecropping, called *mezzadria,* divided cost and labor between landlord and peasant. Commercial leases would specify the land to be worked, the livestock and the tools to be supplied by the owner, along with conditions stipulating the time for ploughing, sowing, and harvesting. While landlords usually advanced capital for oxen, seed, and implements, they generally did so through loans that kept the peasants forever in debt.

When the time came for the division of crops, the peasants had to settle their accounts by adjusting their share of the harvest. During the long period of the year when the city-dwelling owners were absent from the farms, stewards *(fattori)* represented their interests. This system of exploitation of peasants by town investors naturally aroused resentment and distrust among the rural populace. Since Cecchi was a gentleman farmer with a country villa, he understood the bitterness and the misery of the peasantry, who are important figures in several of his comedies. Although the Medici considered themselves the champions of the city's poor against the patriciate, they did not extend their benevolence to the peasantry. Instead, the ducal government perpetuated the division between city and country with sumptuary laws that forbade peasants to purchase clothing and jewelry worn by townspeople. The official efforts to improve agriculture proved to be of little avail at times of natural catastrophe like the great floods of 1588 and the famine of the following year. In all its legislation regarding agricultural affairs, the Medici regime acted to protect and to advance the interests of urban investors.[4]

Through his skill in building a dynasty, achieving independence for his realm, running a complex administration, and contributing to the state's economic recovery, Cosimo succeeded in his program of political restoration. The crowning moment of his career occurred in 1569 when Pope Pius V promulgated for him the title of Grand Duke of Tuscany. But in 1564 a clear sign of declining vigor had become evident when the monarch abdicated command over domestic affairs by naming his son Francesco as regent. A tremendous progressive impetus came to a halt in the Tuscan principality. Although the duke continued to control diplomacy, as when he arranged his son's marriage to the imperial princess Joanna of Austria in 1565, thereby affirming the place of the Medici among the sovereign families of Europe, a sense of vitality had forever passed from him. With the death of the first grand duke in 1574, the last moment of Florentine political grandeur vanished. During the years of Francesco's reign, which lasted until 1587, a heavy burden of taxation drained away the state's resources, so that by the close of the sixteenth century Tuscany had fallen into a condition of stagnation. The highly centralized government with its hierarchical structure of courtiers and professional bureaucrats later served as a model for other, larger modern states like France, just as several cultural institutions that arose during the era of the Florentine grand duchy later became models for academies and schools of art across Europe.

The Florentine Cultural and Artistic Environment

Art fulfilled an instrumental function to glorify the house of Medici. It was also the ruling family's tradition to promote the arts and to maintain a climate suitable for creative endeavors. When Cosimo I ascended to power, most of the prominent artists and writers of Tuscan origin were residing in cities like Venice and Rome or enjoying the patronage of foreign princes like Francis I of France. Cosimo initiated a program to persuade creative personalities to repatriate themselves, promising commissions for major projects or offering profitable sinecures. Among the talented individuals that the duke managed to attract to Florence were the sculptor-goldsmith Benvenuto Cellini; the painter, architect, and art biographer Giorgio Vasari; the poet and rhetorician Benedetto Varchi; and the humanistic historian Paolo Giovio. In painting and sculpture Cosimo's reign became identified with a style of freely imaginative distortions in pose known as Mannerism, the aesthetic principles of which found their theoretical justification in the writings of Tuscan rhetoricians on poetic figures of speech. What took place in the cultural environment made possible by Duke Cosimo was an interpenetration of the arts, with one creative form influencing another through intense, often heated dialogue among leading painters, sculptors, architects, lecturers, and scholars. A creative person living in Tuscany, like Giovan Maria Cecchi, could participate in the "unity of the Florentine cultural and intellectual community" that held together artists and scholars of all classes with Cosimo's encouragement.[5]

Because of his administrative penchant to establish institutional structures, the duke sought to found enduring societies with formal constitutions that would supervise the region's cultural life. On 1 November 1540, a group of Florentine literati, some of them patricians but many of bourgeois origin like the hosier Giovan Battista Gelli, met to found the *Accademia degli Umidi* (Academy of the Damp Ones) for the purpose of discussing works of literature and especially for the promotion of vernacular Florentine tongue to the status of a classical literary language equal to Latin and Greek. For centuries, one of the greatest problems facing writers in Italy was the choice of a proper literary language. This "problem of the language" (*questione della lingua*) had had various solutions: the exclusive use of Latin as an exalted tongue (the humanist approach); the creation of a composite language from several Italian dialects and illustrious foreign languages like French and Spanish (the proposal of Baldesar Castiglione in *Il Libro del Cortegiano,* 1528, with inspiration from Dante's theory of language); the use of living Florentine (Machiavelli's suggestion in his *Dialogo intorno a la nostra lingua*); or the return to a golden age of Italian literature in the fourteenth century, with the Tuscan model of Petrarch for poetry and Boccaccio for prose (the solution of the Venetian Pietro Bembo in his *Prose della volgar lingua,* 1524–1525). Members of the new academy in Florence alternated between the solutions of Machiavelli and Bembo, with a strong and ever-increasing tendency over the years to hold a profoundly puristic approach to exclude neologisms from the literary language. Even though Cecchi did not become formally associated with any of the Italian academies, he shared the love of the Florentine academicians for the vernacular of their city. In later years, however, Cecchi ridiculed the academicians for pedantry, excessive ceremony, and pretentious titles. In the beginning, the "Accademia degli Umidi" was a rather informal association of members interested in discussing language over a pleasant dinner or putting on a comedy during a holiday season. Soon, however, some of the society's members embraced the ambitious program of introducing the general Tuscan public to every major field of knowledge through a series of lectures in the vernacular. At that moment the goals of the academy began to coincide with the duke's plans for the state's cultural regeneration.

From the academy's inception, its membership included

some of Cosimo's officials. As the duke distrusted secret societies and clandestine meetings, he decided to incorporate this new academy into the formal structure of the Tuscan realm. In Winter 1541 the association changed its name to the "Accademia Fiorentina" (Florentine Academy) in accord with its expanding intellectual role.[6] A year later the Florentine Academy received official status as an institution enjoying ducal support. Its officers were to be honored with stipends that usually took the form of awards and prizes. The academy's presiding officer, the consul, was also to hold the post of rector of the University of Florence. Doubtless the chief reason for the prestige and the influence of the Florentine Academy derived from Cosimo's enthusiastic patronage and the privileges and advantages that he granted to its membership. Whereas academies in other Italian city-states disappeared after a brief period of flourishing activity, the Florentine institution lasted until 1783. This academy's authority over the city's cultural life remained undisputed because the monarch decided not to elevate the unpromising University of Florence to an international center of learning and thus saved the academy from the professional competition that destroyed other Italian erudite societies such as that in Padua. Instead, the University of Pisa became the regional university attracting students from across Europe to take classes with distinguished professors whom the duke's agents lured to Tuscany with contracts for lucrative teaching positions.

Among the privileges that the academy enjoyed was a role in supervising instruction in the capital city's schools, where the Florentine tongue soon supplanted Latin as the language of education. Since the duke wished to make Tuscany a center for publication like Venice, he arranged for the founding of the Torrentino printing house in Florence in 1547 and subsequently assigned to the academy supervisory power over the city's book trade. With offices in the Palazzo Vecchio (the seat of government) and representation by its consul on the Council of Two Hundred, the Florentine Academy exerted a major impact on literature and scholarship throughout Tuscany. At its sessions members of the academy would submit their writings (poems, orations, plays, treatises) to their colleagues for correction in style, wording, and grammar. Criticism covered content, literary form, and subtleties of linguistic expression. Vehement debate would arise over questions of etymology, syntactical placement, semantic development, and lexical variations. These academicians were attempting for the first time to fashion a grammar of the Tuscan tongue comparable to the classical grammars of Latin and Greek. But the limits that the Florentine Academy wished to impose on the resources of language, with strict rules of syntax and orthography, worked to the detriment of the creative freedom of expression that had characterized great Tuscan literature in an earlier age. Membership in the academy brought various obligations of a scholarly and literary nature. One of the chief responsibilities consisted in delivering public lectures, or *lezioni*, readings and commentaries on given texts like Dante's *Divine Comedy* or one of Aristotle's treatises. The talks, which drew enormous audiences because they were delivered in a language accessible to every Tuscan, were tours de force with extremely convoluted digressions from the main text into nearly every area of scholarly investigation. Another literary genre that evolved from the academic gatherings was the *cicalata*, the after-dinner speech intended for general entertainment. Giovan Maria Cecchi later used the form of the *cicalata* to parody the ostentatious manner of the academicians in parading their erudition before audiences. Through its promotion of the vernacular, the Florentine Academy left an enduring contribution by reaching out to a far more comprehensive public than ever possible for latinizing university circles. The Florentine academicians had realized still another of Cosimo's dreams for the nation's cultural revival.

During the second half of the sixteenth century, grand ducal Florence began to take on a gracious appearance through the work of leading architects. Chiaroscuro arabesques became the style for facades on older townhouses. The Palazzo Vecchio underwent interior and exterior remodeling, with murals and gold-leaf decorations by Vasari. Government offices moved into the Uffizi Palace, whose stateliness expressed the efficient self-confidence of the Medicean bureaucracy. Between 1559 and 1570 the architect Bartolomeo Ammannati brought to completion the Pitti Palace (the ducal residence since 1550) to make it, with its forceful masonry of great stones, majestic front, and the splendid Boboli Gardens, the largest structure of its kind in the capital city.

Through the construction of the Santa Trinità Bridge, the district along the Arno River acquired a new vitality. The city itself appeared as a work of art to proclaim the magnificence of Cosimo's regime.[7]

Yet behind the elegant facade of Medicean Florence a mood of conservative reaction was starting to manifest its restrictive attitude. The tendency toward institutionalization, already evidenced by the Florence Academy in language and literature and later demonstrated by the new "Accademia del Disegno" (Academy of Fine Arts, 1561) in the plastic arts, was leading to the rigid imposition of codes and standards to replace the freely inventive and experimental spirit that had given impetus to the great art and literature of the Florentine Republic. The various academies and professional associations were beginning to exercise a stranglehold on the region's creative life, compelling every artist to conform to prescribed methods of achieving "perfection" in a given field of endeavor. Florence became a self-conscious society in which the conventional took the place of the imaginative. A sense of excitement and dynamic inquiry passed away in an atmosphere of intimidation and provincial self-satisfaction. Aware of their city's past greatness and complacent about their present state of excellence, the Florentines abandoned their traditional desire to surpass themselves in creative achievement.

As Florence ceased to be a free and independent community, men of letters voluntarily assumed the status of courtiers to the monarchy, prostituting themselves with works in adulation of the ruler and accepting commissions for projects that frequently never found publication. Although some of those ducal commissions included requests for official histories of the Medici accomplishments, scholars had already lost the sense of temporal dimension and the concept of the human being as a unique creature that had characterized the great historiography of the humanistic writers of fifteenth-century Florence. The institutionalized power of state and church caused sensitive individuals in the latter part of the sixteenth century to lose hope in human ability to control destiny. Even in the darkest moments of his exile from political activity, Machiavelli, while writing *The Prince*, never surrendered his faith in man's capacity to withstand at least

half of the capricious assaults of Fortune. During the era of
absolutist monarchy, however, an ever-increasing conscious-
ness of the impotence of individual action to alter fate deprived persons of the will to resist the forces of oppression. In
accepting the general wretchedness of earthly existence and
the limitations of human nature, the generation of the late
sixteenth century succumbed to the autocratic rule of the
secular monarch and the newly reformed Church.[8]

The Religious Reformation and the Moral Climate

Early in his rule Cosimo wished to affirm his sovereignty
over the administration of ecclesiastical affairs in Tuscany,
almost establishing a separate regional Church. The state rig-
orously defended its right to grant benefices, to tax Church
lands and revenues, and to determine whether a person accused of crimes against the faith should be transferred to ecclesiastical tribunals. Most of Florence's hospitals, hospices,
and orphanages, traditionally operated by religious orders,
soon fell under the direction of lay trustees appointed by the
government to see that those institutions actually carried out
their charitable functions. A secular committee was also appointed to supervise all convents and monasteries to compel
inmates to observe their rules. The duke's motivation tran-
scended the purely political desire to integrate separate orga-
nizations into the realm's bureaucratic machinery, for he
seriously intended to uphold the morality of the monastic
and conventual institutions around which a great deal of Tuscany's religious life revolved. When any monastic center
showed more concern with interfering in governmental matters and amassing a vast fortune from private donations (as
the Dominican friars of San Marco did in 1545) than with
conducting pious works of mercy for Florence's large indigent
population, the monarch did not hesitate to expel the negli-
gent members of the order from Tuscany. In the period preceding the convocation of the Council of Trent in 1545, the duke
felt that the correction of the frequently errant Tuscan
Church was incumbent upon him. With his power to select
candidates for the region's religious hierarchy, Cosimo followed his custom of appointing capable administrators as

bishops or their vicars who would scrupulously supervise their dioceses. The principle of efficiency that prevailed in civil matters guided ducal efforts to eliminate abuse and to reintroduce discipline in ecclesiastical affairs.

Strictly enforced state control over the Church in Tuscany led to friction and eventual confrontation between Cosimo and the Farnese Pope Paul III, with the result that, from 1548 to 1567, the Archbishop of Florence, Antonio Altoviti, could not assume his duties at home and had to live in exile in Rome, Perugia, and Padua. With the election of Pius IV in 1559, tension between the papal court and Tuscan government began to relax. Cosimo regularly sent sympathetic delegates to the sessions of the Council of Trent to display his willingness to forward the program of reformation. Finally, after the new Pope Pius V declared in 1566 his firm intention of implementing the comprehensive reforms framed at the council between 1545 and 1563, a new phase of the relationship between Rome and the Tuscan state opened as the two became collaborators in compelling orthodoxy in doctrine and practice. Formal reconciliation came about on 15 May 1567, when Archbishop Altoviti celebrated his first mass in Florence. The Tridentine era of dogmatic application of reform in liturgy, conventual life, and parish administration had at last arrived in Tuscany.

Immediately upon his return to Florence, Altoviti called a provincial synod and carried out a series of pastoral visitations throughout the region's parishes. Synods established the new Tridentine mass, the catechism of doctrine, explanation of the nature and the function of the seven sacraments, while defining exact spheres of duties for clergymen and imposing the strict rule for priests to reside in their parishes. Pastoral visitations provided the archbishop with the opportunity to see precisely under what conditions priests lived in their communities, so as to instruct them to conform in dress, performance of rites, proper maintenance of their churches and chapels, observation of celibacy, and knowledgeable teaching of faith to their congregations. The Church, with the full support of Cosimo's regime, determined to assure uniformity of thought and of action throughout the realm.[9]

In the spirit of cooperation between secular and ecclesias-

tical authorities, Tuscany became an ally of the papacy in its
crusade to combat Protestantism and to defeat infidel nations. The duke's war galleys formed part of the international
fleet under Pius V's Holy League of Spain, Tuscany, Venice,
and the papacy that achieved the naval victory of Lepanto in
1571, thereby ending Turkish domination of the Mediterranean. Within the frontiers of the Tuscan state a working arrangement developed between civil and religious courts in
regard to the program of the Holy Inquisition, restored since
1542, to eradicate heresy from all Christian lands. Although
Florence had always shown itself to be unfriendly to heretical
views (unlike the Lutheran-infested Tuscan town of Lucca),
its onetime tradition of free inquiry and intellectual specula-
tion along with its heritage of Savonarolan scorn of spiritual
corruption contributed to an independent attitude that agents
of the Inquisition considered subversive. The ducal government attempted to exert a moderating influence on the en-
forcement of the Inquisition in order to avoid the large-scale
arrests, torture, execution, and even massacre that took place
in other regions of Italy. Civil courts retained their right of
priority in examining anyone charged as a heretic, carefully
distinguishing between crimes of sacrilege (like blasphemy
and dishonoring sacred objects and buildings) and crimes of
heresy as acts against basic tenets of Catholic dogma. Only
in a clearly demonstrated case of heresy would a defendant be
delivered to the Inquisition. In January 1552 there occurred
the only auto-da-fé in Florentine history. A group of persons
convicted of being Lutheran sympathizers had to march
through the streets, wearing cloaks decorated with crosses
and diabolical figures, to the Church of Santa Maria del Fiore,
where, after an act of public contrition, they were reblessed
into the faith, while outside in the piazza forbidden books
were being burned.[10] Although this unique Florentine auto-
da-fé illustrates the leniency with which the Inquisition functioned in Tuscany, it typifies, nonetheless, the atmosphere of
humiliation and intimidation that repressed original, critical
speech and writing under the Medicean regime. Merely the
awareness of omnipresent police surveillance and the immediate danger of detection and incarceration sufficed to prevent
deviation from orthodox opinion. In the oppressive climate of
Tridentine Italy, in which everyone's faith was put to ques-

tion, self-recrimination readily arose as persons began to doubt the sincerity and correctness of their religious convictions. The anxiety of disturbed conscience spontaneously drove believers to the guidance and consoling forgiveness of spiritual authority.

Exemplifying the gnawing sense of guilt characteristic of Florentines in the last quarter of the sixteenth century, Cecchi underwent a religious conversion late in his life, repenting the erotic fury of his comedies. Besides rewriting some of his first dramas and purifying their language, Cecchi started to write sacred plays at the request of monasteries and convents. Under Altoviti's successor of 1574, Archbishop Alessandro de' Medici (later Pope Leo XI), the Catholic Revival in Tuscany came to concentrate on exalting the piety of the cloistered life while reducing public worship to the passive enjoyment of religious spectacles. Understanding the great extent to which Florentine spiritual life had depended on the religious fervor of monasteries, convents, and lay confraternities, the new archbishop completed the work of institutional reform begun years before by Cosimo. Although the archbishop attempted to shelter convents in particular from the temptations of the outside world, he prudently permitted regular visitations so that the public would have inspiring examples of cloistered virtue. Popular piety in Tridentine Florence looked to glorifying examples of religious rapture in nuns like Maria Maddalena de' Pazzi at the Carmelite convent and Caterina de' Ricci at St. Vincent's in Prato. It was to this conventual community seeking perfection of Christian life that Cecchi addressed his late dramas.

By establishing parallels between the celestial, ecclesiastical, and political hierarchies, the prelates responsible for promoting the Catholic Reformation in the second half of the sixteenth century confirmed the need to accept superior direction as the means to experiencing earthly contentment and spiritual salvation. Obedience to monarch and pope would assure the grace of God. In a world in which Divine Providence determined the outcome of all events, devout Christians were supposed to surrender the vanity of individual initiative to a higher will. Instead of affirming the basic human dignity proclaimed a century before in Florence's humanistic Renaissance, the Catholic Reformation asserted the underlying sinfulness and moral fragility of all persons. Whereas a few dedicated individuals who had retreated to the cloisters might attain in this life a state of mystical transport, those who had not renounced the bonds of this world had to conform to the rigid morality and the external ritual of the Church. Into every person's life was to come a moment of spiritual reassessment in order to recognize errors and limitations, so as to prepare the way to redemption. After a period of anguished self-questioning, there occurred in the life of Giovan Maria Cecchi the moment of conversion that was the moral goal of Florentines during the era of the Catholic Reformation.

Cecchi's Life

A strong sense of family tradition and pride guided Cecchi throughout his professional career as a notary. Born in March 1518 in a Florentine family of old stock that traced its origins to at least the middle of the thirteenth century,[11] Giovan Maria Cecchi always strove to uphold the honor of his ancestral background with its emphasis on public service. In Florentine society it was the family that through its traditions determined the course of an individual's life and eventual position in the community. The Cecchis had long held posts in the government of the Republic. When the Silk Merchant's Guild established the Hospital of the Innocents in 1419 as a shelter for foundlings, the person selected as the institution's first prior was an Antonio Cecchi. For generation after generation, sons of the Cecchi family followed the notarial discipline, which in the city's complex legalistic system functioned as a highly important office to insure the validity of documents that might be called into question at court. Consequently, the title *Ser,* given to notaries, traditionally prefaced the names of male members in the Cecchi family. Early in the fifteenth century Ser Mariano Cecchi participated in the commission to reorganize the statutes of the Commune of Florence. Eight of the Cecchis became chancellors to the priors who governed the Florentine Signoria. This heritage of loyal participation in the affairs of the state inspired

Giovan Maria in his years of service to the Medicean monarchy.

One of the deepest blows to the honor of the Cecchi family came in 1530 when Fabrino del Grilla da Castagno murdered Giovan Maria's father Ser Bartolomeo di Ser Sano. This was a shock to the collective pride of the Cecchi clan from which Giovan Maria never fully recovered, since the crime went unpunished. Although the reasons for the murder have not been explained, the year in which the assassination took place was a particularly violent one because of the siege by imperial forces and the collapse of the Republic. Assassinations, for political and purely personal motives, were happening with some frequency. Neither of the succeeding ducal governments of Alessandro and Cosimo brought legal action against the murderer even though the official book of petitions made to Cosimo in 1537–1538 records Giovan Maria's earnest request for justice.[12] In the code of ethics prevailing in Florence, a family's entire reputation suffered an inestimable loss of standing in society if such a major offense as murder was not punished.

A few years after Ser Bartolomeo's murder, his wife Ginevra di Bartolomeo Sannini also died. As the eldest son, Giovan Maria became the guardian of his two younger brothers, Agostino and Bartolomeo, although he was only sixteen years old at the time of their mother's death. Despite the misfortunes of his youth, Giovan Maria managed to complete the career-designed education that directed sons of middle-class Florentine families into positions that satisfied the needs of society. While mastering the skills of the notarial profession, the future playwright also acquired a love for authors of classical antiquity whose masterpieces he desired to rival one day in compositions of his own in Tuscan. Upon being certified in *notaria*, Cecchi gained membership in the important Guild of Judges and Notaries and all the social prestige that the association brought. For thirty-five years he pursued his notarial career, from 1542 to 1577, reinforcing his guild status by applying his services to the affairs of the Furriers' Guild. With his legal training and public experience, Cecchi very naturally occupied posts in the domain's bureaucracy. Twice he was Proconsul, the Chancellor of the Magistrates of Contracts, and also Procurator at the Tribunal of Commerce. His interests concentrated on commercial litigation, legal agreements, and authentication of documents. Although Cecchi held these various posts of great distinction, he never aimed at acquiring political power. As an honorable civil servant, he could remain an observer rather than an actor in the major political and military events of the times. Cecchi's civic role was that of functionary, one ideally suited for Cosimo's centralized state bureaucratic machine.

Further assaults on the reputation of the Cecchi family troubled Giovan Maria. Early in 1549 his uncle Matteo Cecchi died under somewhat suspicious circumstances. Police investigation later uncovered that Matteo's wife Prudenza had grown impatient with her husband's cruel treatment of her and their children and had poisoned his meals. Found guilty of the murder, Prudenza was beheaded at a public execution on 10 April 1549, in the piazza of Sant' Apollinare. A few years later, in 1553 and 1554, Piero Cecchi (one of the sons of Matteo and Prudenza) found himself convicted of several thefts, for which he was first sent into exile and then, on his return to Tuscany, transferred to Florence's main prison for common criminals, the Stinche. Even though neither of these incidents directly involved Giovan Maria, in keeping with the family morality of Renaissance Florence he had to share in the guilt and the shame that dishonored the name of Cecchi. This notary-playwright was too sensitive to public esteem to remain indifferent to those scandalous events. The sordidness of the crimes left Giovan Maria with a bitter impression of life's misery. Always looking for a quietude of spirit so that he might become a creative author, Cecchi soon began an inward retreat that culminated in his religious conversion.[13]

In the midst of his great personal afflictions Cecchi entered into marriage at the age of thirty-five in 1553, as was customary for men of the professional class who had reached a stage of security and relatively high position. His wife, Marietta Pagni, bore him three children, Baccio, Ginevra, and Niccolò. Within the circle of his immediate family, Cecchi created a protective enclosure into which he could escape from the tedious responsibilities of his official posts and devote himself to literary ambitions. Cecchi's life typified the aspirations of an entire class in the Florentine bourgeoisie: pursuit of a professional career, public service, association with guilds, devotion to family, allegiance to the regime in power, cultivation of scholarly and creative interests.

With the income gained as a notary, Cecchi decided late in life to invest in a commercial venture, and he formed a partnership in the wool trade with members of three of the oldest and most illustrious Florentine families, Marco Antonio Adimari, Mariotto Segni, and Giovan Francesco Baldesi. Since the first document concerning this business enterprise dates from 1 September 1581, it is obvious that the partners were moving against the tide of events in the woolen industry. Increasingly, manufacturers had been abandoning the clothing trade, for the impetus that Cosimo I had given to Florence's economic revival dissipated during Francesco's reign. The leaders of the major guilds refused to accept innovative methods of manufacture and marketing while at the same time they persisted in increasing a burdensome network of functionaries whose chief task seemed to be excluding from participation in commerce anyone who might offer a challengingly new way of diversifying business. However, the partnership of Cecchi, Adimari, Segni, and Baldesi represented all that was most solid and trustworthy in Florence's commercial and legal tradition. At its most vital moment of artistic and intellectual development, Florentine society had joined a passion for mercantile activity with a love for scholarship and creativity.[14]

Cecchi realized still another of the dreams of the middle class by purchasing a villa at Gangalandi in the Tuscan countryside. He apparently visited there with great frequency and took a lively interest in local activities. His financial success enabled him to pay the costs of having the local church of Santa Lucia (later San Michele) restored and of having a modest-sized monastery constructed for the Augustinian Fathers of San Francesco di Paola. Most importantly, this contact with the rustic region of Tuscany gave Cecchi the opportunity for close observation of the conditions, customs, and language of the peasantry. Only one other major sixteenth-century Italian playwright, the Paduan Angelo Beolco (known by his stage and pen name Ruzante), had a more intimate acquaintance with peasant life than did Cecchi. That country villa also provided Cecchi with a retreat where he could devote himself to the study of some of his favorite Latin and Italian authors. In Cecchi's writings, consequently, the countryside appeared as both idyllic refuge and realistically portrayed agricultural area.

It was at the Gangalandi villa that Giovan Maria Cecchi died during the evening of 28 October 1587, having been ill for a week with catarrh. In the *Ricordo* that his son Baccio later wrote about his father, the playwright was stated to be exactly sixty-nine years, seven months, and fourteen days old. Baccio draws attention to his father's religious zeal and dedication to pious deeds. The various misfortunes that had affected his family's honor influenced his conversion and his religious devotion. Through the writings of his later years and his support for religious orders, Cecchi hoped to demonstrate his renewed belief. Even though he usually described his temperament as that of a *"dolcion"* (sweet and pleasant person), the austere spirit of the Catholic Reformation compelled Cecchi to reflect negatively upon the joyous self-indulgence of his early literary compositions and the vanity of relying on his own abilities. An author who had once shown immense delight in satirizing venal and lustful clerics, the playwright determined to exalt the glory of the Church and the history of champions of the Christian faith. Cecchi's death occurred in the same year that Cosimo's son Grand Duke Francesco died. The year 1587 seems to have marked the end of an era.[15]

Although Cecchi's literary fame rests on the dramatic works that he began writing in 1544 and continued to compose until his death, he completed several other compositions in a variety of genres. Living in an academic age when authors were expected to display their ease in executing a wide range of works in prose and poetry, Cecchi conformed to the standard of productivity prevailing among Florentine literati. His poems fall into the categories common to the period: bucolic eclogues (preserved merely in fragments), Petrarchist lyric poems, *capitoli* (satirical poems in terza rima), pieces composed to celebrate a special occasion, and some other works remembered only by rustic titles such as *Fracmezzo di un contadino, Lode della Nencia di Prato,* and *Terzine villanesche.* Typical of the *pièces d'occasion* is a poem commemorating the wedding to a foreign princess of one of the Medici heirs. It would be fair to describe much of Cecchi's verse as pedestrian. Only in his dramas does his verse acquire eloquence and authentic expressivity.

As evidenced throughout his entire literary career, Cecchi had a great love for the actual forms of spoken language ungoverned by the academic imposition of linguistic norms. As a philologist intending to record and to explain the popular language of his home city, he compiled a collection of sixty-four Florentine proverbs, colorful words, and distinctive expressions in *Dichiarazione Di Molti Proverbi, Detti E Parole Della Nostra Lingua.* The author pretended to be composing the work in response to a foreigner who had asked for an explanation of the terms. Cecchi recognized how the richness of a language resided in those proverbs and intricate phrases that were peculiar to one speech area alone. In the text he specifically alludes to earlier Tuscan writers like Boccaccio who made use of some of the same expressions. But in no way is this compilation intended to fossilize the Tuscan language according to a golden model. Instead, Cecchi reveals his fascination with the living dialect that he is glorifying with his study. Many of the same expressions also appear in his own comedies, often in the mouths of some of his most inane characters who attempt to mask their stupidity with the wisdom of proverbs.

Cecchi's notarial expertise in determining the authenticity of documents manifests itself, for example, in his selection of the term *"maccatelle"* (falsified wooden seals used to promote fraudulent schemes with counterfeit letters, and therefore extended in meaning to signify acts of imposture). Falsified documents and imposture occur repeatedly in the complicated multiple plots of several of Cecchi's comedies. The author's attention to visually compelling phrases is reflected in expressions like *"tremare a verga"* (to tremble like a twig in the wind) to describe the condition of someone shivering from the cold or sickness. Cecchi's ear for comic sound combinations shows itself in his choice of the word *"gongolare,"* to rejoice over something that is not altogether proper. Many of the proverbial phrases stress habitual defects, as in the expression *"Questa è la canzona dell'oca"* ("This is the goose's song"), said of someone who repeats the same things. Negative traits and attitudes predominate in this compilation of often picturesque proverbs rather than the positive virtues of honesty, loyalty, industry, and responsibility. Part of the Florentine ethos is the tendency to find fault with others and to state critiques in witty phrases. Cecchi works as a comic artist in the Florentine vein by selecting those terms and phrases that uncover humorous character flaws and ridiculous habits. This collection with its stress on the vivid speech of Tuscany was one of Cecchi's works that contributed in the early nineteenth century to the rediscovery of his significance as a writer after two centuries of neglect. The philologically oriented Accademia della Crusca (an institution founded toward the end of Cecchi's life) recognized in this compilation and in the author's plays a treasure of the Tuscan tongue and began to prepare his works for publication. By 1883 a government decree listed Cecchi's writings as standard texts in Italian schools because of their linguistic importance as documents of Tuscan dialect.[16]

Cecchi's impassioned advocacy of the Florentine vernacular took on a new significance in his religious phase. Like his contemporaries in the Accademia Fiorentina, he wished to make available to as large a public as possible the message of Christianity by rendering the episodes of the Bible into the vernacular. Although Cecchi never went so far as did the other Florentine academicians in proposing to replace Latin with Tuscan in church services, he started but did not complete a series of *Ragionamenti Spirituali*, circa 1558, in which he attempted to refashion in the vernacular the Gospels and Epistles. His avowed aim in this enterprise was to bring to the least sophisticated persons the redeeming lessons of Christian faith. Along with the Gospels and Epistles, Cecchi hoped to execute in Italian the story of David and the *Proverbs* of Solomon. These sermons in the popular tongue relate Cecchi to the vital Florentine tradition of saints' lives, translations from Scriptures, vernacular hymns, and legends of mystics that constituted the folk piety in the capital city toward the close of the sixteenth century. In what was typical humility of the Tridentine era, Cecchi included in the sermons an apology for possible presumption in his undertaking and a request for correction by the Holy Church and its ministers of any error. While employing the "clear and easy Florentine speech" to communicate the good news of Christianity, the author intended to adhere to a strict orthodoxy of view.[17]

As a parody of the *lezioni* and *cicalate* held at the sessions of the various academies of the day, Cecchi composed one of his most humorous pieces in the *Lezione o vero Cicalamento di Maestro Bartolino*, 1582. This burlesque work is presented as a mock-serious erudite commentary on the sonnet "Passere e beccafichi magri arrosto" (roast of scrawny sparrows and warblers) by the comic Florentine poet Francesco Berni (circa 1497–1535). Cecchi's skill as a narrator displays itself here in the suspenseful way that one amusing anecdote interweaves into another before delivery of the entertaining coup de grace. The piece opens with a preface, supposedly by the beadle of the recently founded Accademia della Crusca, in which Maestro Bartolino from the Canto de' Bischeri is described as a man who had never lost sight in his life of the cupola of Florence's Cathedral, a description that would be appropriate to Cecchi. As the preface insists, the language of this *cicalamento* is Florentine, not Italian or Bergamasque or any amalgamation as proposed by philologists like Gian Giorgio Trissino, who wanted to create a composite national language. The main body of Cecchi's work is an exegesis of Berni's sonnet on the theme that, among the many afflictions of life, there is nothing worse than having a wife. Repeatedly, the author satirizes the pretentiousness of academicians by listing lengthy quotations in Latin, by suggesting alternate versions of individual lines in the sonnet, and by citing erudite sources that are frequently altogether fictitious. Among the sage philosophers and pundits that Bartolino includes in his array of references are the Boccaccian characters Maso del Saggio (*Decameron* 8, 3, as the expert on the land of Cuccagna and its province Bengodi) and Friar Cipolla 6, 10, as a consultant on the tribulation of conjugal existence). The very language of this *lezione* mocks the rhetorical devices of academic style with ridiculous plays of antithesis and chiasmus. With proper pomposity the piece has an appendix listing its learned sources, who have names like Porcograsso (fat pig). In an age when literary and artistic endeavors were increasingly coming under the direction of rigid institutions, this burlesque treatise provided an opportunity to ridicule pedantry and academic ceremony.[18]

Even though he never strayed away from his beloved native city, Cecchi produced a travelogue in his 1575 work *Compendio di più Ritratti* with little-known and humorous facts about Germany, Flanders, Spain, and the Kingdom of Naples. The Italian author characterized the religious conscience of German Catholics as one that acknowledged the existence of only five mortal sins because gluttony was considered a virtue and greed a sign of industriousness among the Germans. Many of these stereotypical impressions of foreigners reappear in Cecchi's comedies, especially the gluttonous and heavy-drinking Germans as well as the braggart Spaniards.[19] In contrast to this imaginary travelogue, created out of the author's readings about foreign lands, Cecchi gave a remarkable example of his painstaking exactness as a notary in his *Sommario de' Magistrati di Firenze*, 1562. With all his firsthand experience of the structure and procedures of the Medicean bureaucracy, Cecchi composed this brief treatise in which he described in great detail the various magistracies of the city, their terms of office, and their function. In addition to this report on the civil service, the author permitted his enthusiastic interest in the life of Florence to carry him to digressions on its religious associations, confraternities, and the charitable societies that attended to prisoners condemned to death or arranged for impoverished girls to have honorable weddings. As a bureaucrat intent on assembling concrete facts, Cecchi minutely related information about the administration of these religious societies, their income from private donations, and their relationship to the district of the city in which they were located. Since the life of Florence had traditionally revolved around its districts *(quartieri)*, the author also included some comments of folkloric interest about each zone. The *Sommario* and the *Compendio* show the versatility of Cecchi in documentary reporting and fanciful travelogue.[20]

Throughout his literary career Cecchi enjoyed the praise of his contemporaries because of his success as a dramatist. The title by which he became known was "il Comico," the comic author. Baccio and Niccolò Cecchi remarked on their father's epitaph that he had written wittily, ingeniously, and effectively in the comic style. In two octaves of his *Rime Burlesche* the dramatist Antonio Francesco Grazzini playfully disparaged Cecchi's fame as a writer of comedies, while truly recognizing him as his principal rival in theatrical compositions. One of the most acute observers of the Florentine scene, Anton Francesco Doni (1513–1574), in his *I Marmi* ranked Cecchi as the dramatic equal of Machiavelli, the greatest playwright of Renaissance Italy with his comedy *La Mandragola*. In *The Catalogue of Florentine Writers* by Michele Poccianti (died 1596), the highest level of esteem is accorded to Cecchi as a keen-sighted, urbane, and humorous writer whose plays always had an enthusiastic reception. An example of the popularity of his comedies is the story that the rather melancholy Florentine painter Battista Naldini (died 1591) could be lured out of the solitary retreat of his home only during those occasions in Carnival season when acquaintances of his were holding private performances of the author's plays.[21] Cecchi's use of richly idiomatic Florentine dialect and his portrayal of the foibles of the city's middle class along with their servants and rustic tenants accounted for the immense appeal of his comedies.

Renaissance Comic Genre and Carnival Spirit

By the second half of the sixteenth century literary theorists were debating the nature of the comic genre, finding inspiration in both Aristotle's *Poetics* and Horace's *Ars poetica*. A strong defense of the genre came with Bernardo Pino da Cagli's *Discorso intorno al Componimento de la Comedia de' Nostri Tempi*, 1572, in which the author argued that the aim of comedy was to use the ridiculous to expose the foolishness of improper behavior. For Cagli, comedy possessed moral usefulness by creating laughter as a corrective for the stupidity of dishonest acts. The stage representation of vice could never arouse the pleasure that an audience would experience in beholding a morally uplifting comic drama. In 1585 Antonio Riccoboni introduced the first thorough poetics of the comic genre for that era with his *Ars comica*, stating that marveling at a humorously contrived deception would free an audience of the tendency to succumb to vice. Riccoboni believed that in comedy the performance of a vicious act could be of moral profit to teach the public the ridiculous consequences of commiting stupid deceptions.

The theatrical staging of foolish acts also concerned Nicolò Rossi in his *Discorso intorno alla Comedia*, 1589. According to Rossi, comedy had two ends: the pleasure brought by imitation, and moral instruction to control the strong emotions of the spectators. Comic imitation consisted in showing "badness" of intent and deed, since some foolish or wily acts of badness could arouse laughter. Rossi also recommended the use of intermezzi with music and dance to delight the entire audience. A few years later, in 1593, Frederico Ceruti declared in his *Dialogus de Comoedia* that comedy was a school to give examples of life for people to follow or to avoid. Actors, in Ceruti's evaluation, had a moral obligation even to refrain from the playwright's obscene language so as not to corrupt youthful viewers. All the critics who actively engaged in arguments about comic art recognized that the genre had to combine pleasure caused by the ridiculous with moral utility.[22]

Performance of comedies in the Renaissance took place during public festivals like the carnival season or during major holidays like Epiphany and St. John's Day in June. The two great literary genres of carnival celebration in Tuscany were comedies and the songs *(canti carnascialeschi)* that accompanied and illustrated the themes of pageant floats. Attending merry plays, participating in masquerades, and holding banquets provided a salutary release from the tension of living under an oppressive regime. Even an absolutist government like that of Cosimo recognized the socially therapeutic value of carnival season as a moment of general license for normally conservative and obedient citizens to rebel against the severity of everyday life under the protective disguise of ridiculous masks. Carnival, of course, originated in ancient times with celebrations of life, especially at Springtime with the return of greenery. In Christian times, carnival came to be associated with final madcap revelry on the eve of Lent and its period of abnegation. The rites of carnival could serve the ends of rebelliousness by encouraging disrespectful behavior toward civil authorities, but such activity ultimately reaffirmed established social order to which all citizens had to submit at the end of festive celebrations. After the Catholic Reformation ushered in an era of strict conformity in religious practice, ecclesiastical authorities continued to permit the pre-Lenten frivolity of carnival and comedies as a final opportunity for indulgence of the senses before a season of sacrifice and denial.[23]

Often, the same persons who composed carnival songs and prepared the decorations of the pageant processions were the ones responsible for staging comedies: the *brigate* (informal associations of friends) and, after 1540, members of the formally constituted academies. These were all amateur groups who enjoyed designing and constructing sets, working on costumes, and producing plays. During each week of the pre-Lenten season, one of the duties of a "king" elected by academicians for a seven-day term would be to arrange a banquet with an appropriate celebration such as a verse competition or performance of a comedy by members of the academy, who acted both male and female roles.[24] In addition to the theatrical activities of the *brigate* and academies, religious mutual aid societies known as lay confraternities occasionally mounted productions of profane comedies along with their usual sacred dramas until late in the century when Archbishop Alessandro de' Medici forbade them to stage plays of a secular nature.

Among the forms of popular entertainment in late Renaissance Italy that usually accompanied plays were court ballets, tournaments, and formal balls. While entire streets and piazzas served as the setting for large-scale carnival processions and pageant-jousts, plays had their productions in spacious halls during Winter and in courtyards and gardens during good weather. The grand hall of the Palazzo Vecchio, the Salone dei Cinquecento, was turned into an improvised theater to honor major state affairs. At the Pitti Palace, the hall generally reserved for dramatic productions became known as the "sala delle Commedie." Finally, a permanent theater for the Medici and their guests opened in 1586 at the Uffizi, just over the offices of city magistrates.[25] Although the resources for public spectacles and courtly events might be lavishly expended to assure the splendor of productions, the *brigate* and academies that staged most plays had to operate with limited budgets depending on the good will of volunteers. The enormous number of plays written and actually produced attests to the enthusiasm of the participants working in their improvised theaters.

During Cecchi's lifetime, the Florentine court sponsored several politically significant celebrations that included the staging of comedies. Some of those events concerned state weddings, celebrations of life that festive comedies ideally suit.[26] On Cosimo's marriage to Eleonora of Toledo, the comedy *Il Commodo* by Antonio Landi was performed on 9 July 1539, in the courtyard of the old Medici palace on Via Larga. When the grand duke succeeded in having his son Francesco wed Joanna of Austria in 1565, the festivities featured a Christmas Day production of Francesco d'Ambra's comedy *La Cofanaria* in the Salone dei Cinquecento by members of the Confraternity of St. Bernardino and St. Catherine. During a state visit to Tuscany in the Spring of 1569, Joanna's brother Archduke Karl attended several theatrical performances, among them the comedy *La Vedova* by Giovambattista Cini at a command production in the Salone dei Cinquecento and the sacred drama *La Coronazione Di Saul* by Giovan Maria Cecchi with staging by the Confraternity of the Evangelist.[27] Two years after the deaths of Duke Francesco and Cecchi, the new monarch, Ferdinando, married Christine of Lorraine and celebrated the occasion with processions, concerts, soccer matches, religious ceremonies, and productions of three comedies throughout May 1589. To honor Ferdinando's wedding and to commemorate Cecchi's role as an author of sacred plays, Baccio Cecchi, the playwright's son, arranged for the Company of the Evangelist to present *L'Esaltazione Della Croce* together with its intermezzi. Dramatic productions thus played an integral part of the pomp of courtly ceremonies during the Medicean Restoration.

Performances of comedies occupied the attention of bureaucrats, courtiers, and leading artists in Italian Renaissance society. Throughout the sixteenth century, artists like Raphael, Vasari, Cellini, and Bronzino participated in comic performances by designing scenery, costumes, and stage properties. Writers of distinction composed comedies: the Ferrarese poet Ariosto, the political theorist Machiavelli, that "scourge of princes," Pietro Aretino, the assassin Lorenzino de' Medici, the Florentine statesman Donato Giannotti, the hosier Gelli, the heretical theologian-philosopher Giordano Bruno. The full social significance of comic theatrical activity in Italy during the close of the Renaissance is only beginning to be appreciated.[28]

Critics have often attempted to disparage this form of comedy by denying it any claim to originality or insight into individual psychology or societal structure. Because the inspiring model for the Italian plays comes from the twenty surviving plays of Plautus (circa 254–184 B.C.) and the six of Terence (circa 185–159 B.C.), the dramatists of the sixteenth century would appear no more than imitators of an ancient theater that in itself was imitating the Greek New Comedy. The numerous Renaissance comedies would be merely variations on the Latin plays, with combinations or "contaminations" of two or more plots from ancient dramas. Therefore, the epithets for classicized comedy, "observed," "learned," and "erudite," must assume negative connotations as if opposed to popular forms like the farce or sacred theater. The unvarying outdoor stage set, representing a street often with the incongruous proximity of church, merchant's home, and house of ill fame, might be judged the unhappy result of slavish imitation of a convention that was justified by the attitude in ancient times that the interior of a home was a nearly sacred enclave whose privacy would be violated by its being shown on the stage. When some of the characters in Italian comedies meet on the street and start to communicate secrets, they almost seem to be apologizing for not speaking indoors. Strict imitation of the ancient Roman theater might explain the falsity of the fixed outdoor scene. For its detractors, learned comedy could never represent the life of its times.

However, Renaissance authors wanted not so much to imitate as to emulate the ancients. Moderns could demonstrate their talent through the innovative way they reworked classical plots or altered ancient character-types to make them reflect the contemporary Italian scene. By following what were held to be models of equilibrium and mastery of form, vernacular writers hoped to achieve the near literary perfection of authors of antiquity. The unchanging outdoor scene constituted a deliberate choice, for the Italians possessed the most advanced stagecraft in Europe and could have easily switched sets from act to act or scene to scene. In most Italian

cities of the period, life remained street-oriented. Merchants
passed part of the day strolling around porticos, encountering
business associates, and closing negotiations for a contract.
Many shops opened out onto the street, so that there was a
constant communication from interior to exterior.[29] The
stage set for Italian Renaissance comedy is not a monotonous,
uninspired, slavish re-creation of ancient Roman life; instead,
it reflects the actual scene of a modern Italian city street,
with the artistry of vanishing-point perspective as developed
by the painters and architects of that period. In fashioning
their comic theater, Italian writers were following Cicero's
observation that comedy was an image of truth, an example
of customs, and a mirror of life. The life that Renaissance
comedy mirrored was that of an urban bourgeois civilization.

This modern comic theater with its aspiration toward classical perfection resulted as the culminating moment of a century and a half of striving to achieve the formal order and
balance of the ancient Roman comedy. Humanistic scholars,
by the second half of the fifteenth century, had abandoned
writing Latin comedies on the model of vernacular sacred
plays and had adopted the pattern of Plautus and Terence. All
this humanistic research and experimentation encouraged
authors to compose vernacular comedies according to the
classical model. Three generations of writers of learned comedies arose during the sixteenth century and the beginning of
the seventeenth. Bold pioneers at the start, like Ludovico
Ariosto with his five plays and Niccolò Machiavelli with *La
Mandragola* and *La Clizia,* established the form of the erudite
comedy in absolute adherence to ancient models. As a second
generation of playwrights emerged throughout central and
northern Italy, an elaborate theory of comic composition was
being formulated following publication, translation from
Greek to Latin, and explication of Aristotle's *Poetics* in the
1530s and 1540s.

Cecchi and fellow playwright Antonio Francesco Grazzini
belonged to that second wave of dramatists who became exposed to the increasing canonization of theatrical practice by
neo-Aristotelian critics like the Ferrarese rhetorician Giambattista Giraldi Cintio with his *Discorso Intorno Al Com-
porre Delle Commedie E Delle Tragedie,* 1545. While
Grazzini attempted to rebel against servile imitation of the

ancients, Cecchi tranquilly accepted prevailing theory. One of the salient facts to realize about Italian Renaissance theater is that even before critics began to change Aristotle's observation about drama in the light of Horace's *Ars Poetica* to form a rigid system of rules, the early playwrights such as Ariosto and Machiavelli had already succeeded in creating a perfectly classical theater. Because of its adherence to rules, this form of drama is also known as "regular" comedy. By the close of the sixteenth century and the start of the seventeenth there arose the last generation of comic dramatists, in the South at Naples with Giordano Bruno and Giambattista Della Porta. Three currents ran through Italian Renaissance comedy: a conservative tradition of imitating ancient plays, an innovative trend of incorporating themes and situations from the novella, and a candid portrayal of contemporary society. The learned comedies of Cecchi represent all of those currents, making him the most representative playwright of his times.

The Dating and Classification of Cecchi's Plays

It is very difficult and often nearly impossible to determine the dates for the composition of Cecchi's learned comedies. Although the author boasted about the rapidity with which he wrote his plays, never dedicating more than ten days to finishing any single drama and frequently completing one in only four days, Cecchi was in the habit of returning to his works and refashioning them to the extent of altering entire scenes and rearranging the sequence of events. He also followed the example of the Italian dramatist whom he admired most, Ariosto, in recasting some of his plays from prose to verse and often using that author's preferred proparoxytonic hendecasyllabic verse (the limping sdrucciolo). Other times Cecchi chose as his verse form the normal hendecasyllable line. Renaissance dramatists being preoccupied with using a verse form that was poetic and verisimilar at the same time, Cecchi wrote blank verse without rhyme, since this metric style most closely resembles the everyday cadence of prose. Not only are there both prose and verse renderings of some of Cecchi's plays but certain dramas also have multiple versions

with significant differences in structure. Because the impact
of the Catholic Reformation on Cecchi also led him to revise
his thinking about the use of satire in his plays and the inap-
propriateness of risqué language, in the reworkings of his
comedies after the late 1550s, the portraits of lecherous, venal
clerics are altered to make them innocuous while the double
entendres and erotic wordplay become blunted. With all the
variant versions of Cecchi's plays circulating in manuscript
form, scholars must assume the perplexing task of preparing
definitive editions and arriving at an accurate chronology of
composition.[30]

Some of the learned comedies were published within the
author's lifetime. The Venetian publishing firm of Giolito de'
Ferrari issued the first edition of six of the erudite comedies
in 1550: *La Dote, La Moglie, I Dissimili, Gli Incantesimi, La
Stiava,* and *L'Assiuolo.* While all the plays in that first edition
were prose versions, another issue released in 1585 by the
Giunti Press contains versions of *La Dote, La Moglie, Gli
Incantesimi,* and *La Stiava* in verse. Individual comedies like
La Dote, La Moglie, and *Il Servigiale* underwent separate
printings, in 1556 for the first two plays by the Giolito de'
Ferrari Company and in 1561 for the third comedy by Giunti.
Except for one edition in 1750, Cecchi's comedies had to wait
until the nineteenth century for full-scale publication, and
even at the present moment two of the plays, *I Contrassegni*
and *Il Debito,* have not yet been printed. Manuscripts of Cecchi's plays, with often strikingly different versions of the
same work, exist in public and private collections at Florence,
Siena, and elsewhere. For a dramatist whose plays enjoyed
enormous popularity in his own times, the comedies of Cecchi have undergone a problematic fate since the author's
death.[31]

One fairly reliable way to discover the date for the writing
of Cecchi's plays is to look for internal evidence within the
dramas. Few authors have delighted in discussing their own
works more than he did. He used the prologues to his plays
as a form of conversation about his literary pursuits. In some
of the prologues Cecchi actually indicated the date of composition or first performance for a particular play. In other
instances Cecchi mentioned the sequence in which he had
written certain dramas. Reference to a recent military expe-

dition provides a clue for the chronology of still another drama. Since the author was fond of using counterfeit letters as a plot device, the fictional date that is specified within a play for one of those letters might disclose the very time of the work's composition or first performance. The examination of such internal evidence and the assemblage of external evidence about details of presentation by amateur groups provide the following chronology for Cecchi's learned comedies.

1544	*La Dote*
1545	*La Moglie*
1545 or 1546	*Il Corredo*
1546	*La Stiava*
1547	*Gli Incantesimi*
1548	*I Dissimili*
1549	*L'Assiuolo*
1549	*Lo Spirito*
1550	*Il Donzello*
1550 or 1551	*La Maiana*
1555	*L'Ammalata*
1556	*Il Servigiale*
1556	*I Rivali*
1557	*Il Medico*, reprinted 1585 as *Il Diamante*
1558	*Gli Sciamiti*
1561	*Il Martello*
1567	*Le Pellegrine*
1574–1579	*Le Cedole*
1585	*Le Maschere*
1585	*I Contrassegni*
circa 1587	*Il Debito*

From this chart, which excludes his sacred dramas, moral plays, and farces, one can gain an idea of Cecchi's considerable productivity.[32] The intense theatrical activity of the 1540s, when in certain years Cecchi completed two comedies, is immediately noticeable. That period also marked the beginning of his notarial career. A significant falling off of dramatic composition occurred between 1551 and 1555, when a series of misfortunes struck the Cecchi family. After 1555 the author entered a period of stability in his personal affairs and resumed writing dramas. By 1562 Cecchi had largely moved to writing religious plays in preference to comedies. Repeated entreaties by acquaintances caused him to

write *Le Cedole* during the 1570s. Cecchi liked to project an
image of himself as a *dolcion* who would not refuse the appeals for him to furnish new plays. Even at an advanced age,
when he admitted to being ill and feeble, Cecchi produced
the comedy *Le Maschere*. For forty-three years Cecchi devoted his energies to contributing play after play to the theatrical life of his native city.

As the most productive playwright of his times, Cecchi
addressed his dramatic works to a public consisting of the
professional Florentine classes of lawyers, notaries, merchants, clerics, and nuns who all looked to the theater as a
source of instruction and entertainment. In developing his
artistry Cecchi fused learned and popular literary traditions
to produce a body of dramatic works that reflected all the
facets of sixteenth-century comic theater: emulation of the
ancient Roman comedies of Plautus and Terence; the influence of the Italian novella (especially Boccaccio's *Decameron*) with its themes of love as a natural right and fortune as
the arbiter of human destiny; the sacred plays *(sacre rappresentazioni)* from the fifteenth and early sixteenth centuries
with their stress on satirizing the vicious tendencies of everyday life; and the Tuscan folk farce. Through his comic works
Cecchi intended to present his society with a portrait of its
daily existence, pointing out the ridiculous excesses of the
morally blind while offering hope of a happy outcome to
those who would recognize their own foolishness.

Cecchi's plays are generally divided into four categories:
commedie osservate, drammi spirituali, commedie morali,
and *farse*.[33] These categories are somewhat arbitrary since in
content and in form several of Cecchi's dramatic works display characteristics from across the four divisions. The *commedie osservate* are the twenty-one secular plays written in
five acts and following the unities of time and space in observation of the practice of Plautus and Terence. Cecchi's son
Baccio employed the term *commedie osservate* in his *Ricordo*, whereas his father had referred to his classicizing plays
as being "osservate di stil comico" (observed according to the
comic style). In the prologue to his play *La Romanesca*, 1585,
the dramatist defined *farce* as a theatrical form intermediate
to tragedy and comedy, with the exalted characters of the
tragic stage and the everyday figures of the comic style and

with the freedom from unities of time and place. Farces contain fewer acts than observed comedies, frequently three acts. The line of distinction between *commedie morali* and *drammi spirituali* grows particularly blurred because both types may be moralizing in tone and may be of a sacred nature. As an example of the "moral" drama, *Il Figliuol Prodigo*, 1569–1570, takes the biblical parable of the prodigal son, sets the events in the mercantile environment of contemporary Florence, and observes unities of time and place within a five-act frame. By *dramma spirituale* or *dramma sacro* was intended a high-style sacred play like *L'Esaltazione Della Croce*, written in verse, derived from the *Legenda Aurea*, with a setting in Jerusalem at the time of warfare between Christians and infidel Persians, and accompanied by six elaborate intermezzi to express the drama's grandiosity. For this present study I wish to devote one chapter to some of the observed comedies that closely follow ancient Latin models, one chapter to observed comedies inspired by novella traditions and illustrating modern Italian life, and one chapter to religious and moral dramas that will include farces.

Few writers have reflected their era and milieu as thoroughly as did Giovan Maria Cecchi. The goal of this book will be to study the explosive political, religious, economic, and domestic tensions of late Renaissance Italy, as reflected in Cecchi's dramas. His work as a playwright will be the subject for this examination of the author who most comprehensively represented the age of the Medicean restoration in Florence. In its critical methodology, this book will follow Northrop Frye's theory of comedy as a renewal of society, Susanne Langer on comedy as festive celebration, and Wylie Sypher on the comic victory over mortality. Contemporary Renaissance theories of comedy, especially those of Giraldi Cintio, will also be cited for their reflection in Cecchi's stage works. Both the dramatist's secular and religious plays will come under study as mirrors of Renaissance society.

2

COMEDIES OF ANCIENT INSPIRATION

Several of the learned comedies are adaptations of dramas by Plautus or Terence. Although Cecchi set his plays in contemporary Italy and used typical Italian names for his characters, he adhered closely to the plots and character-types of the ancient plays from which he drew inspiration. Throughout his writings, usually in prologues, Cecchi acknowledged that he enjoyed an especially warm rapport with Plautus, his "good companion" and "very dear friend," as stated in the play *Il Martello.* One can therefore speak of "friendly borrowing" by the Renaissance author from the comedies of ancient Rome. It was Cecchi's avowed intention to render the ancient comic material a living experience for contemporary Italian audiences.

Marriage as a Financial Arrangement: La Dote

Cecchi's first drama draws attention to one of the most abused practices in Florentine society: the dowry. As a social institution, marriage among the Tuscans functioned for an economic and political end, and Cecchi chose in *La Dote* to stress the obsessive pursuit of monetary advantage that frequently was the determining factor in concluding a marital alliance. Marriage without a dowry provided by the bride-to-be's family seemed abhorrent to the bourgeois mentality of merchants who always sought profit even in the most intimate of relationships. A father's ability to give his daughter or daughters the cash, government bonds, and town and country property to make up a suitable dowry testified to a family's prosperity. Because as time passed and dowries grew increasingly larger due to competition among families, the Florentine government in 1425 created the "Monte delle Doti," an investment institution whereby families could accumulate sufficient interest from a moderate principal in order to provide a daughter with a respectable dowry upon her reaching marriageable age in early adolescence. But even with the success of the "Monte delle Doti" in enabling many middle-class families to build the dowry sum, those households that wished to enjoy the greatest prestige continued to undergo considerable expenditure with dowries. There also existed the danger that a family might compel a daughter to enter a convent in order to avoid the disastrous expenses of a dowry. An observant critic of his society, Cecchi opened his career as playwright with a comedy exposing the venal dowry practice and its threat to family honor.[1]

Although the Italian writer derived the main plot of his drama from Plautus's *Trinummus*, Cecchi situated his play in sixteenth-century Florence instead of ancient Rome. In Plautus's play dramatic conflict arises from the efforts of the profligate youth Lesbonicus to preserve family pride by rejecting the chance to have his sister married without a dowry to his idealistic friend Lysiteles.[2] Conflict shifts in the Italian comedy from the economically unrealistic viewpoint of the young to the greedy calculation of the old. The value system behind Plautus's play rests on the prestige that comes to a family able to provide a dowry, while in *La Dote* focus falls on the monetary loss that would result from allowing a marriage without a substantial dowry. Although the dowry practice prevailed in both ancient Rome and Renaissance Florence, the two comedies approach the consequences of an identical situation with different emphases. To the ancient Romans, a woman who married without bringing her husband an acceptable dowry would have appeared more of a concubine than a wife deserving respect. Plautus's comedy presents the idea of the disgrace to the *genus* (the clan, the family name) if a marriage came about without proper financial agreements. Cecchi instead directs critical regard to the predominant custom of valuing a large dowry over other considerations in arranging a marriage.

In Renaissance Tuscany money made possible honor, personal defense, and social adornment. As Cecchi complains in

the prologue to the 1544 version of *La Dote*, marital negotiations always concentrated on determining the amount of a
dowry rather than on paying attention to the qualities that
could contribute to the union's success and happiness: the
bride's character, her education, her family's background and
reputation. Within the play those very qualities attract young
Ippolito to wed the sister of his impoverished friend Federigo.
In act 2, scene 4, Ippolito attempts in vain to convince his
father, Fazio, that the only worthwhile dowry is the bride's
good manners. To the somewhat misogynistic Fazio, money
alone compensates men for the pain of entering into conjugal
life, since all women, rich or poor, will display their haughty
nature on escaping the prison of their parents' homes. With
his acquisitive merchant psychology, Fazio urges his son to
take advantage of the demographic situation in Florence,
where eligible bachelors are in short supply as compared to
women of marriageable age. The moral outlook that Cecchi
holds up to ridicule in this play is one of exploitation and
victimization for profit.

After exposing society's mercenary values, the playwright
proceeds in the original prologue to confide to the audience
his debt to Plautus for dramatic material. The function of a
prologue in many Italian Renaissance plays was not to introduce the work's argument but to serve as a vehicle for the
author to justify reliance on inspiration from antiquity as
well as to defend innovation. Cecchi defends abandoning the
use of an argument by commenting that the keen intelligence
of modern minds renders superfluous the recourse to a prologue that relates the plot. Along with his candid admission
that he is following the ancient Latin model of Plautus, Cecchi also asserts the "newness" of his work because he has
adapted a comedy from antiquity for the vernacular tongue
and represented in it modern customs. Just as Plautus and
Terence turned to the Greek New Comedy for inspiration,
Italian playwrights, according to Cecchi, must find their
sources in Latin authors. The Florentine dramatist defends
his right to borrow from writers of an earlier epoch by citing
Terence's observation that, since everything has already been
said, authors should be free to repeat the same material in a
newly refashioned guise. From acknowledged imitation of the
classics would appear the creation of new works in a modern

spirit.³ As Cecchi declares, the time will come for another
generation of dramatists to look to Tuscan playwrights for
models of excellence.

In what was to become a typical feature of this writer's
dramatic style, the opening words of the first scene in act 1
of *La Dote* seem to be the continuation of a conversation
initiated offstage. The elderly merchant Bindo functions as a
protatic character to advance the plot exposition as he reprimands his friend Manno for apparently greedy actions in ad-
ministering the estate of his young wards, Federigo and
Camilla. In the eyes of Florentine society, Manno took advantage of Federigo's lack of experience by convincing the youth
to sell his house to the guardian. The general community has
interpreted that sale as a betrayal of the trust that Filippo
Ravignani, Federigo's father, had placed in Manno on leaving
on a voyage to England that, according to widespread opinion,
ended in a fatal shipwreck. Bindo's accusatorial attitude reflects the Florentine insistence that wealth must be acquired
by honorable means. Manno easily demonstrates that appearances are deceiving; instead of exploiting Federigo's inclina-
tion toward profligacy, he bought the Ravignani home to
safeguard a treasure of three thousand ducats that Filippo had
buried there and whose existence was known to Manno
alone. After news of the shipwreck and Filippo's supposed
death reached Florence, Federigo began to squander his inheritance and would have sold the house to a stranger had
Manno not intervened to save the treasure and provide a
dowry for Camilla. Manno thus proves to Bindo his great
trustworthiness. While this initial scene of the play belongs
to the two old men, the second scene presents the youths
Federigo and Ippolito.

This symmetrical balancing of scenes with characters of
different age groups does not occur in the first act of Plautus's
play, where two scenes present old Megaronides and Callicles
who correspond, respectively, to Bindo and Manno. In the
1585 revision, in verse, Cecchi added an intermediate scene
to create variety, a dialogue between the maids Tessa and
Crezia, who also appear in the second act for the same purpose of setting off the weighty conversations of the main
characters. Neither the addition of the two dialogues between
the maids nor the introduction of Crezia as a wholly new

character succeeds in hastening the rhythm of the comedy's expositional sections. Those opening two scenes succeed best by themselves with the contrast in the interests of two generations.

As a model for a comedy's formal structure, Giraldi Cintio, in his *Discourse on the Composition of Comedies and Tragedies,* published about the same time as the first performance of *La Dote,* made these observations: the first act should deal with the argument; the second act should set in motion the issues presented at the play's start; complications would characterize the third act; by the fourth act a solution should come into sight that the final act would bring to a proper conclusion. Just as Giraldi drew his theories from studying ancient comedies, Cecchi took Plautus's material but rearranged it in a taut structure to achieve the maximum effect of complications and disturbances. Consequently, Cecchi advanced what corresponded to act 2, scene 4, of the *Trinummus* to act 3, scene 3, of *La Dote,* in which Federigo's double-dealing servant Moro betrays his master by dissuading Ippolito's father, Fazio, from accepting the Ravignani country villa as partial payment of Camilla's dowry. Whereas the third act of *Trinummus* ends with a promise of hope, Cecchi closes his third act in a mood of catastrophe where one impediment after another appears to block the wedding of Ippolito and Camilla. Not only will Fazio reject the villa, but Manno does not succeed in locating the treasure's burial place in contrast to the situation in Plautus's drama where Callicles knows the exact location of Charmides' hoard. Cecchi displays his perception of comedy as a dramatic structure built on plot entanglements that entrap young and old characters in an involved succession of events.

In the beginning of act 4, the Italian author further complicates his plot by resorting to *contaminatio,* interweaving a comic situation from Plautus's play *Mostellaria:* the motif of a haunted house. In the *Trinummus* the return of the trader Charmides from a business trip to Seleucia comes as no surprise, but the sudden reappearance from death of Filippo Ravignani, whose presence threatens to interfere with plans for Camilla's wedding, causes astonishment. To remove Filippo from the scene, Moro invents the ruse of telling the old man that his house is haunted by malevolent spirits and that Federigo is at the villa recovering from an illness brought on by the supernatural invasion of their home. Moro's ruse and Federigo's later complicity in the deception figure as a *beffa*, a trick or joke played on a victim, which is a recurring theme of Italian Renaissance literature. In literary works of an earlier period, like the *Decameron*, the *beffa* represents the triumph of a superior intelligence over an inferior mind. But in this situation the ruse will be of no avail since Filippo's concern over loss of his treasure prevents him from seeking out Federigo at the villa and impels him to return to the house with a locksmith. Already at this initial moment in Cecchi's career as a dramatist, the *beffa* results in frustration of intelligent effort rather than in victory. This attitude of the futility of inventiveness eventually predominated in the writer's works after he came under the influence of the Catholic Reformation.

Cecchi returns to his chief source in the *Trinummus* by using impersonation, one of the favorite situations in ancient Roman comedy. Just as Megaronides and Callicles hire a sycophant to pose as Charmides' messenger bearing letters of credit for his daughter's dowry, so, too, do Bindo and Manno arrange for a servant to arrive disguised in a Levantine costume with written assurances of the payment of Camilla's dowry from the treasure that Manno has at last uncovered. In both comedies the elder merchant's arrival at his home leads to a comic encounter between the impersonator and the enraged individual who is supposed to have written the letters. While the fourth act of the *Trinummus* ends with Callicles proving his good faith to Charmides, Cecchi sustains dramatic suspense until the last act when Filippo learns that Manno has not betrayed him and stolen the treasure for himself. A mood of comic reconciliation will reunite Filippo with his children; restore harmony in the households of Ravignani, Manno, and Fazio; and create a future society in the marriage of Camilla to Ippolito with the dowry appropriate to her status.

This play follows the preference of ancient Latin comedy for doubled characters, with the pair of older men Bindo and Manno opposed to the youths Federigo and Ippolito. In the 1545 prologue Cecchi anticipates possible objections that he might have erred in describing a friendship between two such

dissimilar individuals as the irresponsible Federigo and the
dutiful Ippolito. He explains how the two became friends
some time before Ravignani's disappearance and the period of
Federigo's dissipation. Above all, Ippolito's tolerant attitude
sustains the relationship despite the difference in personalities. In act 5, scene 2, Ippolito sadly comments that the
change in Federigo has strained their friendship. Ippolito also
declares that it is love for Camilla and not friendship with
Federigo that impels him toward an unprofitable marriage.
Lysiteles' failure in Plautus's comedy to distinguish between
love as an emotional attachment and love as an expensively
passionate distraction reflects a classical view of love as an
aberration from the norm. By contrast, Ippolito expresses the
Renaissance idea of love as the fulfilling moment in the relationship between a man and a woman.

Federigo displays none of the noble spirit that eventually
redeems the Roman *adulescens* Lesbonicus from his original
profligacy. The verb that occurs repeatedly to describe Federigo's behavior after news of Filippo's death is *"consumare,"* to
consume, as he has wasted his estate. With all his propensity
for squandering, Federigo remains a scheming individual always seeking expedients to futher his own purposes and perfectly willing to subject Camilla to the humiliation of being
married without a dowry. By contrast, Lesbonicus is determined to sacrifice his one remaining source of income, a
farm, rather than damage his sister's reputation and future
marital happiness. In *La Dote* Federigo follows a self-destruc-
tive course that would lead him to enlist as a mercenary
soldier were it not for Filippo's return, and to achieve his ends
he agrees to deceive Fazio about the villa's inflated value.
Federigo's most reprehensible act is his part in the *beffa* of
the haunted house because the victim is his father. Although
by the play's conclusion Federigo receives Filippo's forgiveness, the youth does not enter that new society formed by
Ippolito's marriage to Camilla. In the Latin comedy, Lesbonicus is to wed Callicles' daughter. The differing fortunes of the
youths in the ancient and Renaissance comedies result from
the moral attitude and conduct of the characters.

In presenting pairs of morally opposing characters, Cecchi
was employing a technique of ambivalence that, according to
Giraldi Cintio, constituted a "double drama" *(commedia dop-*

pia), in which individuals of equivalent social status (two old merchants, two middle-class young lovers, two servants) act as foils to set off each other's fundamentally different traits. The purpose of Plautus in doubling characters like Lesbonicus and Lysiteles was a pedagogical one to demonstrate the solid moral education that Lysiteles gained from his father Philto, who regarded proper conduct as a reward in itself. By exploring the contradictory aspects of the relationship between Federigo and Ippolito, the Italian writer wished to pose to his audience that dual choice confronting young men: dissoluteness and corrupt manipulation by Federigo; the decision by Ippolito to follow a love based on reason, esteem, and affection. The technique of ambivalence in Cecchi's double dramas succeeds in pointing out the rewards of moderation and loyalty as well as the dangers of profligacy and treachery.

Even if Cecchi did not aim at transcending the commonplace in characterizing Bindo as the moral conscience of the Tuscan bourgeoisie and Manno as the embodiment of trust, in the arch-miser Fazio, the dramatist created a compelling portrait of materialistic calculation to the exclusion of regard for family name and bonds of friendship. Although Fazio was once Ravignani's confidant, the merchant would not later agree to a liaison between Ippolito and apparently penniless Camilla. While Fazio functions as the classical *senex iratus*, the wrathful old man who becomes the *alazon*, or figure blocking the love of two young persons, Cecchi's character has no counterpart in the *Trinummus*, where Philto consents to his son's wedding without financial advantage and actually seems to welcome the connection with a family of noble background.[4] Fazio prizes wealth above fine birth, youthful beauty, and gentle manners as the criterion for selecting a daughter-in-law. This character's outstanding feature is the vehemence of language with which he resists in act 2, scene 4, his son's respectful entreaties, reducing every consideration to a crude ledger of debits and credits. Cecchi attempted in Fazio to penetrate the psychological obsessions of an individual preoccupied with venal interests. Fazio would judge Ippolito's wedding to Camilla as both a moral offense and a financial loss, failing to recognize in human relationships any possibility other than profit. In this miser Cecchi deliberately carried a flaw of the Florentine bourgeois temperament to its

most grotesque distortion. Fazio exemplifies a ridiculous pretentiousness with his mercantile mentality that almost has
vicious consequences for the young. In his effort to free himself from the shackles of human commitments, this character
makes himself the slave of monetary pursuits. Only the generous gesture by Filippo to grant a dowry rescues the drama
from Fazio's comic obsession.

   This play's most morally ambiguous character is the servant Moro. Usually in Renaissance comedies the clever servant schemes to overcome the obstacles to his young
master's amorous desires. Although Moro recalls Boccaccian
characters like Friar Cipolla *(Decameron* 6, 10) for his linguistic ability to talk himself out of compromising situations,
he uses his talents only for his advancement, at the cost of
damaging the interests of Federigo and Camilla.[5] As his nick-
name indicates, Moro is of Moorish origin, the slave Giam-
pagolo, whom Ravignani purchased sixteen years prior to the
time of the drama at the slave-market in Tunis. Moro's status
as a slave in Renaissance Florence raises the question of Cecchi's excessive imitation of ancient Roman comedy, in which
the servant subclass is always held in slavery. As will become
evident in later discussion of the play *La Stiava,* slavery did
exist in sixteenth-century Italy. Moro's cynicism derives from
awareness of his precarious existence as an article of property
that can be sold or put to death at the owner's will. This
servant's chief act of betrayal toward Federigo occurs when
he dissuades Fazio from accepting the villa by lying about the
decrepit conditions of the farm buildings and poor harvests.
Even though Moro's counterpart, Stasimus, in the *Trinummus* similarly endeavors to prevent loss of the family farm,
the Plautine slave acts primarily out of terror that he and his
young master will lose their last economic resource. While
realizing that his action may result in Camilla's being forced
into a convent, Moro caustically declares that he has perhaps
saved her soul for Heaven. With his wickedly inventive imagination Moro improvises the *beffa* of the haunted house and
thereby implicates Federigo in deceiving his father. This
slave's self-assertiveness renders him a character in his own
right and not merely an instrument of his youthful master or
the stock figure of the wily, devoted servant.

   Cecchi's predilection for creating doubled characters appears in the foil to Moro's selfishness: the faithful maid Tessa, who thinks only of protecting the Ravignani family. Occasionally, Tessa and Moro engage in verbal skirmishes, debating over the issues of devotion to service and loyalty to oneself alone. Tessa longs to see Camilla married to Ippolito, fearing that the penniless girl may fall prey to a social climber who will wed her without a dowry because of her family's connections. The play's 1544 prose version remains artistically superior to the poetic recasting as it presents Tessa alone (without the other maid, Crezia) as Moro's spiritual antagonist, highlighting her faithfulness and his disloyalty. It is Tessa who opens the door of the home to Filippo and reunites him with Camilla. Through her joyful description, the audience is enabled to behold the tender scene in which Filippo greets his children, scolds Federigo, and permits his anger to subside. This guileless maid, rather than the resourceful Moro, is the one who sets in motion the events that lead the drama to its happy conclusion.

Terence, more than Plautus, provided Cecchi with models for Filippo. Generally, the Plautine father restrains his son's passionate impulses by strictly controlling family finances, and Fazio's miserliness is just an exaggeration of that paternal tendency. But the Terentian father also shows himself to be a sensitive, reflective parent deeply concerned about his children's welfare. At the start of act 4 in *La Dote,* Ravignani's thoughts center on his beloved home rather than on his treasure. As a master of suspense, Cecchi so constructs events that it requires the entire time span of the fourth act for Filippo to overcome the obstacles of deceit and at last to enter his home. On first meeting Moro, the merchant immediately inquires about his children's well-being. This intense family affection leaves Filippo vulnerable to disappointment over his son's participation in the *beffa* of the enchanted house. In act 5, scene 1, Ippolito reprimands Federigo not so much for his extravagance but for trying to trick a man like Ravignani with all his admirable qualities of intelligence and discretion. The notion of the *beffa* required a moral judgment on a victim whose stupidity merited the punishment of the jest played on him.[6] Ravignani always showed good judgment, as in his choice of Manno, instead of Fazio, to guard his estate during his voyage to England. With commercial enterprises that involved loans to the royal court of Scotland, Ravignani was too worthy a figure to have deserved victimization with his son's complicity. All of Filippo's wounded pride explodes in the fifth scene of the last act when he reproaches Federigo for ingratitude, for disgraceful conduct, and, most of all, for allowing a vile servant to abuse a person of Ravignani's social stature. At the close of the *Trinummus*, Charmides quickly accepts Lesbonicus's perfunctory apology and promise to mend his ways. Because of his profound devotion to his family, the merchant will forgive Federigo for the anguish he has brought him and will even include Moro in the general amnesty for the household. Like Terence before him, Cecchi recalls a past time of love in the Ravignani home, describes present distress, and projects a hopeful future of restored harmony.[7]

In the verse rendering of *La Dote*, the restraining influence of the Catholic Reformation caused the author to examine the comedy with a self-inquisitorial scrupulousness to delete or to alter every morally and religiously objectionable passage. Although the 1585 version is a thorough revision, it is not an emendation comparable to Torquato Tasso's transformation of his epic poem *Jerusalem Delivered* to *Jerusalem Conquered* in conformity with reformist sentiment. Instead, Cecchi looked to refining language and eliminating passages satirizing clerical abuse. Consequently, some of the entertainingly vulgar interchanges between Moro and Tessa lose their vivacity and take on an inoffensive tone. In this version somewhat equivocal references to the Virgin and certain saints vanish altogether. Derogatory remarks about priests as lazy and covetous creatures are removed along with comments about the rapacity of monks. In all, the writer made every conceivable effort to bring his play into line with the chastened tastes of the Tridentine era, and, in so doing, he diminished that mischievously irreverent spirit that enlivened the original version.[8]

While Latin playwrights chose to situate their plays in cities of the Hellenistic world like Ephesus, Epidamnus, Thebes, Cyrene, and especially Athens (the setting of the *Trinummus*) instead of Rome, Cecchi selected his native Florence as the locale for this first drama. Throughout the comedy there abound references to local landmarks like the New Market and the convent of the Most Holy Annunciation. Among the buildings lining the onstage piazza are Ravignani's house and a church where some of the characters occasionally seek refuge. The constant opening of doors, the appearance of servants at windows, the spying behind columns all contribute to creating a sense of stage spaciousness. In act 3, scene 6, a scenic counterpoint develops between two separate groups of speakers, Tessa with Moro, and Fazio with Ippolito, moving toward a tense crescendo during which the miser attempts to draw Moro into his circle. Cecchi's feeling for exact, familiar place also carries his drama beyond the confines of the stage set and even beyond those of the city to the countryside in the horror story that Moro relates to Fazio about bad crops and poor labor conditions at the villa. Along with the contempt that the urban slave Moro expresses for ignorant peasants, one gains an insight into the tyranny that a proprietor like Federigo could exercise over rustic tenants. The scenic space of this drama is a bourgeois world whose economic interests extend into the Tuscan farmland and over to distant countries through international finance.

When *La Dote* appeared in its first performance by the company of San Bastiano de' Fanciulli in 1544, it proved to be a delightfully captivating comedy through the exuberant freshness of the Florentine dialogue and its feeling for local texture. Cecchi further enriched the repartee with colorful proverbial expressions that produce concretely rendered analogies. Fazio conveys his misogyny with this remark: "Women have as much abundance of injurious words as May abounds in leaves." After Manno has purchased the Ravignani house, Moro expresses his scorn: "Filippo left ducks to protect the lettuce." The trick of creating a false impression is stated in this way: "He showed him the moon's reflection in a well." When the jig is up for Moro, and he has to seize an opportunity, the slave remarks, "The ball has bounced on my roof." In spite of his foreign origin, Moro is a master of the Florentine dialect. In this play, use of proverbs does indicate quick wit and linguistic resourcefulness instead of intellectual vacuousness. Since one of the oldest comic devices is arousing laughter by introducing a character who speaks a language or dialect different from that of the main characters, the locksmith whom Filippo hires to open the haunted house speaks a peculiar language that resembles Venetian dialect. This employment of a non-Tuscan dialect serves to plunge the drama into a modern era of linguistic rivalry among the various Italian regions. The fact that in this play the non-Tuscan dialect is spoken by a person carrying out a menial task indicates the way Florentine society perceived certain roles. Certainly, the brief appearance of the frustrated locksmith muttering in his twisted Venetian dialect provides a moment of relief from the monotone of the Florentine vernacular.

In this first comedy, Cecchi cast ridicule at the practice of the dowry that discriminated against young women of limited economic means but admirable personal traits. The playwright probed the acquisitive psychology of the Florentine bourgeoisie and exposed in Fazio its venality. Not wishing to create a drama of underlying conflict between an unreasonable generation of parents and amorous, impetuous youths, the writer revealed the basic shortcomings of characters like Federigo. Doubtless, the character that becomes the hero of this initial comedy is Filippo Ravignani, who personifies the wisdom, affection, and discretion of Florentine society at its strongest. Rather than being a defender of a social status quo, Cecchi upheld in the loving father and brave entrepreneur an ideal of personal integrity that overcomes greed and prodigality.

An Italian Comedy of Errors: La Moglie

A carnivalesque mood of amusement caused by confusion over mistaken identities pervades Cecchi's second comedy, *La Moglie.* In the prologue to the original prose version, the author expressly refers to the performance of his comedies for the carnival season. The same company of San Bastiano de' Fanciulli also produced this Italian rendering of a comedy of errors arising from the appearance in Florence of twin brothers separated from each other since childhood. Even the time span of this drama takes place during the carnival season when foreign visitors to the Tuscan capital find themselves swept into the public madness of masquerades and practical jokes. The victims of this play's farcical situations blame their poor fortune on the "carnival tricks" *(burle carnascia-*

lesche) devised by the mocking Florentines. An astounding succession of events characterizes a festive sense of life as the routines of bourgeois commercial activity give way to the frivolity of carnival time.

Plautus's *Menaechmi* inspired both Cecchi in *La Moglie* and William Shakespeare in *The Comedy of Errors,* 1592, to write highly farcical dramas about the bewilderment created by identical twins. While Cecchi follows Plautus by introducing only one set of twins, Shakespeare compounds already confusing situations by adding twin servants for the twin masters. Puzzlement over double identity and ignorance of true parentage predominate in the Italian comedy. Plautine intrigue as well as Terentian lyrical sentiment contribute to the complexity of *La Moglie,* since Cecchi practices *contaminatio* by combining the story of identical twins with Terence's drama of clandestine love, the *Andria.* By drawing on several sources of inspiration from antiquity, the Italian dramatist interwove multiple levels of vision to create an ambivalent drama of confused identity and troubled marital commitment whereby he could represent the clash between reality and appearance as well as the collision between the world of commerce and the world of romance. The presence of identical twins overturns the conventional reality of the Florentine middle class, and restoration of social order will come about only after the goals of the mercantile group coincide with those of the romantic young characters.

In the expository first act, the Florentine youth Ridolfo explains to his servant Fuligno how during a trading expedition to Ragusa he fell in love with and married a beautiful and modest slave-girl named Spinola, who claimed to be the daughter of a Sienese merchant, Silvano de' Silvani. Her father had wed the sister of the Genoese tradesman Alberto Spinola in Alexandria, Egypt, where there was a flourishing community of Italian merchants. After the birth of twin sons and a daughter, Silvano set sail on a journey to Marseilles and disappeared in a shipwreck near Corsica. Upon his sister's death, Alberto Spinola decided to return to Italy with the three children, but, on their way home, Turkish galleons seized their ship and caused the family's separation. Spinola and one of her brothers, Alfonso, were taken as slaves to Ragusa where later the Italian merchant Ruberto Amidei pur-

chased Alfonso and trained the boy as a managerial appren-
tice. Eventually, Alfonso married Amidei's daughter
Margherita and took charge of the family's business in Florence. For the background of his drama, Cecchi wove a highly
novellistic adventure tale of vicissitudes and separations that
eventually find their resolution in the hectic events of a single day in Florence.

Evidently Cecchi once again delighted in satirizing the Tuscan custom of arranging marriages solely for reasons of financial gain and political alliance. In *La Moglie*, young Ridolfo is
afraid to admit to his socially ambitious father, Cambio, that
he has wed a penniless slave-girl of dubious parentage. Consequently, Ridolfo, on realizing that Spinola must be the sister of his friend and neighbor Alfonso, enlists that youth's aid
to bring the girl to Florence on the pretext of her fulfilling a
vow to enter a convent. Alfonso tells his wife that Spinola is
the daughter of a prominent Ragusan businessman and that
it is to their economic benefit to receive the girl temporarily
as a guest in their home. The author stresses how most of his
characters act out of primarily commercial motives and remain insensitive to the romantic aspirations of individuals
like Ridolfo and Spinola. When Cambio grows suspicious
about his son's frequent visits to Alfonso's house, the old
man plans to discourage a liaison with the Ragusan girl by
arranging for Ridolfo to wed the daughter of the successful
entrepreneur Pandolfo Agolanti. Even after Agolanti with-
draws from the marriage agreement because of doubts about
Ridolfo's relationship with Spinola, Cambio continues to exert pressure on his son to consent to the wedding with the
purpose of determining the young man's true sentiments. It
is to his resourceful servant Fuligno that the troubled Ridolfo
turns to find a solution to his predicament.

Understanding Cambio's devious mentality, Fuligno sees
through the scheme and advises Ridolfo to call his father's
bluff by agreeing to sign the marriage contract. Though astonished by his son's sudden eagerness to cooperate, Cambio
hastens to Pandolfo and persuades him to reconsider the
match. Just as Ridolfo is becoming hopelessly entangled in
the net of his own deceptions, the drama shifts attention
away from the Terentian comedy of endangered love to the
Plautine farce of confused identities when Alfonso's brother

and exact double, Ricciardo, arrives in Florence. For some years this twin and his uncle have been living in Siena, and out of respect for his supposedly dead brother the young man has assumed the name of Alfonso. Again and again, most of the Florentine characters take the increasingly perplexed Ricciardo for Alfonso until at last Madonna Margherita concludes that her husband must have lost his sanity. On two occasions, Margherita's servants drag first one and then the other twin into the Amidei home. All the chaos resulting from the remarkable resemblance between the twins thwarts Fuligno from executing a stratagem by enlisting the servant Nibbio to pose as Alberto Spinola newly come to Florence to provide his niece with a dowry that would remove Cambio's objections to his son's marriage to the former slave-girl. As a final desperate effort to dissuade Pandolfo from accepting Ridolfo as a suitable son-in-law, Fuligno contrives to have a public messenger proclaim that Ridolfo is indeed married to Spinola and that any other wedding would seriously violate ecclesiastical laws.

All complications and conflicts vanish at once after the actual Alberto Spinola arrives in town and encounters his long-lost nephew, Alfonso. With the revelation of identity, social harmony is restored. The comedy's festive spirit of reconciliation includes not only the uncle's reunion with his wards but also the surprising discovery that Pandolfo Agolanti is none other than Silvano de' Silvani, who fled his native Florence over twenty years before for slaying a Bolognese. Surviving the shipwreck, he returned to Florence under a false name, entered trade, and remarried. As all masks of feigned or mistaken identity fall, an atmosphere of concord reigns in which Silvano's daughter by his second marriage participates, since she will be wed to her ardent suitor Alessandro Rustichelli. Events have brought to Cambio everything that he wanted for his son: marital alliance with the household of a prosperous merchant. In typical Cecchian style of ambivalence, this play looks both to the past and to the future as it celebrates the renewal of earlier family bonds and the coming promise of two weddings.[9]

Since *La Moglie* exhibits a fundamental dualism in its structure, the author seeks to introduce disorder into the drama's playworld without permitting it to be torn asunder into

irreconcilable halves. The dramatist realizes that stage time
must flow at different speeds so that the deliberately confusing intricacy of various plot devices contribute to developing
the play's themes rather than to distorting them. Cecchi
frames the three tumultuous central acts with a slow-paced
opening act and the concluding act with its traditional *agni-
zione*, or recognition scene. The strategic positioning of
scenes especially serves the function of advancing major
themes of personal identity, family bonds, and romantic attachment. Already by act 2, scene 2, the whirlwind stirred by
the twins has started to disrupt the patterned behavior of
bourgeois life. At the play's center, in the third scene of act 3,
the perspective shifts to the discouraged viewpoint of Fuligno, who sees all his efforts to aid Ridolfo in total disarray.
Because Cecchi builds his comedy on dramatic contrasts, he
has Fuligno shake off despair and attack catastrophe with the
intrigue of Nibbio's impersonation as Alberto Spinola. The
servant's rational design to rescue the romantic situation
fully collapses by act 4, scene 9, with the frustrating encounter between the faltering impostor and the uncomprehending
Ricciardo. Although certain minor discrepancies of comic
movement are to be attributed to Cecchi's imitating the *Andria*, Terence's first play and the weakest in construction, the
Italian writer endeavors to fashion a comedy in basic blocks
of scenes that give scope to the interplay of personalities, the
conflict of social values, and the duality of romance and commerce. The play's flawed design becomes evident in its purely
mechanical reliance on the expedient of a discovering agent,
Alberto Spinola, with his eleventh-hour arrival in Florence.
Through the recognition scene, however, underlying contin-
uities of parentage and relationship are immediately dis-
cerned. With the recognizing of long-existing natural ties, the
disparate elements of the drama enter into formal unity.

In the playworld of Cecchi's drama Florence appears to be
a place of challenge, petty harassment, and frustration for
strangers. By contrast, Plautus in the *Menaechmi* depicts the
city of Epidamnus as presenting no greater perils than ridiculous prices and the swindling propositions of parasites and
courtesans. The dangers awaiting travelers in the setting for
La Moglie never arouse the sense of marvel and fascination

that distinguishes the exotic city of Ephesus in *The Comedy of Errors*. For although Ricciardo justifiably feels assailed at every doorway around the piazza where the Italian comedy unfolds, since an increasing number of persons mistake him for Alfonso, he never has to face a sentence of death as occurs at the opening of Shakespeare's play for the twins' father, Egeon. Cecchi prefers to hold harassment to a minor degree, following the example of Ariosto's comedies by directing satire against abusive petty officials like the customs agents who confiscate Ricciardo's personal silverware as criminally undeclared articles of import. In his exasperation Ricciardo protests that someone in authority ought to instruct strangers on the correct procedures for entering Florence, but the only lessons he receives are expensive ones in the fines levied against him. Cecchi allows his audience to glimpse at a great remove the ultimate source of authority and justice for the Tuscans in the person of Duke Cosimo, but, because of the oppressive Florentine administration, the author would never include the ruler as a dramatic character, in contrast to Shakespeare, who even in the farcical *Comedy of Errors* introduces in the cast a duke to act as enforcer of institutional justice. Instead, Cecchi obliquely refers to Duke Cosimo's hunting expeditions in the Tuscan woods and mentions that some of the courtiers lodged at Cambio's villa. To rectify abuses of power by minor officials, there existed, according to the playwright's assurances to the members of his audience, a supreme agent of legal order embodied by Cosimo de' Medici.

Traditionally, Florentine writers portrayed the Sienese as dolts lacking the urban sophistication of their rivals in the metropolis on the Arno. In Florentine popular speech, the term *Sanese* (Sienese) equated *sciocco* (stupid), *bestia* (beast), or *matto* (mad). As soon as Ricciardo identifies himself as Sienese, the Florentine characters assume he is insane. Ricciardo therefore finds himself the unwitting victim of a centuries-old city-state rivalry in Tuscany, a competition not to be settled until Cosimo's conquest of Siena in 1559. With an ironic sense of justice, Cecchi, the arch-Florentine patriot, employs the comedy's recognition scene to redeem Ricciardo, Alfonso, and Spinola when they learn that they are actually the children of a Florentine native. In the game of appearance and reality, the formerly orphaned trio not only regain their father but also acquire the saving grace of a proud civic identity.

Cecchi represents the hierarchical structure of daily life in Florence by introducing characters from a variety of classes. A moving chronicle of urban life crosses the stage space. Servants run off to drink at the Three Corners' Tavern. A neighborhood baker assists in the attempt to lock up Margherita's apparently insane husband. Cecchi's comic artistry passes across different planes, from the worlds of romance and commerce to the workaday spheres of action for minor characters in the artisan and professional classes. Cambio's retainer and confidant, Valenzo, typifies economic dependence on membership in the guild system, obtained only through his patron's influence. Registration in the tapestry weavers' guild makes possible for Valenzo various commissions to decorate the homes of wealthy merchants for weddings and banquets. As with the company of tradesmen in *A Midsummer Night's Dream*, the many servants in this comedy, with picturesque names like Mosca (fly), Nibbio (kite), and Noce (walnut), contribute to a burlesque sense of farcicality as they become caught in the disorder caused by the exact likeness between the twins.[10]

Whatever their social class, few of the characters in this drama feel that they have any control over the circumstances of their lives. Although a perpetual failure like his ingeniously inept counterpart Davus in Terence's *Andria*, Fuligno never permits defeat to crush his spirit and readily accepts responsibility for his reverses. His master, Ridolfo, appears as the conventional lover in prey to the captivating charm of Spinola's beauty while remaining in fear of his father's anger. Indeed, old Cambio reveals a meanness of spirit as he tries to thwart his son's liaison with the slave-girl in order to favor a profitable match with Pandolfo's daughter. In the character of Pandolfo Agolanti, the author studies the difference between mask and reality, for, in Cecchi's ambivalent perspective, that model citizen and entrepreneur Agolanti turns out to be the ultimate outsider with a criminal past. Representing the Florentine professional class in this play is the physician who comes to treat Alfonso's supposed madness. Even though Cecchi had a model for his pedantic physician in the *Men-*

aechmi, this Latin-spouting character who sounds like a priest displays the pretentiousness of an entire group of Florentines who went around town vaunting their university education in medicine or law. Boccaccio, in the *Decameron* 8, 9, derides the vanity of the judges, lawyers, notaries, and physicans with their advanced degrees from Bologna. Through a wide range of characters like servants, tradesmen, members of professional groups, shopkeepers, and international entrepreneurs, Medicean Florence emerges as an active force in this drama.

Ironically, *La Moglie* is inspired throughout by misogynistic sentiments. Although Ridolfo is already married at the drama's start, his need to conceal the conjugal relationship from Cambio has prevented him from experiencing the disillusionment that characterizes Alfonso's married life, in which all romance has died. Alfonso's marriage conformed exactly to the conventions of commercial alliances in Florence, here for the purpose of securing the young man's continuing service as manager of the Amidei business. Knowing and dreading his wife's greed, Alfonso can never summon the moral strength to make the generous gesture that would free Ridolfo from the necessity of subterfuge: publicly acknowledging Spinola as his sister by granting her a substantial dowry. In the tedious bourgeois situation of Alfonso's marriage, the youth makes a definition of wives that is part of Italian folklore, equating the word *donna* (woman) with *danno* (harm) and *ruina* (ruin). These equations bring to mind the title of the seventeenth-century Milanese comedy *Chi Ha Donna Ha Danno* (he who has a wife has trouble) by Tommaso Santagostino.

It is obvious in this play that the tensions between Alfonso and his wife began long before the confusing arrival in town of his twin brother. When Margherita asks her uncle to reason with the seemingly deranged Alfonso, the old man expresses sympathy for the husband, whom he perceives as being constantly harassed by nagging. Even the family maid blames Margherita for pushing Alfonso over the brink into insanity with her unending criticism and jealous recriminations; the only thought in Margherita's mind other than financial utility is jealousy that explodes in domestic fury after Spinola comes as a guest to their household. Cecchi never develops

the marital tension beween Alfonso and Margherita to the
point of total separation reached in the *Menaechmi,* where,
at the play's end, Menaechmus of Epidamnus prepares to
abandon his wife like an unwanted piece of old property in
preference to rejoining his twin in Syracuse. For Plautus, fra-
ternal bonds were more enduring than matrimonial vows.
Cecchi instead left Alfonso in the situation of having to restore peace with his wife even though the underlying causes
for discontent have not been fully explored and admitted. In
a play that deals with the desire of men to take wives, Cecchi's misogyny might seem pessimistically incongruous except that his comedy celebrates the rejoining of a family; and
marriage, with all its shortcomings, is indispensable to the
creation of the family.[11]

A certain accumulative structure distinguishes *La Moglie*
as error over confused identity continues to spread across the
play. In scene after scene, the number of persons who mistake
Ricciardo for Alfonso grows greater and greater until the stage
becomes a site of complete anarchy. At the start in act 2,
scene 4, Ricciardo has to contend only with Ridolfo, who
turns to him for assistance to forestall the wedding with Agolanti's daughter. Despite their mutual lack of comprehension,
the two youths end their puzzling encounter with gentlemanly civility. Then, in act 3, scene 4, Ricciardo's patience is
tried still further by baffling confrontations with Margherita's
maid and Fuligno as they attempt to remind him of family
relationships that the Sienese visitor of course cannot recognize: the marriage to the Amidei woman, the bond to Ridolfo
through Spinola's marriage. Cecchi demonstrates in these
scenes of bewilderment how physical likeness implies relationship and responsibility. Coming to Florence places the
unsuspecting Ricciardo in a whole series of connections with
strange individuals who make demands on him. Confusion
intensifies because he also goes by the name *Alfonso.* It is in
the illogical nature of farce that Ricciardo never realizes others might be addressing him as his twin. Curiously, Cecchi
does not choose to lead Ricciardo to a mirror confrontation
with his twin, unlike other versions taken from the *Menaechmi* plot. Instead, the two brothers suffer in isolation from
each other, and their reunion will occur offstage after the
play's conclusion.

Cecchi's carnival comedy *La Moglie* provides relief from the rigid order of life in Florence under ducal administration. The comic dislocations of speeches set in a mistaken context, the misunderstandings brought about by physical likeness, and the duality of structure between the commercial and romantic spheres all accomplish the author's goal of demonstrating the fragility of human relationships. Although the Italian dramatist does not seek the copiousness of effect to be achieved later by Shakespeare with his matched pairs of twins, the use of *contaminatio* between Plautine intrigue and Terentian sentiment has permitted Cecchi to investigate domestic discord, the need to re-create a social identity, and the contradictions between family and matrimony. By mingling a variety of verbal styles and character-types, the Florentine playwright depicts life as a comedy of continual surprises and unending errors.

The War between Generations: La Stiava

The play *La Stiava* belongs to a comic tradition that represents the conflict between two contending generations, the old and the young, to triumph in love. Cecchi's comedy closely resembles in plot and in characterization the play *Il Vecchio Amoroso*, written between 1533 and 1536 by the senior Florentine statesman Donato Giannotti, since both works derive from the *Mercator* of Plautus. The Italian versions follow the ancient comedy in presenting the struggle between an elderly merchant and his son for mastery over a slave-girl whom the son purchased on a commercial voyage. Each of the Florentine dramatizations differs from the Latin model through use of a recognition scene in which the slave-girl is discovered to be the long-lost daughter of a close friend of the father's. The young woman will be reintegrated into society with the payment of a dowry to make legitimate her marriage to the merchant's son. In his prologue, Cecchi abandons exposition in order to announce the two themes of this play: the tribulations that Love inflicts on its followers, and the need to have a faithful friend. For both competing generations of old and young, love will prove a source of anguish while friendship provides sound advice and physical assistance.

As the drama concentrates on the disputed slave-girl of the title, it therein displays unity of action in spite of all the entanglements into which the various contending parties involve themselves. Cecchi's desire to reconcile classical imitation with an attempt at contemporary realism results in the play's being set in Genoa, and not ancient Athens, on a street between the homes of the merchants Filippo and Nastagio. The life of that Italian port with its harbor appears prominently in the action of *La Stiava,* for the characters are constantly running down to the ships that bring the merchandise on which their livelihood depends. While deriving his plot from an ancient play and accepting the conventions and the rules of classical theater, Cecchi sought here to fashion a drama that would reflect the values and customs of his own society. Did the author commit an anachronism by centering his plot on a slave-girl in a social setting in which slavery was not a recognized institution? For Plautus's *Mercator,* there was no problem of an anachronism, since slavery was a widespread practice in the Graeco-Roman world. Cecchi admits his boldness, commenting in the prologue, "Nor should the name of Slave-girl cause fright." Although the situation of the slave-girl in Cecchi's play could be explained as an expression of the author's devotion to the Plautine comic heritage, his efforts to orient the slave-girl's background to the historical circumstances of his own times demonstrate the writer's artistry in fusing classical antecedents with a portrayal of the scene in sixteenth-century Italy. Slavery was indeed an institution in Renaissance Italy. Most of the slaves in Italian cities were females of Tartar blood who were purchased by Italian merchants sailing to Black Sea ports. Prior to the stage action in *La Stiava,* the young merchant Alfonso bought Adelfia at the slave-market in Constantinople. The fact that the slave-girl is not of Tartar extraction but is Italian-born has enormous importance for the outcome of the play. Genoa was one of the ports through which foreign slaves entered Italy just like the harbor town of Pisa, the scene for Giannotti's comedy. Even though the general enthusiasm to see classical comedy revived on the Italian stage would have made the anachronism of a slave-girl acceptable to the audience at the play's first performance by the San Bastiano de' Fanciulli group in 1546, the author aimed at historical plausibility.[12]

Through their titles, the three similar dramas by Plautus, Giannotti, and Cecchi indicate the social focus desired by the respective playwrights. In the *Mercator* a tug-of-war takes place between the merchant Demipho and his son Charinus, from which the youth emerges victorious. Giannotti attempts in *Il Vecchio Amoroso* to stress how, because of erotic frenzy, an elderly man loses his dignity and appears a totally ridiculous figure. Cecchi's title shifts emphasis away from the pretentious blocking figure of the angry old man to the pathetic slave-girl heroine.[13] Unlike both the *Mercator* and *Il Vecchio Amoroso*, the slave-girl never makes a stage appearance in *La Stiava*, not even after her identity has been established; for Adelfia is not so much a person in her own right as an object of conflict for possession. As a slave-girl, Adelfia figures at the center of the drama, an object of disputed ownership. When the son refers to the slave-girl as his possession ("my merchandise and my property," act 2, scene 2) that he can sell to a young acquaintance of his, Filippo asserts his paternal authority and invokes a biblical tradition wherein the goods of the son are those of the father. Throughout the play Adelfia is no more than a creature, designated by the term "fanciulla" (girl),[14] whom others manipulate. Only with the discovery of the girl's true identity comes the transformation of her status from that of a slave outside of regular society to membership in the Genoese bourgeoisie as Nastagio's daughter and Ippolito's sister. Cecchi has adapted the ancient model of Plautus's comedy to the mercantile value system of Renaissance Italy.

Love, much more than a contest of authority, unlike the situation in Giannotti's play, is the inspiring force of this drama of the slave-girl. Toward the center of the play, old Nastagio comments (act 3, scene 5) on the power of Love to transform a miser like Filippo into an extravagant suitor. What Cecchi has done is infuse the classical plot material from Plautus's play with a Boccaccian love atmosphere. Although no particular earlier novella could be cited as an antecedent for *La Stiava*, its spirit is modern as it follows Boccaccian models like *Decameron* 2, 10, on the vanity of an elderly judge who loses his young wife to a virile pirate. Similarly, in *La Stiava*, old Filippo has to surrender Adelfia to his son, who had previously married the girl. To bring about that

socially correct surrender and to establish Adelfia's identity,
the Italian author resorts to the classical dramatic device of
the recognition scene. Whereas in ancient comedies the long-
lost daughter is usually a victim of abandonment by parents
who at first did not want a girl to inherit their estate, infant
exposure was not a practice in Renaissance Italy; dramatists
like Cecchi would relate the recognition to circumstances of
warfare or piracy. In *La Stiava*, Adelfia's identity is determined by the objects in a box she carries with her, containing
a chain, a pendant, and a notation of the date Turkish pirates
seized her in the sea near the island of Ischia. The recognition
makes possible the change in status for Adelfia from a slave
with no rights to a daughter-in-law whom Filippo must
respect.

This Florentine comedy appears as a markedly original
drama rather than as a pallid reworking of the *Mercator*. In
minor details of characterization, as with Nastagio's maid,
Nuta, and Filippo's servant, Gorgolio, the Italian writer succeeds in enriching the comic material of the Plautine model.
Nuta is a compassionate friend of the young characters and
an outspoken advocate of the equal right of wives to take
lovers just as their husbands do. While Gorgolio's name
recalls that of the Plautine character Curculio, his well-
intentioned ineptitude resembles that of the servants in
Ariosto's comedies who complicate already entangled plots.
Although Cecchi deliberately avoids writing comically long
and suspenseful soliloquies for Gorgolio, in contrast to the
lengthy speeches of his counterpart in the *Mercator*, he has
the servant disrupt the action in the final act by abducting
Adelfia as the girl is being transferred from Nastagio's home
to the establishment of the procuress Apollonia. The girl's
unexplained disappearance provides Filippo with his last
vindictive gesture to separate his son from Adelfia. But Gorgolio ends the complication he has caused by revealing that
the girl is on board a ship in the harbor. As is typical in
Cecchi's dramas, Gorgolio's attempt to be a dynamic character has merely boomeranged and temporarily halted the play's
action. Another character who contributes in creating a sense
of milieu is Nastagio's farm steward, Meino, a rural adminis-
trator who is zealously devoted to land and to animals but
out of his element in the city.[15] All of these figures from the

servant class are foils to Adelfia because their servile status does not deprive them of the political freedom that is denied to the slave-girl. Nuta in her household affairs, Gorgolio on the open street with his ill-fated schemes, and Meino coming from the countryside enjoy a liberty of action that the title character will not know until she is recognized as a member of the middle class.

Of the entire cast in *La Stiava,* old Filippo shows the most outstanding characterization, not as the love-crazed Demipho of the *Mercator* nor the domestic tyrant Teodoro in *Il Vecchio Amoroso* but as a crafty merchant who briefly falls prey to desire to recapture the erotic joys of his vanished youth. From the moment that the seventy-year-old merchant first sees Adelfia on board the ship, Filippo abandons the dignity of his age to become a grotesque figure who calls himself a boy ready to have a love affair. Falling prey to an uncontrollable passion, the old man feels compelled to snatch the girl from his son. This obsession prevents him from admitting that he does not have the strength to initiate or to sustain intimacy with Adelfia. Cecchi describes Filippo's transport in terms of the senses of vision and touch wildly aroused by immediate contact with Adelfia. Filippo's frenetic engrossment is reminiscent of the passionate preoccupation of the father-figure Nicomaco in Machiavelli's comedy *Clizia,* 1525, with a similar desperate attempt to experience the final complete gratification of erotic longings. Even in the most intense stages of his fascination, Filippo still behaves as a calculating merchant, regarding the girl as an article of merchandise that should be handled to appreciate its value. Adelfia is a victim subjected to Filippo's will. For, although the father lacks the sexual prowess of the son, Filippo's greater experience and his social might as a father and as a leading figure of the Genoese middle class put him at an advantage over Alfonso.

Cecchi depicts in Filippo's preoccupation a domestic crisis that threatens to destroy the happiness of the old and young generations. The senior merchant has come to define old age in terms of his wife's wrinkled and jaundiced face because her appearance offers a mirror to his own deterioration. Adelfia's refreshingly lovely face with all the bright hues of youth awakens Filippo's dormant sensuality and stirs him to a fever pitch of emotions until he is prepared to destroy the harmony of his household. Given the vehemence of his feelings, this mentally alert merchant does not hesitate to manipulate and to betray whatever filial trust is left in the somewhat naive Alfonso. Filippo also plays on Nuta's suspicions, letting her believe that Nastagio has brought Adelfia into his house for his own sexual pleasure rather than to accommodate his long-time friend. No sentiment, whether of family or of friendship, remains inviolate before the passion that dominates the elderly merchant. Cecchi adds a dimension to Filippo's character not present in any of the other similar treatments of senile erotic frenzy: hypocrisy. This man would prefer to maintain a surface appearance of respectability while satisfying his unseemly desires. In the midst of scenes in which he treats other persons as objects of his own utility, Filippo hypocritically remembers that he has to go to mass. This merchant is a portrait of calculation, accompanied by an all-ruling yearning for sensual possession, always continuing to assume a mask of social propriety.

As Filippo's confidant, Nastagio provides a rational counterbalance to his friend's senile obsession. With the wisdom of his years, Nastagio understands the irrationality of Filippo's feelings and actions. In an effort to introduce clarity to his friend's darkened thoughts, Nastagio resolutely reminds him again and again of his advanced age and the decline in vigor that must accompany the passing of time. Like many of Molière's characters, Filippo is resorting to rationalizations in the midst of his irrationality. Since he considers friendship to be an obligation, Nastagio will yield to Filippo's entreaties for him to receive Adelfia into his home and to arrange a banquet for the merchant and the slave-girl. That generous act produces a situation of embarrassment and compromise for Nastagio in the central scenes of the play's third act after his wife, Giovanna, unexpectedly returning from their villa, discovers the slave-girl, and confronts the understandably confused cooks who come to prepare Filippo's banquet. Nastagio's loyalty to his friend has merely brought him domestic discord. By placing the scene of Giovanna's return at the middle of the play, in contrast to Gianotti's version, in which the friend's wife comes back in the fifth act, Cecchi wishes to stress the centrality of the consequences that Nastagio suffers for letting friendship prevail over his own wise advice. In his dialogues with Filippo, this character always shows himself to be in command through his discretion and cool rationality. However, beginning in the scene where he is forced to explain his actions to the not-so-easily-convinced Giovanna, Nastagio's sense of detachment collapses. Like his counterpart Lysimachus in the *Mercator,* he suffers greater censure than does Filippo. As Cecchi demonstrates, when a supremely rational person commits himself to supporting the follies of a friend, he must bear the full responsibility of his acts without the mitigating excuse of following a mad passion.

Alfonso and Ippolito function as agents of comic reversal against the conspiracy of the two old men. Just as Filippo relies heavily on the all-suffering Nastagio, in parallel fashion, Alfonso tests his friend's patience. Beginning in Alfonso's soliloquy of act 1, scene 1, it is obvious that passion and blind jealousy dominate this youth. Between the erotic attachments of Alfonso and his father to the slave-girl there lies a basic difference. Even though Alfonso originally knew Adelfia as a slave in Constantinople and regarded her as his own precious commodity, he still granted her the dignity of marrying her. Affection redeemed an initially sensual attraction, and a long period of living together as legitimate spouses sanctions their passionate relationship, in contrast to the immediate sexual violence that dispossesses Filippo from the first time he beholds the girl. Adelfia's existence serves initially as a barrier between father and son and then later as a bond between all generations. Without knowing it, Alfonso has been in in love with the sister of his lifelong friend Ippolito and the daughter of his father's closest confidant, Nastagio.

By tradition, children like Alfonso and Ippolito should obey their parents, carrying out whatever duty requires of them. But in order for society to survive, children must rebel against their parents' will and marry the object of their affection. With Ippolito's assistance, Alfonso attempts to circumvent his father's schemes to claim possession of Adelfia while avoiding a direct confrontation with Filippo. After the father adroitly turns down Alfonso's false offer of the slave-girl as a servant in their home, the youth tries to remedy the situation by stating that he has a buyer (Ippolito) for Adelfia. Filippo counters that simulated exchange with the announcement that he has a close friend and therefore more authoritative buyer (Nastagio) for the girl. In the struggle between father and son, Ippolito displays the same degree of faith and devotion that Nastagio shows to Filippo. At times Ippolito actually echoes his father's very words of counsel. Similarity in attitude and situation between Ippolito and Nastagio also appears in the way failure to secure the slave-girl for the friend results in recriminations. In act 4, scene 2, after Alfonso learns that some older man has taken Adelfia away from their ship, Ippolito has to endure the verbal abuse that his disappointed friend hurls at him. Whatever defense that Ippolito offers is taken up by Alfonso in a tour de force of accusations and remonstrances.[16] Since friendship makes forgiveness possible, however, Ippolito will accept Alfonso's apology for the madness that caused him to rail at his ally. Finally, as brothers-in-law, the two friends have gained a kinship tie to hold together their relationship within the structures of family and society.

With the recognition of Adelfia's true identity, the lovers cease to be victims of circumstances as a new society emerges from the integration of the young with the old. A reality principle triumphs as Filippo reluctantly renounces the illusion of youthful vigor so as to inaugurate the new social order. As in other comedies, Cecchi has chosen to represent the family as a milieu threatened by strife but capable of reconciliation before compelling events like the agnition. Through the parallel interrelations of characters, on the levels of either servants and masters or young and old, this drama proceeds to a final condition of social stability. To illustrate this mood of renewed harmony, Cecchi breaks with classical tradition by having Filippo, instead of one of the servants, deliver the play's farewell *licenza*. In the spirit of comic appeasement, the dramatist permits the defeated father to enjoy the last words that bring to a close this play of youthful ardor, friendship, and ridiculous passion.

Rival Brothers: I Dissimili

Along with adding to the merriment of holiday seasons and festive occasions, dramatic productions by Florentine *brigate* and confraternities often had a moral purpose to provide the young with an edifying spectacle that would instruct them to avoid the attractive appearance of vice and instead to follow virtue. A concern for virtuous conduct in family life had characterized many of the sacred dramas written and produced in Florence during the fifteenth century. In his comedy *I Dissimili,* first presented by the Company of San Bastiano de' Fanciulli for the carnival of 1548, Cecchi continued this moralizing tradition but placed it in an altogether secular context by deriving his plot from the most didactic of Terence's works, the *Adelphoe,* a play about conflicting systems of education. It is evident from the title of his play that Cecchi hoped to represent the clash between individuals of greatly dissimilar characters competing with each other in the rearing of children. Following Terence, the Florentine playwright explored what should be the relation between fathers and sons: whether one of unquestioning obedience by the young or one of affectionate companionship and gentle guidance. The collision of values between a strict and a lenient education motivates Cecchi's drama in its study of the middle-class Florentine household.

In the prologue to this prose play, Cecchi freely acknowledges his debt to Terence for the portrait of two dissimilar brothers. The dramatist states that he has intended this play for fathers and young men of marriageable age, since the work's central concern with its stress on the correct method of education would interest both of them. Understanding the psychology of his public, Cecchi suggests that his play will convince fathers to choose a golden mean between strictness and leniency. His play will give food for thought to the older generation while entertaining the young, who will profit from a middle course between rigid discipline and pampering. By showing the comically ridiculous effects of two extreme systems of education, this play will point to an ideal way of treating the young with sympathy and firmness in order to safeguard the tranquility and prosperity of the Tuscan family.

Set in Florence during the era of Duke Cosimo, this comedy contrasts two brothers of advanced age, Filippo and Simone. Years before, their father left each one the means to lead an independent existence. While Filippo chose to frequent sophisticated courtly circles like those found in the Vatican un-

der the Medici Pope Leo X and in France under Francis I,
Simone preferred to retire as a farmer to his villa in the most
Spartan of circumstances. Returning to his home city in 1538,
Filippo obtained guardianship of one of Simone's two sons.
Though remaining single all his life, Filippo attempted to be
a model father by adopting a highly permissive and generous
attitude toward his charge, Alessandro, whereas Simone
reared his other son, Federigo, with the greatest severity. At
the play's beginning, it appears that Filippo's nonchalance has
contributed to Alessandro's delinquency, since the youth has
just tried to knock down a neighbor's door and carry away a
girl named Fiammetta. Subsequent events reveal, however,
that both Alessandro and his brother are equally involved in
the unsuccessful break-in inasmuch as it was Federigo who
was in love with Fiammetta and Alessandro who was merely
taking the initiative to secure the girl for him. In fact, Alessandro is secretly married to Ginevra, the daughter of the
impoverished widow Madonna Gostanza; and the girl has recently given birth to a baby boy. With his usual irony Cecchi
demonstrates how two entirely opposed systems of education
in different environments have produced similar results: both
youths are facing disaster as they break the law to pursue an
amorous intrigue.

Neither the impetuous Alessandro nor the timid Federigo
can act effectively without the assistance of Filippo's servant
Sfavilla. But not even that masterful rogue can persuade Simone to entreat Fiammetta's guardians Pietro dall'Acquila
and his wife, M. Dorotea, to release the girl to her supposedly
long-lost brother Roberto Burlamatti from Lucca. Simone's
probing questions soon unmask the purported brother as an
imposter endeavoring to unite Fiammetta with Federigo.
Sfavilla meets defeat a second time when he instructs Alessandro to write a letter in the name of the absent Pietro
dall'Acquila in order to frighten Dorotea with a story of her
husband's sudden illness and an urgent request for her to join
him in Pisa. Seeing the letter and guessing who probably
wrote it, Simone arranges for Dorotea to place Fiammetta
temporarily in the safety of a convent while the older woman
sets out for Pisa. Neither the device of a disguise nor the
recourse to a forged letter occur in Terence's *Adelphoe*. Writing in the final phase of the Italian Renaissance, Cecchi dram-

atizes the result of reliance on quick wit and imaginative improvisations. Those individuals who would aspire to achieve their fortune through deceit become victims of their own duplicity.

After discovering the truth about Alessandro's clandestine wedding and recent paternity, Filippo finally overcomes the youth's sense of shame and receives a full confession from him with a plea for forgiveness that is readily granted. Until the last act Filippo enjoys ascendancy over events, as his liberality merely seemed to err in generosity while his brother's sternness has alienated everyone from him. Although Simone's acuteness of mind might protect the old man from the entrapments of astute servants, he decides to abandon his severity in order to win the affection that has always escaped him. Outdoing himself in kindness at Filippo's financial expense, Simone astonishes the servants by lavishing gifts on them and overwhelms his sons with unusual fatherly understanding. In the meanwhile, Fiammetta has become reunited with her mother, who withdrew years before to the convent after the death of her husband and the loss of their daughter. Fiammetta's uncle, Alberto, a friend to both Filippo and Simone, will provide a dowry to bless the girl's marriage to Federigo. Preparations for a double-wedding banquet bring to a close this comedy of misunderstanding and reconciliation in which two older men come to recognize the inherent limitations of their antithetical systems of educating the young.

Both Filippo and Simone display need to secure the love, esteem, and gratitude of the sons in their charge. Whereas Simone equates reverence with fear, Filippo confuses liberality for the firmness that a parent should assert over a child. Like his counterpart in Terence's play, Filippo advocates a worldly ethic that reflects his experiences as a courtier. Yet, even though Filippo's easy philosophy of life excuses youth for most of its mistakes, this man's belief in dignity and trust does cause him to regret Alessandro's apparent foolishness in trying to abduct a girl. This urbane character upholds a hedonistic view that values inner tranquillity over purely sybaritic satisfactions. In regard to rearing children, Filippo perceives a certain temporal progression that irrevocably alters the basic relationship between generations: at first the parent treats the offspring as infants dependent on his guid-

ance, then as brothers of equal consideration, and finally as
peers worthy of admiring respect. This sophisticated character understands that wealth has permitted him the luxury of
experimenting with the role of father but that the passing of
time will compel him to surrender the supervision that he
has attempted to exercise with generosity and compassion.

Filippo's consummate sense of tact permits him to confront Alessandro in act 4, scene 9, by playing a gently teasing
trick on the youth with a false story about a Pisan gentleman
who is supposed to be wed to Ginevra. Even though this scene
has an exact equivalent in the *Adelphoe,* act 4, verse 639 and
following, Cecchi subtly represents the growing distress in
young Alessandro, who increasingly stumbles over his words
as he endeavors to continue his deceit and to prevent the
wedding with the Pisan all at the same time. Filippo is admin-
istering the most loving kind of punishment to the errant
youth as he forces Alessandro to become more and more fran-
tic before the impending loss of his wife and their child. Now
that the youth has become a father, it is imperative for Alessandro to admit what has happened and to act as a responsible
adult. At last, after leading the young man through several
tortuous debates about the correct sense of obligation, Filippo
almost hurls the truth in Alessandro's face and compels him
to acknowledge his ungentlemanly behavior. The young man
must experience the growth in character necessary to achieve
independence in his role as an adult in society. Filippo interprets his responsiblity as a parent as one of guiding his ward
to act honorably. Cecchi, however, carefully depicts the contradictions in Filippo's character that show him to be flawed.
Although reluctant to exercise authority in a highly visible
and imperious manner, the older man wishes to remain in
command of every situation by imposing his will in the most
subtle way possible. As a well-to-do bourgeois, Filippo displays a readiness to promote the cause of love and marriage
over the financial advantages of the Florentine dowry system.
When the greedy Simone objects that Ginevra will not bring
any dowry to Alessandro, Filippo replies that all that matters
is the girl's loveliness, good character, and fine breeding. This
man's social ideal is that everyone should strive to be a *"per-
sona dabbene,"* a worthwhile individual, without regard to
property or to wealth. Such liberality born of substantial

means can also take a condescending tone when Filippo deals with persons of a class lower than his. Money then becomes a means to manipulate others and to hold them in their proper place of social inferiority. On learning of the attempted break-in and abduction, Filippo contemptuously comments that Pietro dall'Acquila and his wife are *"genterelle"* (people of little account) whose feelings of offense can easily be remedied with some money. This wealthy former courtier accepts and supports social hierarchies determined by financial power.

Simone demonstrates that he understands his brother's use of money to secure command when the old farmer decides to take revenge for the loving respect that generosity always brought Filippo. Simone destroys Filippo's property by ordering the garden wall that separates his brother's home from that of Gostanza Aldobrandi to be torn down so that Ginevra may be brought over to comfortable quarters. Cecchi does not carry revenge to the full extent in the *Adelphoe*, in which Filippo's counterpart, Micio, is persuaded at age sixty-five to marry a widow. Instead, in the Italian play, Filippo's decline merely brings him to the realization that wealth and gentle manners cannot always succeed in managing the lives of others. With both sons married, Filippo will have to retreat from the foreground of action and control. Even though his brother Simone acts as a rigid authoritarian parent, the old farmer never serves as a major blocking force against the young. Freedom of action has always seemed to Simone to hold the danger of anarchy, as when Alessandro tried to knock down the door to Fiammetta's home. Not only concern over scandal causes Simone's alarm, for the farmer also respects the property of other persons and fears civil authority. Trying to direct people with money would appear a waste of one's resources to Simone. Through four entire acts this character has to sustain the role of the heavy father whom everyone criticizes for frugality and tyranny. Evidence of Federigo's corruption and complicity in the misdeeds of Alessandro eventually weakens Simone's convictions about the certainty of his views. Pain also provides him with useful lessons about his own conduct as Simone sees himself ridiculed by Filippo, scorned by both his sons, and made a fool of by servants. This character's strength is that he will profit by those experiences. As with Demea, the corresponding brother in Terence's comedy, Simone will overcome his false illusions. The turning point of the Italian drama occurs in act 5, scene 2, during Simone's soliloquy, in which the farmer reflects on the years of sacrifices and obedience to paternal duties that have left him pathetically isolated from the immediate family of his sons and his brother and the extended family of their servants. Although Filippo is ten years older than Simone, he could almost pass as the son of his younger brother since a life of ease and insouciance has protected him from the stress that has aged Simone. By appropriating Filippo's tactics and carrying generosity to an extreme, Simone begins to win the respect and the gratitude of others. This character's triumph arrives when he delivers the *licenza* and admits to the lesson he has learned. Cecchi illustrates with Simone that comic reversal need not render a self-deluding character a ridiculous figure but can redeem him with the light of self-understanding.

While both of the elderly brothers carried their opposing views to an excess, their mutual friend Alberto takes that golden middle way that the author holds up for his audience to emulate. Before Filippo's smug confidence, Alberto diplomatically recommends against indulging a child's every whim. Alberto emphasizes in his conduct a strong sense of family obligation as he negotiates with Filippo to safeguard the interests of his kinswoman Gostanza and her daughter Ginevra after the baby's birth. With the discovery of Fiammetta's identity, Alberto joyfully assumes his responsibilities to his niece. Through this sage character the author reveals how one may ease the tensions of bourgeois existence. Alberto's instrumental function as mediator becomes that of representing the conscience of the middle class as he struggles to restore harmony. This diligent citizen contributes to a comic conclusion by lessening parental concern over material preoccupations and working toward an enduring commitment of loving mutual responsibility.[17]

Despite the difference in their education, Alessandro and Federigo are remarkably similar in their desires but diverge in the vigor with which they try to realize their longings. Alessandro resembles Filippo in generosity, spending his allowance to further Federigo's amorous designs on Fiammetta.

In contrast to the youth Aeschinus in the *Adelphoe,* Filippo's ward has not ravished Ginevra in a fit of alcoholic intoxication. Seduction in Italian Renaissance comedies varies greatly from the acts of violence characteristic of ancient Latin comedies, because writers like Plautus and Terence could not criticize the institution of the Roman family, for in the moral tradition of the *Decameron,* young women of Italian society yielded of their own free will to the impetus of love. Alessandro does not have to live with the feelings of shame and guilt that oppress the Terentian Aeschinus, nor does he display the furious determination that drives the youth in the Roman comedy to storm a procurer's establishment in order to carry off a music-girl for his timid brother. Even though he does not possess the explosiveness of his classical counterpart, Alessandro with his bold spirit acts as a foil to Federigo's fearful hesitancy. Federigo walks around town with his face partially covered by his coat, warning Sfavilla not to call out his name in dread that Simone might recognize him and punish him. Cecchi portrays Filippo's ward as lacking the frankness to confess freely his transgressions to his adoptive father. Loyalty to his brother only partly explains Alessandro's unwillingness to admit to his wrongs; to a large extent Filippo's leniency has led the youth to believe he can get away with anything that pleases him. Federigo emerges as the most passive and least imaginative figure of the play, precisely as a result of the repressive education he received from Simone. In a monologue at the start of act 4, Federigo laments his utter helplessness before circumstances created by his apparently intransigent father. It is only through a stroke of good fortune (the recognition of Fiammetta as Pagolo's daughter), the financial support promised by Alberto, and Simone's unexpected conversion that Federigo will succeed in his romantic hopes. Significantly, since decisive events take place independently of him, Federigo does not make a stage appearance after the third scene of the fourth act. This comedy examines how the nature of youthful desire impels two brothers of profoundly diverse education in the identical passionate direction.

Intervention favorable to the romantic designs of the two young brothers comes from their resourceful servant Sfavilla, whose name means the "spark" that will fire their schemes to defeat Simone. Unfortunately, the spark of inventiveness never rises to a flaming success, for Sfavilla's attempts to prove himself a brilliant strategist both with the aid of an impostor and with the use of a forged letter result in complete routs for him. His failure as a tactician derives from the haste with which he proceeds instead of planning his campaigns down to the most minute detail. Sfavilla's greatest strength is his ability to understand the psychology of the individuals with whom he must deal. With his youthful masters this servant alternates between sympathetic counsel and imperious directions, especially toward Federigo, whom Sfavilla literally shoves on and off stage. Even after the setbacks with the impostor and the false letter, this continually creative schemer plays a countertrick on Simone while he protects Federigo from his father's suspicions about the boy's involvement with Fiammetta. It is only in the final act that this keen-witted servant ceases to be a major participant in dramatic events and becomes a passive witness as Simone makes Sfavilla a recipient of his newly assumed generosity. In act 5, scene 5, Sfavilla stands as a perplexed observer before the astounding spectacle of Simone's kindly acceptance of Alessandro's marriage and paternity. No longer able to play an active part in the development of the young protagonists' love, Sfavilla is relegated to the sidelines, for this drama's secondary characters eventually assume the role of confused witness, offended victim, or mere instrument of communication.

By following the Terentian contrast between a benevolent uncle and a harsh father, Cecchi employed a duality method in constructing his comedy on rival systems of education. The Florentine playwright presents the double-sidedness of this ambivalent situation by carefully balancing the virtues and the failings of the two elder brothers against each other until the converted Simone becomes a *signore dabbene*, even in the eyes of Filippo's servants. The extreme views of two brothers serve as a corrective to each other, as youths will attain their maturity by overcoming corrupting influences.[18] Artistically and ethically, the opposition of doctrines never obscures the comic movement to relieve the tensions of bourgeois life in a harmonious realignment of social units through celebration of double weddings. Through reference to contemporary institutions, use of vigorous idiom, and physical structuring of scene, the author succeeds in demonstrating those pressures and operations of the social world on its members in their frenetic pursuit of illusory and often ridiculous goals. The actual projection of life, with the birth of Alessandro's son, expresses the triumph over isolation and alienation that the final wedding banquet will honor. Simone's joyous *licenza* speaks of the spirit of fellow feeling prevailing at that very moment of carnival when the festive comedy is being performed for the delight of Florentine audiences. From the domestic despotism of the severe father and the refined hedonism of the indulgent uncle there will come a new loving commitment to restore the texture of family and social life. Within the stage space, Cecchi has represented a complex urban world at the midpoint of the sixteenth century.

The Torments of Jealousy: Il Martello

In contrast to the traditional portrait of a harsh, initially unyielding father in *I Dissimili*, Cecchi presents in his comedy *Il Martello*, 1561, a parent who prefers being loved to being feared by his son. Although the title of the play literally means "the hammer," during the Renaissance the term *martello* signified jealousy or amorous torment, an emotional state that the elderly father, Girolamo, not only understands in his son Fabio but also continues to experience himself. Cecchi developed this play from an earlier farce, *Gli Aggirati*, in three acts. In the expanded verse comedy father and son are both victims at the mercy of Girolamo's second wife, Madonna Papera, who keeps a tight rein on the family's finances. For some time Fabio was frequenting the establishment of the courtesan Angelica, who afterward barred entrance to the youth at the request of a well-to-do client named Captain Lanfranco Cacciadiavoli. Fabio may return to Angelica's favor only at the price of thirty ducats.

Meanwhile, the young man has fallen passionately in love with the courtesan's ward, Emilia, without Angelica's being aware of his changed feelings. Unable to assist his son with funds, Girolamo appeals to the family servant Nebbia to de-

vise some strategem to secure the desperately needed cash.
Knowing that Papera is to receive eighty ducats for payment
on a grain transaction, Nebbia arranges for Girolamo to impersonate his wife's chief steward and for Angelica to play the
part of Papera in order to swindle the peasant Tognon Di
Bartolo out of the money. Without hesitation, Fabio's father
cooperates with the scheme but on the condition that he may
visit Angelica's establishment for two weeks and share with
his son the courtesan's attentions. After ousting the captain
from Angelica's graces, Fabio immediately undertakes to
elope with Emilia while his father and the courtesan are holding a banquet with food provided by Lanfranco Cacciadiavoli.
Girolamo's joy soon turns to terror when his wife, her steward, and the enraged Tognon burst on the banquet, acting on
information supplied by the captain's parasitic companion,
Sparecchia, about the old man's shameful conduct. Fortunately for all parties concerned, Fabio learns that Emilia is
actually Papera's daughter Selvaggia by her first husband,
Cambio dello Scalza. A wet-nurse abducted Selvaggia as an
infant and carried her to Genoa, and Angelica's sister took
charge of the girl upon the nurse's death with the understanding that one day Selvaggia would be returned to her rightful
family. In Papera's jubilation over recovery of her daughter, a
general amnesty pardons all the guilty parties. Once Tognon
has a receipt in hand for the grain payment, the peasant leaves
in satisfaction. Fabio will wed Selvaggia with all the wealth
that Papera will bestow on her daughter. At the sight of such
legitimate happiness, Angelica undergoes a moral conversion
and renounces her meretricious life in preference for marriage
to the captain. Lecherous old Girolamo will avoid the wrath
that his scandalous behavior merits. In the excitement of impending wedding festivities, Nebbia closes this comedy of
deception and reunion with an envoi expressing his eager
expectation of a just reward for his labor to advance the cause
of youth and romance.

  Unlike many of this author's plays, with their intricately
developed plots and secondary intrigues, *Il Martello* remains
one of Cecchi's least complicated comedies due to its firmly
constructed and symmetrically balanced composition. The
opening two acts serve a purely expository function to represent Fabio's dilemma and his resolution to persist in his at-

tempt to escape with Selvaggia. One of the play's most visually compelling scenes occurs at the end of the second act when the door to Angelica's establishment is shut in Fabio's face after Sparecchia and a porter carrying food enter in preparation for a dinner in the captain's honor; the playwright depicts exclusion in all its physical sense of personal injury. With the third act, the momentum of the play shifts to Nebbia, as the wily servant creates the *beffa* to cheat Tognon and Papera of the eighty ducats. By the close of act 3, victory apparently belongs to the triumphant Nebbia and Fabio, after Tognon falls into the trap that has been set for him. In ten quick-paced scenes of act 4, events reverse themselves again and again until the vindictive Sparecchia seems on the verge of causing disaster for Fabio and Girolamo when he steals into Angelica's home to spy on the revelers at their triumphal feast. However, as this play repeatedly demonstrates, appearances do indeed deceive; the backstairs flight by the young lovers suffices to set in motion developments that will lead to the unexpected agnition and the consequent reconciliation. In its formal patterning, Cecchi's comedy progresses from a vicious status quo of youth corrupted by lust, paternal dignity degraded by indecent desire, maternal love devastated by loss, and feminine honor exchanged for mercenary advantage to a new order of moral conversion and societal correctness. Composed at the time of the author's own religious awakening, the play expresses hope for regeneration.

In the verse prologue Cecchi remarks that, although his inspiration is Plautus's comedy *Asinaria,* his intention remains to readjust the ancient material in the light of modern times and altered social conditions. In addition to the one Roman comedy that Cecchi openly acknowledged as his source, there is also definite influence of *contaminatio* from Plautus's portrayal of a venal courtesan in the play *Truculentus* and the braggart warrior in the *Eunuchus* of Terence. Plautus does not resort to the plot device of the rediscovery of a long-lost daughter. Instead of the reconciliation that brings harmony to everyone in Cecchi's play, the ancient Roman comedy presents the enraged shrew Artemona abusing her husband, Senator Demaenetus, and leading him home, while their son Argyrippus is left at a bordello to enjoy the company of a lovely girl who is devoted to him. Cecchi wishes, however, to bring conflict to a peaceful settlement in which tensions are eased and solid bonds for the future are created. By transferring classical plot motives and character-types from ancient comedies to the Tuscan mercantile world, the modern author endeavors to introduce novelty without violating Plautine and Terentian sources.

Among the classical character-types that Cecchi adapted most successfully to a modern environment is the braggart warrior Captain Lanfranco Cacciadiavoli da Mantova. The origin of the braggart as a stage figure derived from the mercenary soldiers of ancient Hellenistic times who would return home wealthy with spoils from the Oriental wars of their Macedonian generals. Authors of the Greek New Comedy like Menander satirized these opulent soldiers for pretensions to lofty social position, maintaining an entourage of parasites and courtesans, the claims to military victory unsubstantiated by fact, and actual cowardice before a genuine challenge. Plautus created the most complete portrait ever made of the braggart in his *Miles Gloriosus,* a comedy that exposes the mercenary warrior as a contemptible poseur trembling in fright when menaced by personal injury. Italian Renaissance playwrights like Cecchi could look to the military situation in their warworn land to find a modern equivalent to the Hellenistic braggart in the mercenary soldiers who sold their disloyal services to the various contending Italian communes.

In the Italian erudite comedies, the braggart soldier is often impoverished despite his claims to have acquired booty from the ruins of demolished cities. Another original feature of the Italian braggart warrior appears in his literary affectations, speaking in an ultrarefined Petrarchist language and flaunting a knowledge of military tactics and dueling ceremonies. The characteristic that the Renaissance figure shares with the Hellenistic and Roman braggart is an overriding cowardice that unmasks all their pretensiousness to noble rank, prowess, and amorous seductiveness.[19] From his very name the captain of *Il Martello* recalls fierce military figures whose cruelty Dante cites in the *Inferno:* the Lanfranchi leaders of the Pisan Ghibellines in canto 33, verse 32. But the surname Cacciadiavoli ("he who hunts devils") is reminiscent of the Dantesque pander Venedico Caccianemico ("he who hunts

the enemy") of *Inferno*, 18. Cecchi's character also inclines to
lascivious vice, permitting himself to become Angelica's
plaything and always struggling to meet her demands for gifts
and cash payments. To stress this warrior's infernal associations, Cecchi gives the name *Farfalla* (butterfly) to the captain's lackey after one of the evil demons called Farfarello in
Inferno, 21, who torment grafters. With all his boasting about
the numerous opponents that he has vanquished, Captain
Lanfranco appears a fop playing a gallant role and trying to
impress a prostitute by greeting her in florid Spanish. The
Florentine author fashions in the Mantuan captain a strutting
caricature who brags of his familiarity with the crowned
heads of Europe, but who is actually most at home in a
brothel. In all his swaggering bravado, Cacciadiavoli dis-
courses with pedantic boorishness about the gentlemanly
honor code and its expression in the ritualistic art of fencing.
Yet when this expert on dueling is faced with single combat,
he readily accepts his parasite's suggestion for strategic withdrawal and recourse to intrigue. Even though Cecchi's character has some traits in common with braggart soldiers in
ancient plays like Captain Diabolus in the *Asinaria*, the slow-
witted officer Stratophanes in the *Truculentus*, and especially
the not-very-bold warrior Thraso in the *Eunuchus*, Cacciadiavoli reflects the troubled political and military situation
in sixteenth-century Italy with its mercenary officers blustering over their exploits in battle while shamefully fleeing honorable confrontation.[20]

Angelica and her maid Agnola form a predatory team that
takes advantage of free-spending soldiers and impassioned
youths. Prostitution has taken them to Genoa and Rome and
now to Florence, forever in pursuit of clients. Contemporary
society offered Cecchi actual models of courtesans, many of
whom were intellectually and artistically accomplished figures who earned the respect of poets, painters, sculptors, and
high-ranking clerics that frequented their establishments,
where banquets served as occasions for cultural events, especially the performance of comedies at carnival time. Angelica, however, shows herself to be a rather commonplace
harlot without any particular gifts other than the ability to
arouse the captain's licentious ardor. Despite the fact that her
name describes her angelic face, this prostitute's character

recalls the bewitching Princess Angelica of Boiardo's *Orlando Innamorato* and Ariosto's *Orlando Furiosi* with the spell she casts over the warrior Roland. Cecchi portrays this greedy team from a brutally realistic and mercantile viewpoint as two entrepreneurs working as quickly as they can before the onset of old age deprives Angelica of the one capital she possesses: her attractive body. In act 3, scene 5, Agnola delivers a speech in which she compares the labor of a prostitute to that of a fowler setting the trap for a bird. Angelica's very being is the bait that catches the victims. The Italian author derived the source for Agnola's analogy from a passage in the *Asinaria* in which the procuress Cleaereta calls herself a fowler. As Cecchi illustrates, however, the prostitute also becomes a victim.

Unlike many of the courtesans and the procuresses in ancient plays, Angelica does not have a string of well-to-do clients fighting their way to her door with presents. For six months Fabio was her sole source of income until the captain arrived to oust the youth from her affections. Angelica cannot allow sentiment to govern her relations with clients, or else she would be ruined economically. One of the features implicit in Cecchi's portrayal of harlots is the similarity of their lot to that of mercenary soldiers. Consequently, the ensuing marriage between Angelica and Captain Lanfranco seems a necessity; neither one has found any other suitable partner. This oppressive existence of always having to anticipate the displeasure of clients, the pressure of ecclesiastical and secular authorities, and the certainty of retirement at the loss of youthful attractiveness contribute to Angelica's sudden decision to quit her profession and to insist on wedding the captain. Fortunately for Angelica and Agnola, the carnival season occurring during this drama has been one not of venal licentiousness but of redeeming experience.[21]

Renaissance dramatists found the classical figure of the parasite one of the most challenging to adapt to comedies intended to represent modern life (parasites had formed a professional group in Hellenistic and Roman times, serving as letter writers and enlivening banquets with jokes and humorous anecdotes). In Renaissance times, a modern equivalent of the parasite arose in the accomplished jesters who traveled from one commune to another and often participated in diplomacy and political intrigue. By the end of the fifteenth century those jester-parasites belonged to bourgeois as well as aristocratic circles. Since one of the chief responsibilities of those hangers-on was to handle preparations for banquets, Italian comic authors chose to emphasize the gluttony of the supposedly insatiable parasites. The pleasures of the palate and the stomach assume an existential dimension for Sparecchia, who dreams of visions of pheasants and capons. Gluttony eventually overcomes the cowardice that usually prevents Sparecchia from intervening in the combat between the captain and Fabio. When the parasite sees himself cheated out of a meal, he abandons his timidity and initiates the actions that will undo all the ruses of the wily Nebbia. With the ambivalence typical to Cecchi's plays, Sparecchia refuses to remain the victim of a *beffa* and takes revenge for his lost meal by exposing Girolamo's improprieties to Papera. Hunger achieves results unobtainable by characters of cunning far superior to Sparecchia's. As this parasite's very name signifies, he is the "one who wants to clear dining-tables" of their delicious repasts. Yet it is this voracious caricature who brings about the drama's resolution.[22]

While the classical character-types of braggart warrior, courtesan, and parasite all share ancient antecedents, the peasants in Cecchi's plays reflect the contemporary reality of life in the Tuscan countryside. At the arrival onstage of Tognon di Bartolo near the play's exact center in act 3, scene 6, Cecchi presents the first of the gallery of peasants to figure prominently in his plays. Except for a certain brusqueness of speech, Tognon, who hails from a village near Pisa, does not stand out linguistically from the Florentine characters. In later dramas Cecchi developed the use of dialect and rustic jargon to distinguish the farmers from their urban critics. Because of his desire to introduce a peasant character, Cecchi deviated from the *Asinaria,* in which the victim of the thieving transaction is designated as a *mercator,* a merchant dealing in donkeys. Interestingly, that other Italian Renaissance dramatist who also excelled in portraying rural life, Angelo Beolco, retained the merchant figure in his own adaptation of the *Asinaria* entitled the *Vaccaria,* 1533. Tall as a bean pole, reddish in face, with a voice like that of a braying ass, Tognon draws to himself the derisive attention of city servants who regard him as an easily duped fool. Despite some difficulty in expressing himself and remembering unfamiliar names and terms, Tognon surprises the swindling conspirators with his suspicious air of reserve. The clever charade by Angelica and Girolamo as Papera and the steward succeeds only because Nebbia can produce an authentic letter from one of the woman's overseers charging Tognon to make the grain payment. Even Nebbia must acknowledge that Tognon is not the simpleton he appeared to be. With a single-mindedness characteristic of persons leading an uncomplicated life, this peasant preserves his dignity by pressing his claim of payment until the real Papera and her adminstrator verify his assertions. At this point the farmer triumphs over the ruses devised by sophisticated town-dwelling masters of deceit.[23]

As a representative of the servant-class, the rather nebulous Nebbia shows his greatest strength to be his willingness to take advantage of good Fortune, as when he accidentally discovers the letter that convinces Tognon to hand over the cash to the impostors. Nebbia's weaving of a *beffa* to obtain funds for the youthful pair in no way displays the insight into the hidden motives of the human psyche that distinguishes the greatest practitioners of artful ruses in Italian literature. The servant even underestimates his intended victims, as when he judges Tognon to be a countrified dolt. All Nebbia succeeds in doing is acting on a superficial level to manipulate other persons by appealing to their base emotions, like Angelica's greed and Girolamo's lust. Nebbia has to rely on fortuitous happenings to promote the success of his schemes. Neither intellect nor intuition operate to any great extent in the servant's undertakings. In devising a trap for the cautious peasant with the ready cash, Nebbia consistently ignores Fabio's wise observation that persons are not as naive as they might seem to be. This rather crafty character lacks the joy of gameplaying that inspires the greatest strategists to defeat their opponents by arousing the most profound longings and apprehensions. Nebbia's temporary success results from the merely mechanical seizing of the opportunity offered by Fortune rather than from the victorious affirmation of inventive intelligence.[24]

In this drama of amorous torment and misdirected deceit, Cecchi created a carnival play on the theme of the opposition between appearance and reality in the bourgeois milieu of the city that the author most adored: his native town of Florence with its economic sway over the surrounding countryside. The prologue declares the playwright's linguistic pride as a Florentine by explaining that some of the comedy's non-Tuscan characters will speak in the city's noble tongue, which many writers have long aspired to master. To suggest the civic background for this masquerade-drama, the author had various conspirators refer to the omnipresent police spies and the danger of violating local laws safeguarding the sanctity of convents. Even in her lowly status as an alien courtesan, Angelica trusts in the justice of ducal authority to defend her from abuse. This comedy demonstrates how living in Florentine society often necessitates donning a mask as a person of business and credit to achieve the visibility that assures success.

Frequently repeated words like *maschera* (mask), *volto* (face), and *immascherarsi* (to put on a mask) express the ruling motif of carnival disguise to advance the interests of erotic passion. Comic structure, however, points to the controlling of disorderly and socially dangerous emotions within the institutions of matrimony and the family, as with the concluding announcement of the double weddings to be celebrated in Florence's cathedral, the Duomo. In the new era of the Catholic Reformation, the solemn occasion of the marriages takes place not as the result of a triumphant human intelligence designing artful *beffe* but as the consequence of an ascendant Fortune that brings life into harmony with divine will. While working with classical character-types from ancient tradition, Cecchi endeavored to represent the contradictions, stresses, and aspirations of Medicean society.

Conclusion: Toward a Comedy of Ambivalence

Other plays of direct emulation from antiquity include *La Maiana,* after Terence's *Heautontimorumenos,* and *I Rivali,* modeled on Plautus's *Casina* or Machiavelli's reworking after the Latin in *La Clizia.* Throughout all these comedies of classical inspiration Cecchi employed a technique of ambivalence to reveal the forever shifting state of reality and the

deceptiveness of appearances. As a literary method, ambivalence functions in two ways. The term may signify the nature
of what holds two elements in opposition between their positive and negative features. Ambivalence may also apply to
duality in nature or meaning without opposition but often in
parallelism. In the second, extended function, the five comedies under study in this chapter all seek to entertain and to
enlighten at the same time, as explicitly stated in some of the
prologues. The time for the action in the plays usually occurs
during the very same carnival season as at the initial performances, and this "nowness" of a moment of revelry and trickery
must soon give way to a period of sacrifice when all the
masks of merriment will be discarded in an atmosphere of
commercial realism and domestic tensions.

Structurally, the comedies display a duality in symmetrical
blockings of scenes with paired characters such as old men,
youths, or servants of different sexes, in either opposing or
parallel relationships. Characters of dissimilar backgrounds
scrve as foils to highlight each other's basic traits, as when
peasants and town servants confront each other. Double weddings generally close the dramas, especially after a recognition scene has brought contending parties into the unity of
unforeseen family alliances. Yet for an author who celebrated
the family and matrimony, Cecchi introduced into his stage
works the disquieting theme of misogyny whereby husbands
try to flee the ceaseless recriminations of their shrewish
mates. Also as a writer who participated in the Boccaccian
tradition of exalting the power of intelligence over stupidity,
Cecchi readily portrayed the limits of an inventive imagination before an arbitrary Fortune. This comic theater im-
presses on its viewers the duality that one finds in life.

By recourse to *contaminatio* the dramatist combined Plautine intrigues of disguise and deception with Terentian sentiment. Along with exposing the acquisitive psychology of the
adult Florentine bourgeoisie in *La Dote,* the playwright tried
to represent the contradictory inclinations of the young generation: prodigality and vitiating self-indulgence or moderation and constancy of purpose. Seemingly solid reality
collapses in *La Moglie* on account of the confusion over the
striking resemblance between twin brothers, and the return
to order takes place only after mercantile calculation comes

into accord with youthful amorous desire. A long-standing friendship in *La Stiava* finally prevails in the triumph of rationality over senile passion, with the preservation of a family from the potentially destructive struggle between a father and son for the same woman. Dualism lies at the core of *I Dissimili* with its antithetical systems of educating the young as advocated by brothers of radically unlike temperaments; here Cecchi in particular demonstrated how apparent leniency and gentleness could prove a subtle and extremely effective form of restraint. Attraction to feminine beauty discloses its contradictory consequences in *Il Martello* with the play's emphasis on the pain of love: erotic slavery and meretricious debasement with Angelica, honorable devotion and renewed family harmony with Selvaggia. By selecting comedy over tragedy the author in all these plays investigated how life in its oppositions and parallel situations could arrive at moments of redemption and restoration. In his comedies of modern inspiration from the Italian novellistic tradition and the example of contemporary reality, Cecchi continued his study of a bourgeois world torn between the conventions of commerce and the ideals of romance.

3
COMEDIES OF MODERN INSPIRATION

Modernity and the Novellistic Tradition

It was the tradition of the Italian novella and especially Boccaccio's *Decameron* that encouraged comic playwrights to describe their world and the values of their own period. Boccaccio and the masters of the brief tale who followed him proved to be a rich source of plots, themes, jests, and ridiculous as well as admirable characters for the authors of comedies. The short Italian narrative of the late Middle Ages and Renaissance showed the contemporary scene as a spectacle full of dramatic possibilities that sixteenth-century playwrights transferred to the stage. The comic writers saw in the *Decameron* a proclamation of a revolutionary morality of the rights of Love and Nature. In the world of Boccaccio's novella collection the dominant principle is the force of physical Nature against all social institutions. In the *Decameron* priests and nuns are portrayed as humans with erotic needs that must be satisfied. Whenever superior authorities like parents or judges try to impose artificial standards of restraint, Nature in the Boccaccian world eventually takes revenge with resulting disaster. The comic playwrights who derive inspiration from Boccaccio aim their dramas at the avoidance of disaster for troubled lovers. Although many of the tales in the *Decameron* end in marriage, the author did not hesitate to represent adultery as the most intelligent course for a sensitive person entrapped in an unhappy domestic situation. Comic stage writers of the Renaissance readily echoed Boccaccio's sentiments on adultery as a perfectly justifiable act.

Boccaccio celebrated an ideal of *saviezza*, a situational wisdom to which a hero or heroine resorts with intelligence and self-control to defeat bestial stupidity and social intolerance. The comic theater featured the heroic figure, male or female, of superior and quick wit triumphing through a cleverly designed *beffa* or with brilliant, inventive verbal skill. Capricious Fortune appeared as an antagonistic force in the *Decameron* to lovers and brave characters, just as it later became an arbitrary power in Renaissance comedies.

With other dramatists of his period, Giovan Maria Cecchi shared the admiration for Boccaccio and the novellistic tradition. Like the author of the *Decameron*, Cecchi wrote in the colorful and expressive Florentine tongue and represented a remarkably similar Tuscan environment with its ambitious merchants, love-distressed wives and maidens, scheming servants, and awkward peasants. Through direct picturing of the customs and character-types of his century as well as drawing comic themes from the tradition of the novella, Ser Giovan Maria endeavored to produce comedies classical in form but thoroughly modern in subject matter.

Erotic Fury: L'Assiuolo

A novellistic erotic fury predominates in the drama generally regarded as the author's masterpiece: *L'Assiuolo*, 1549. In the prologue of this prose play Cecchi asserts the work's independence from classical models: ". . . the spectacle of a brand-new comedy . . . derived neither from Terence nor from Plautus . . ." The playwright stresses his innovation by writing the adjective *nuova* twice, to affirm not only that the drama had never before appeared onstage but also that its subject matter was to depart strikingly from the plots of ancient comedies. One of the claims the writer makes, that the events occurring in the play actually took place in the town of Pisa, the drama's setting, is quite common to Italian Renaissance theater but probably does not correspond to reality. The most superficial examination of the plot reveals its obvious sources in the novella tradition rather than in chronicle. Cecchi's affirmation of the play's originality continues in the prologue as he states that the background for dramatic situations does not come from the sack of Rome in 1527 or the siege of Florence, with resulting kidnapings and breakup of families to be reunited in a recognition scene. Significantly, the play will not conclude with any weddings. This drama's bold modernity, expressed in licentious language, becomes apparent in its major theme: adultery in the Boccaccian spirit of revolt against inhibiting social conventions.

Cecchi structures *L'Assiuolo* on a series of deceptions and disguises. The device of false letters leads different characters, like the elderly lawyer Ambrogio and his young wife, Oretta, into situations of entrapment. While in ancient comedy false letters are rarely used to advance the plot, false letters abound in Cecchi's works, reflecting the novellistic recourse to *beffe* played on individuals who permit their passions to prevail over the intelligence that ought to recognize the forgery. In *L'Assiuolo* vanity causes Ambrogio to accept as genuine a letter, supposedly written by the lovely widow Anfrosina but actually composed by her son Rinuccio, inviting the old man to visit her at night while Rinuccio and his friend Giulio are expected to be out of town. While Rinuccio is hoping to steal into Ambrogio's home and into bed with Oretta, the equally enamored Giulio counters his friend's plan by sending Oretta a letter purportedly by Anfrosina urging the lawyer's wife to come to the widow's home and to surprise her husband in attempted adultery. Jealous anger impels Madonna Oretta into believing the letter's contents and hastening to Anfrosina's house, where Giulio is scheming to take Ambrogio's place in bed. The mechanical device of false letters becomes a psychological tool in Cecchi's plays whereby characters like Ambrogio and Oretta allow strong emotions rather than reason to guide their actions.

In this drama the author deliberately fuses the device of disguise with the motif of masquerade, since the time of the play's action occurs during the carnival season. When the lawyer is about to set out for his ill-fated rendezvous at Anfrosina's home, he and his servant Giannella leave dressed as pages, and they refer to the convenience that carnival time lends to disguise (act 4, scene 2).

Another form of disguise that takes place prominently in the play is the figure of the transvestite character. In the Italian novella as well as in the early erudite comedy the transvestite is an individual who has fallen so much in the sway of amorous passion that he or she will don the clothes of the opposite sex to reach the beloved one.[1] Three examples of the transvestite appear in *L'Assiuolo*. When Giulio lures Ambrogio to a courtyard where the attorney is to be locked for several hours hooting in vain like an owl (hence the play's title) to signal to Giannella to release him, the young man is waiting by the courtyard gate dressed as a maidservant. Jealousy, rather than love or erotic desire, convinces Oretta to don male garb and to follow her lecherous husband to Anfrosina's home. Cecchi shows sympathy for Oretta's complaint (act 4, scene 3) that while society permits Ambrogio to deny her pleasurable activities, she has to place herself in grave peril to confront him at his adulterous pursuits: "and thus (poor Oretta! you did not lack for anything else) you have to stay in a prison for life; have an elderly, jealous, love-sick husband fallen into his dotage; so . . . I have to go dressed as a man climbing a garden wall late at night to get out of my house and wander disguised throughout Pisa . . ." The final transvestite figure appears at the play's end when Ambrogio attempts to expose Oretta and her lover to his brother-in-law Uguccione. But the "paramour," whom Oretta defiantly introduces to her brother and her husband as the youth Fabio, turns out to be her sister Violante with a false beard and masculine attire. Again, with the transvestite disguise, the dramatist succeeds in integrating a traditional comic expedient into the psychological motivation and the social situation of his characters.

Boccaccio's *Decameron* inspired Cecchi with plot situations and character-types as well as delightfully salacious language. Ambrogio's involuntary and frigid vigil in the courtyard recalls the nocturnal torment of the unhappily amorous scholar, Rinieri, in *Decameron* 8, 7, with none of the painful consequences of Boccaccio's tale. The trap with which Giulio leads the unwitting Oretta into a sexual encounter has its model in the fate of the jealous wife Catella succumbing to the desires of Ricciardo Minutolo in *Decameron* 3, 6, when he lures her to a public bathhouse expecting to find her unfaithful husband. Rinuccio's discovering himself in bed with the wrong woman brings to mind *Decameron* 8, 4, except that the Pisan youth fared better than Boccaccio's canon of Fiesole, who forever suffered public ridicule for lying with an ugly maidservant. Oretta's intelligent defense of her honor and success in humiliating Ambrogio before her brother has a counterpart in the astute stratagem of adulterous Monna Sismonda in *Decameron* 7, 8, to cast shame on her husband in the presence of her angry brothers. Some of Boccaccio's characters are expressly mentioned in this play to point to parallels in temperament and in situation, as in act 4, scene 6, where Ambrogio's sexual limitations are compared to the lack of vigor in the elderly Pisan judge Ricciardo di Chinzica of *Decameron* 2, 10.

Ambrogio belongs to the same group of jealous husbands in the *Decameron* who deserve to be cuckolded when their unjustified suspicions become reality. This attorney appears even more ridiculous than the merchant Filippo in *La Stiava* because he has a wife who is young and beautiful. Ambrogio's physical faculties have declined so much that he barely recognizes persons on the street, but he vainly believes he can satisfy his wife and a mistress. Jealousy dominates his actions to the extent that he has banished tradesmen from his premises and shuttered the ground floor of his home from contact with the street, placing Giannella as a sentinel by the bolted front door. Cecchi here participates in a long literary tradition going back to early medieval narrative *exempla*, in which it is demonstrated that barred windows and locked doors cannot protect a husband from a wife's betrayal. The author creates in this attorney more than a stereotype as he portrays Ambrogio's multifaceted personality. His jealousy is matched by miserliness, for even in his obsession to seduce Anfrosina this lawyer carefully controls his expenses in dealing with the go-between Madonna Verdiana for her services to win the widow over to Ambrogio. When pressed for compensation, the old man attempts to make Verdiana accept his old shoes as payment.

Although jealousy keeps him at home a great part of the day, Ambrogio's desire for wealth would not permit him to abandon his legal practice completely. The author especially desires to represent this character in all his professional pretentiousness discoursing on court procedure before his client Rinuccio and trying to manipulate Giannella by awing the servant with unintelligible Latin phrases. Ambrogio's pedantic recourse to Latin terminology recalls another supremely pretentious attorney from an Italian Renaissance comedy:

Messer Nicia Calfucci in the *Mandragola,* except that Machiavelli's character possesses none of Ambrogio's jealousy or lasciviousness. What Ambrogio holds in common with Messer Nicia and countless other attorneys all through the later tradition of the Commedia dell'Arte is vanity, which causes all of them to believe themselves irresistible either in love or in their professional careers. Ambrogio also displays another typical flaw of the pedant's character: cowardice as he enlists Giannella's aid before entrusting himself to the streets late at night merely to walk a short distance to Anfrosina's house.

The usual reward for the cowardice, vanity, miserliness, and jealousy of such an individual is a humiliating defeat, as when Oretta disgraces Ambrogio before Uguccione. The old man's abasement becomes complete when this attorney has to turn to his victorious adversary Rinuccio to act as a mediator in the domestic conflict. As Ambrogio once stated to Giannella, every labor claims its reward; and the reward to be exacted by Rinuccio will be Oretta's freedom from her husband's domination. Fundamentally insecure in his relationship with his wife and clients, Ambrogio, the wealthy and successful lawyer, endeavors to convince himself of his abilities as lover and jurist only to meet shame before family and neighbors.

Although the elderly attorney attempts to pass himself off as a sexually attractive individual, he remains so unsure of himself that he has to enlist the aid of M. Verdiana, the *pinzochera* or falsely pious go-between who bears the same name and characteristics as a venal figure in *Decameron* 5, 10: " . . . an old woman who seemed to be a St. Verdiana . . . always going around to church services with beads in hand reciting the 'Lord's Prayer,' and she never talked about anything other than the lives of holy Fathers and the stigmata of St. Francis; and almost everyone thought her a saint . . ." The author has behind him a novellistic and theatrical tradition in which the procuress conceals her greed and ruthlessness under an appearance of religious zeal, counting her beads while persuading young women to gratify her clients. Unlike several other examples of the go-between, Verdiana does not practice witchcraft to bolster her arguments with love potions. Even though this character permits no one to swear in her presence, she casts lewd aspersions about the sexual activities occurring in monasteries and convents. Her major scene takes place in act 2, scene 2, where the bigot confronts miserly Ambrogio and has to employ all her rhetorical skills to force him to make adequate payment for her services on his behalf to Anfrosina. As will be demonstrated shortly, this comedy reflects in the dealings of characters like Verdiana and Ambrogio an attitude of commercial calculation that figures eros and cash as equivalent exchanges.[2]

Every character in *L'Assiuolo* is continually calculating his profit and advantage. Rinuccio and Giulio as students at the University of Pisa do not particularly bring to mind the inept *adulescentuli* (youths) in ancient Roman comedies; rather they are Goliards intent on enjoying themselves. Their prototype is to be found in fifteenth-century humanistic plays like the *Comedia Bile* about a jolly but hungry wandering student securing a good meal for himself or *La Commedia Elettorale* about a student election at the Univesity of Padua. Charm and quick wit are the chief resources of the Goliards in humanistic comedies. Giulio finds himself torn between intense desire to possess Oretta carnally and the eagerness to help his friend Rinuccio, in whose home this Florentine is lodging. Were it not for his servant Giorgetto, it is doubtful if Giulio would have seized the opportunity to trap Oretta in Anfrosina's home. Erotic conquest does not completely quiet Giulio's guilty conscience in deceiving Rinuccio until he prevails upon the woman to share her favors with his friend. This willingness to include Rinuccio proves that carnal desire rather than true love always motivates Giulio. Rinuccio emerges as by far the more sympathetic member of the two companions in amorous adventure. This youth's flexibility before changing circumstances becomes apparent in his accepting the turn of Fortune that placed him in bed with Violante rather than with her sister. Instead of consuming himself with vindictive wrath at Giulio's deception, he forgives the Florentine student and consents to the arrangement wherein he will become Oretta's part-time lover and Violante's full-time consoler. Rinuccio, like Giulio, reveals a vehemence of erotic yearning rather than a depth of loving attachment to an individual woman. Because of his discretion and adaptability, the Pisan youth enjoys a total triumph after Ambrogio has to appeal for him to intervene in the domestic

dispute and to resolve the family strife. Toward the two amorous young men Cecchi shows an indulgence that he does
not grant to the foolish attorney.

Around the central characters of the old and young generations revolve their servants as satellite figures. Although
loyal to his master, Giannella is a bungler. Ambrogio would
castrate this servant rather than keep him in the same building with Oretta except that the lawyer believes his valet to
be impotent. A coward by nature, Giannella is something of
a braggart warrior, as in two scenes where he claims he has
had to fight off from one hundred fifty to as many as three
hundred assailants when in reality only Rinuccio and Giorgetto frightened him away from his sentry post outside Anfrosina's house during Ambrogio's night of torture. Giannella's
appetite matches that of any parasite in ancient Roman comedy. His stupidity functions as a foil for the intelligence of
Giorgetto, who masterminded the device of the letter to lure
Oretta away from her home and into Giulio's arms. Giannella's obtuseness contrasts with Giorgetto's self-confident inventiveness as he accurately judges Giulio's libido to be
stronger than his friendship for Rinuccio. Giorgetto's success
in accommodating his master's desires resembles the clever
stratagems of the parasite Ligurio in the *Mandragola* in unit-
ing his client Callimaco with Madonna Lucrezia. Giulio's
servant clearly proves he is an accomplished rogue, to whom
falls the honor of delivering the play's envoi admonishing old
men for taking young wives and afterward displaying jealousy. All these servants participate in the comedy's festive
spirit, each seeking his utmost enjoyment. Like the male servants, Agnola also joins in the merriment as a reward for
assisting Rinuccio and contributing to Oretta's liberation
from a prisonlike existence almost completely devoid of happiness. Even though Agnola accepts payment from the young
man, her intentions do not reflect Verdiana's savage greed but
rather a desire to correct an unjust situation of feminine subjugation. The maid acts on her own initiative, independently
of her mistress, who remains unaware of the schemes perpetrated upon her person until after Giulio's seduction. Agnola
follows an ethical attitude favoring love as the rightful domain of the young. With the play's resolution in success for
the four young characters, Giorgetto and Agnola find them-

selves in the ascendant party, while Giannella has rescued himself from Ambrogio's disgrace by confessing to his complicity before Uguccione and is permitted to take part in the comedy's carnival celebration.

Oretta must doubtless be regarded as this play's target character. Ambrogio considers her a possession that should be locked away from the world. Rinuccio and Giulio alike long to know her carnally, but it would be a distortion of this play's significance to state that either youth loves her. The lady's maid profits by facilitating an adulterous situation that Oretta never sought on her own. Oretta sees herself as a victim of society, as she laments in act 4, scene 3, since men impose a harsh tyranny over their wives, who, unlike the husbands, did have the freedom to choose their spouses. This lack of equality with men places Oretta in the humiliating situation of having to masquerade in masculine apparel to chase after her faithless husband. Her initial act of adultery occurs involuntarily as she falls victim to the *beffa* devised by Giorgetto for Giulio. But after her passionate encounter with the Florentine youth she becomes converted to a new morality of pleasurable self-interest, as expressed in a speech to Giulio at the start of act 5: "Since his madness, my jealousy, and your cunning have led me to do what I would never have done on my own, I cannot say anything other than that this was destined by the One who can dispose of us: since we must not resist the will of That One, I do not wish to be in opposition."

Cecchi modeled Oretta's declaration of adulterous intent after a speech in the *Mandragola* attributed to Lucrezia, who, like the wife in *L'Assiuolo*, commits an act that she would never have made on her own initiative. Both women appear as ethical pragmatists who adjust to the novel situation in which they experience erotic joy for the first times in their lives. Like fanatics they move from one extreme to another. The Machiavellian wife does not have to defend her honor with the resentment that inspires Oretta to expose Ambrogio before Uguccione. There remains, however, a fundamental difference between the moral conversions of the two wives. Lucrezia enters into only one relationship, with Callimaco, who sincerely pledges to marry her whenever her husband dies. Lucrezia has therefore the assurance that matrimony will redeem the adultery one day. By contrast, Oretta will form liaisons with two men, Giulio and Rinuccio; as she soon learns, one of those youths will also be her sister's lover. Longing for vengeance and newly awakened sexual desire rather than serious commitment bring about Oretta's conversion to adultery.

While Oretta's growth toward freedom comes about through pain and shock, Violante displays from her initial stage entrance at the play's center in act 3 that she is already an independent creature whose flexibility permits her to set in motion a series of crucial events. In act 3, scene 4, on encountering Giannella and Giorgetto in an argument outside Ambrogio's house, Violante comes to the aid of Giulio's servant by taking the letter supposedly from Anfrosina and some male clothing described as costumes for a play to be performed by a group of nuns. Only Violante could have overcome Giannella's opposition to introduce the letter and the clothing into the attorney's household. Fortune *(l'occasione)* placed this willful young woman on scene at a decisive moment. Later, through Fortune, it is Violante and not Oretta that Rinuccio finds in bed with him. Fate also destined this passionate maiden to be with the very person for whom she had felt a strong attraction. This modern woman, whose one restraining concern is to protect her reputation, will readily accept the arrangement to share Rinuccio with her sister so long as discretion guides the actions of all the lovers. Violante possesses such a dominant personality that in her final stage appearance she has assumed the semblance of masculine aggressiveness in her disguise as Oretta's "lover" Fabio in order to denounce Ambrogio as a lecherous hypocrite. For in a male disguise a woman can succeed when she intelligently seizes the opportunities created by Fortune.

Although the author derived many of the motives for this modern drama of amorous frenzy and feminist revolt from novellistic sources, he structured it within a classical framework. In the prologue Cecchi referred to the unity of time, designating the play's action as "an event that occurred in ten hours or less." The unchanging scene is a Pisan street where the houses of Ambrogio and Anfrosina and a church are located. The church serves as a convenient meeting place and as a site for strategic withdrawal whenever characters like

Giulio believe their presence might impede the progress of amorous conspiracies. Statements about scaling garden walls, climbing in and out of windows, and breaking out of locked courtyards create the oppressive atmosphere of a prisonlike setting from which inmates are seeking release. References to the local university and student life, Ambrogio's comments about court schedules, and Verdiana's descriptions of her visits to churches and to saints' shrines all give the audience an impression of the entire Pisan scene beyond the restrictions of the immediate setting. Male characters like Ambrogio resent the totally feminine domains of the convents where their wives ostensibly gather to watch performances of sacred plays but actually for the purpose of exchanging items of gossip. Various linguistic devices also contribute to the sense of the physical scene as achieved by highly descriptive proverbs, striking phrases adapted from the writings of Boccaccio and Machiavelli, and carefully cued interchanges between characters rapidly dashing on and off stage as they communicate their passionate desires. Working within the spatial and temporal confines of classical drama, Cecchi fashions a complete urban environment for his comedy of erotic conspiracy.

Social relationships within the playworld of *L'Assiuolo* reflect a mercantile attitude that inextricably links money to sex to dominate romantic affairs. The word *amore* becomes confused with the exchange of goods and services. Sexual subjugation follows from economic subjugation. In the play's opening scene Giulio reprimands Giorgetto for thinking of Oretta as nearly a common prostitute whose favor he might acquire with some coins. The youth acknowledges that Ambrogio's financial success now allows the elderly man the leisure to stand guard over his wife. In its structure, the bourgeois family as represented in Cecchi's comedy perpetuates the husband's control over the wife. Only a widow like Anfrosina could enjoy a degree of independence comparable to that of males.

Money in this drama can be a means to achieve one's amorous goal, and it can also be a force to obstruct the desires of another. For Ambrogio, money is an inert commodity that must remain with him, and the scenes between the attorney and Verdiana center on the word *pagare* as the two argue about the kind of payment the old bawd will receive for her efforts with Anfrosina on Ambrogio's behalf: his discarded clothing or gold coins. In contrast, Rinuccio uses cash freely to promote his amorous schemes, generously paying Agnola for information about her mistress. The ultimately inferior socioeconomic status of women appears most evident in a conversation of act 5, scene 2, in which Rinuccio and Giulio describe their romantic adventures respectively with Violante and Oretta as resembling the sampling of new goods that might be acquired and used in common by partners in a commercial enterprise. Giulio's willingness to share Oretta with his friend would constitute a joint business venture.

The metaphorical language employed by Cecchi to draw the parallel between cash and eros reveals the ambivalence at the heart of this comedy where Violante with her independent spirit and Oretta with her newfound attitude of rebellion are considered as commodities that could be shared by friendly male partners. Terms of monetary exchange prevail in the language of this drama, which reflects a bourgeois mentality equating eros with commerce.[3] This reduction of the bonds of affection to shared business transactions illustrates the profound difference between Cecchi's play and that ideal of loving commitment that inspired the *Decameron* and the *Mandragola.* There is a depth of understanding of the human need for tender devotion in Boccaccio and Machiavelli that is absent in *L'Assiuolo's* amorous partnerships for the satisfaction of mere sensual desires that underscore male economic and social supremacy over women.

After this comedy's original performance in 1549 by the Company of the Monsignori and the Fantastichi, it became one of the most popular and highly admired plays in its era. Regarded as a companion piece to the *Mandragola,* this drama, along with Machiavelli's, expressed a general longing for release from the constraints of the bourgeois marriage. Anton Doni relates in the *Marmi* a gala occasion in the Sala del Papa at the Palazzo Vecchio when both plays were performed with acts of the one drama alternating with those of the other to serve as each other's intermezzi. The spontaneous, impetuous, and often insolent spirit of erotic fervor in *L'Assiuolo* appealed to a public seeking the temporary escape of carnival-season licentiousness.

The Comedy of Chests: Lo Spirito

Pretense to occult powers, deception of the gullible, and false possession by spirits figure in the complex verse play *Lo Spirito*, which finds unity in the central theme of the triumph of intelligence over adverse Fortune. As in *L'Assiuolo*, Cecchi asserts in the prologue that he derived the subject matter of his drama from actual occurrences in Florence except that he altered them somewhat for aesthetic purposes. The prologue explains the comedy's title from the mad little spirits that invade persons' bodies, especially those of attractive young women, to take possession of them. From this fable, which is based halfway on fact, the audience is supposed to gain a double benefit: the pleasure of laughter and the usefulness of seeing how spirits take sway and then depart, as well as the lesson of allowing oneself to be duped by a fictitious story of possession. The author illustrates here how his play conforms to the Horatian dictum of the utile dulce to produce delight and advantage. As frequently in his prologues, Cecchi makes some autobiographical comments in describing himself as neither old nor young (he was thirty-one years old in 1549), neither highly lettered nor without letters. Rather than calling himself a comic poet, the playwright prefers to think of himself as someone who writes chiefly to please his friends.

Unlike *L'Assiuolo*, which did not conclude in any weddings, *Lo Spirito*, with its division into doubled pairs of lovers, results in the public declaration of four marriages equally distributed between the young and old generations. At the play's opening the youth Napoleone relates how he had to enter into a clandestine marriage with the former slave-girl Emilia, since he feared angering their common guardian, old Neri. Difference in social rank between the bourgeois Napoleone and the penniless freed woman Emilia would have prejudiced Neri against granting them permission to wed. Deception comes about on the part of the young lovers not as a willful act but as the result of the domestic coercion imposed on them. Not long after the wedding, Napoleone undertook a commercial voyage to the Levant, and an inaccurate report soon reached Florence of his death. Meanwhile, Neri arranged for Emilia's marriage to still another former slave, Aldobrando, the adopted son and heir of the well-to-do merchant Anselmo. Before Aldobrando could consummate his wedding to the girl, Napoleone returned home and easily persuaded the young man to yield his conjugal rights to him. Aldobrando's willingness to consent to an agreement whereby Napoleone could visit Anselmo's household and meet secretly with Emilia came from his passionate interest in the niece of a foreign physician who was taking up temporary residence in the city before assuming a professorship at the University of Pisa.

Paralleling the imperiled amorous relationships of the young are the marital commitments of the old. Anselmo lives with a feeling of guilt and sinfulness because years before he and Neri's sister Laura were once lovers, until her brother compelled her to marry another man. Out of their illicit relationship was born a child that died, and, now that Laura has become a widow, Anselmo hopes to redress past wrongs by marrying her. Following continued opposition to the family alliance, Anselmo retaliates by shutting the door of his home to every member of Neri's household, including Napoleone, who can no longer visit his wife.

Although Neri is under constant pressure to marry some suitable partner from the Florentine bourgeoisie, he explains to an acquaintance that he already has a wife who might be dead or alive. The playwright introduces a political note here from recent Tuscan history because Neri had to flee Florence in 1530 as a rebel against the Medici forces. After killing a nobleman in Venice, this republican partisan left Italy for refuge in Romania, where he married a noble but impoverished widow whose family had moved from Constantinople at the time of Turkish occupation. When the Vatican lifted the banishment of most of the rebels, Neri returned to Italy to assume the post of papal envoy on a mission to France. During the period of separation from his wife, the forces of Barbarossa invaded Romania and carried away scores of prisoners. All that Neri has managed to learn is that his wife was seven months pregnant at the time of her disappearance. The burden of the past weighs heavily on the two old men and affects their treatment of the young.

In order to advance the plot from its romantic stalemate, the author presents in the cast of characters a resourceful outsider, the Greek magician-astrologer Aristone, who plays on the superstitious nature of the supposedly sophisticated

Florentines to demand high fees for his miraculous services. Anselmo, Napoleone, and Aldobrando all seek the necromancer's assistance so that they can reach their beloved ladies. The magician persuades each romantic aspirant to hide in a different chest that is to be transported to the bedchamber of the desired woman. This device of using a chest derives from the novella tradition, as in *Decameron* 2, 9, or 9, 2, in which persons are hidden in trunks for one reason or another.[4] In addition to these novellistic sources, Cecchi also had the example of recent Italian comic theater to inspire him. In *Il Negromante* the sorcerer Giacchelino commands the slow-witted youth Camillo to conceal himself in a trunk that he claims will magically transport him to the object of his romantic passion. Equally important to Cecchi's drama is the situation of a chest whose transfer is interrupted by civic officials, as in Bibbiena's *La Calandria*, in which customs agents intercept a trunk bearing the simpleton Calandro to what he believes is an assignation. Similar disaster befalls the encased lovers of *Lo Spirito*.

Acting on Aristone's instructions via a servant-woman, Emilia has been pretending that a spirit had possessed her and caused her to speak in Latin. The magician convinces his admirer Anselmo to quarantine Emilia in her bedroom, to which Napoleone comes conveyed in a trunk. Aldobrando also holds trysts with the niece of the physician Maestro Antonio. Hoping to elude the spies with whom Neri surrounds Laura, the gullible Anselmo also agrees to the stratagem of his being carried to her room in a chest. By the end of act 4, every one of Aristone's ruses with the coffers has ended in failure. Aldobrando's latest visit to the doctor's house meets with one setback after another when by chance the trunk in which he is concealed is first placed in Antonio's studio and then mistakenly conveyed to the Customs Office to be declared as a shipment of books intended for a professorial post at Pisa. On his discovery by the customs officials Aldobrando is immediately arrested. Anselmo meanwhile never reaches Neri's house, as the presence of sheriff's deputies there to collect the debts of Laura's deceased husband forces the servant transporting the chest with the old man in it to deposit her charge temporarily in Antonio's house, where a domestic uncovers the elderly suitor and chases him away with a thrashing. On returning to his house, the frustrated Anselmo finds Napoleone with Emilia and expels him from his house. This unfortunate series of events leaves Aristone exposed as a fraud by the fourth act's finale.

Cecchi resorts to agnition to rescue this drama from total defeat for the romantic parties and their families. Maestro Antonio identifies Aldobrando and Emilia as coming from a noble and wealthy lineage before the Turkish occupation of the Balkans. With Aristone's revelation of the secret marriage between Napoleone and Emilia, parental approval is secured for public acknowledgment of the match. Neri also discovers that Antonio's sister, Maria, is the merchant's long-lost wife and that the physician's niece Laldomine is none other than the old man's daughter. Aldobrando receives permission to wed Neri's child. In the mood of peaceful resolution and family reunion, Neri at last agrees to Laura's marriage with Anselmo. Both old and young generations participate in the joy of marital alliances that unite their families.

With the device of three trunks and the recourse to just as many recognitions, it might appear that Cecchi unnecessarily complicated this comedy's plot to the point where it becomes nearly impossible to trace events and intricate relationships. But this play's interior structure, like that of other dramas by the same author and his contemporaries, reflects the Manneristic style of art during the Medicean Restoration. The crossed relations of Napoleone/Emilia/Aldobrando/Laldomine correspond to the rhetorical figures like chiasmus that academics such as Varchi were resurrecting from Quintilian's treatises on oratory.

Viewed in the rhetorical practice of its era, a complex play like *Lo Spirito* no longer seems to be heavily muddled in its plot development.[5] As in Mannerist painting, there is a continual movement back and forth over the work of art as Cecchi compels the members of his audience to reexamine certain relationships and to anticipate the recognition of originally undisclosed identities. To appreciate the entangling and unraveling of the threads in the plot of *Lo Spirito* one must accept the conventions that guided the dramatist in building the framework of events. With what Cecchi considered as heightening comic delight, he tried to push imagination beyond logical limits so that his audience would be impressed by the plot's inventiveness and continual surprises.

Throughout this comedy various characters accuse Fortune or Destiny of acting as their enemy. Napoleone's prolonged illness during the trip to the Levant is attributed to the caprice of *"fortuna"* or *"sortaccia"* (evil fate), which just as arbitrarily cured him of the mysterious malady that had almost killed the youth. In act 5, scene 5, Aristone blames Fortune for the simultaneous collapse of his schemes with the three chests. Although Dr. Antonio can trace his ancestry to Byzantine aristocracy, fate *(la sorte)* has so impoverished him that he must prostitute his education by rendering medical services for payment. This negative attitude toward Fortune as a cruel force that destroys the human dream of realizing perfection on earth is a recurrent theme of Renaissance literature as compared to the medieval vision of Fortune in works like the *Divine Comedy* as an impartial power distributing wealth and might among individuals and nations.

In the fifteenth and early sixteenth century, Italian writers like Poliziano and Castiglione spoke of a direct antagonism between Fortune and human beings. Ariosto, too, saw Fortune as arbitrary and envious of the human aspiration to accomplish extraordinary deeds. Machiavelli also recognized the enormously important role of Fortune in human affairs, but in *The Prince* he stated that one should avoid a fatalistic attitude since Fortune usually determined no more than half the results of man's endeavors. When Cecchi composed *Lo Spirito,* he had not yet embraced the religious fatalism that was to characterize his conversion during the Tridentine era. The author's optimism would leave the possibility for human intelligence to alter destiny.

In the figure of the fraudulent magician Aristone the audience could behold the gift of natural wit to combat foreverchanging Fortune. As a model for the false sorcerer, Cecchi looked to the magician Ruffo in the *Calandria* and especially to the title character Giacchelino of *Il Negromante.* Ruffo appears in Bibbiena's play as a rather lowly swindler who professes to have power over spirits but in reality laughs at his patrons' credulity. With Giacchelino one finds a master criminal-type leading a gypsy existence across Europe in search of victims to defraud. Like Giacchelino, the magician in *Lo Spirito* exploits the tensions within bourgeois households, where he succeeds in making everyone reward him for the miraculous results that he merely promises to achieve. Aristone's greatest offense consists in betraying the trust that unhappy persons place in him, but he differs from Giacchelino in not being a common thief.

Cecchi's character reflects the very practical approach of sorcerers in Renaissance Italy to study the black arts not for the pure love of magic but solely for the profit that could be won from a gullible public who wanted quick results.[6] Aristone excels by taking advantage of individuals whose rational faculties have yielded to amorous distress. Rather than actually practicing magic, Aristone merely seeks to create the reputation of being a wondrous sorcerer. To that end he seeks to win the esteem of an influential citizen like Anselmo, whose faith in his powers would win still more clients for the false necromancer. Aristone confesses his limitations to his servant Sollectico:

> Believe me that all
> these enchantments and the knowledge of Spirits
> are only jests today: that art which once
> existed (if indeed it ever did exist) is lost,
> and whoever wants to make a show of it as a profession
> has to be astute and stay alert so as to dupe everyone.
> (act 3, scene 2)

Fearing a summons from the Holy Inquisition on charges of black magic, this wily character officially calls himself an herbalist rather than a necromancer. Aristone even fabricates credentials by claiming to be a graduate of the University of Padua in logic, physics, and astrology, with special training from a Calabrese alchemist. Since this charlatan constantly quotes Aristotle, the unlettered Anselmo asks him if he is related to that sage, and Aristone appropriates the great philosopher as one of his ancestors. Composure at a time of angry confrontation and tactfulness in dealing with aggrieved parties enable Aristone to achieve victory over hostile Fortune. That affirmation of intelligence gains for the magician at the play's close an invitation to become Neri's guest during the rest of his stay in Florence. To this charmingly resourceful rogue falls the honor of delivering the comedy's envoi. The triumphant quality of character for which the author expresses admiration is an urbanity that pacifies contending interest groups.

Cecchi strives to create a vivid impression not just of the immediate scene onstage of Florence with its cathedral dome and its townhouses but also of the vast Mediterranean world that serves as a background for this drama of the antagonism between Fortune and intelligence. Political flight to Romania, commercial voyages to the Near East, diplomatic missions to France, and enslavement in North Africa and Sicily indicate the broad geographical experiences of some of the play's main characters. Several members of the cast—Aldobrando, Emilia, Maria, Antonio—are refugees from the fall of the Byzantine Empire. Maria's description of the respectful treatment she received from her Turkish captors arouses amazement in the Florentines, who live in terror of being impaled by Ottoman invaders.

Contrasted to the worldly sophistication of this comedy's international characters is the parochialism prevailing in Florence. Not only does a merchant like Anselmo reveal his ignorance of Greek philsophy, but servants like Maria's maid Menica believe Palermo is a man's name and Sicily is a town like Fiesole. Cecchi carries his drama from the macrocosm of the Mediterranean basin to the microcosm of the Tuscan capital, which here appears as a constricting society dominated by mean-minded shopkeepers, scheming lawyers, and disgruntled physicians.[7] A few sly representatives of the servant class, like Solletico and Antonio's errand-boy, Rondine, manage to parody the vain dissimulation of knowledge and respectability by the bourgeoisie. Cecchi fashioned in *Lo Spirito* a playworld moving across international frontiers to the restricted social order of a provincial center.

First performed by the Company of the Fantastichi, this play in the Giunti edition includes a series of verse intermezzi that announce the crucial developments of each act. The intermezzi work to engage the public directly in the drama by pointing out parallels between their condition and that of the theatrical characters. In the intermezzo preceding act 1, actors costumed as dreams, chimeras, and spirits sing a madrigal proclaiming that their role is to cheer *The Spirit* which is coming to the audience in the form of a play that will demonstrate Love's might. The second intermezzo analyzes the state of lovers, drawing attention to the condition of living between fragile hope and certain pain similar to the vacuousness of the spirits performing these interludes. To prepare the public for Aristone's stratagems to assist the lovers, the third intermezzo urges the spectators to employ the gift of intellect to see through chimerical appearances and to behold the danger of errors. By the fourth act, when the main plot devices are growing increasingly complicated, the errant spirits of the intermezzo declare that neither their nebulous form nor the illusions that they produce are as distorted and confusing as the experiences that befall the lovers in the audience.

These intermezzi point out how Cecchi was creating a drama not of detachment but of engagement for his public. After the catastrophic close of act 4, the final interlude sets the audience at ease by explaining that love is often severe in testing the constancy of lovers but now a joyous time is about to arrive when Faith and Chastity will fulfill every amorous expectation. Cecchi's Florentine spectators could regard themselves mirrored in the intermezzi with their representation of love's distress and the eventual reward for loyalty. With its multiple weddings for members of both the young and old generations, *Lo Spirito* becomes a festive celebration of love's triumph over the hardships of international warfare and the prejudices of class and caste.

The Portrait of Greed: Il Servigiale

Portrayal of the greed prevailing in the bourgeois and ecclesiastical circles of Florence distinguishes the comedy *Il Servigiale*, originally produced for the carnival of 1556 by the Company of San Bastiano de' Fanciulli. Marriage appears here as a commerce of family interest negotiated by parasitic brokers. In act 4, scene 3, of this verse drama the corrupt lowclass shopkeeper Geppo remarks that whoever has money is the ruler over other persons. Members of the servant class, like the errand-boy Giannicco, impudently reproach their masters for starving the domestic staff while trying to im-

press their social peers. Having ready cash substitutes for erudition, as a university graduate remarks in act 3, scene 6, that
a horse could receive a doctorate if enough money were paid.
At the time of this play's composition, Cecchi had not yet
abandoned satire of the clergy, whom he characterizes here as
greedy priests demanding gifts of shirts and handkerchiefs or
nuns, called "house-emptiers," never tiring of asking for
donations.

Charlatans and fools dominate the scene in Florence as
they parade along the streets in rich velvet attire to mask
their worthlessness. Distinctions of class bring about the major actions in this comedy because the wealthy but miserly
entrepreneur Domenico Ciuffagni has always forbidden his
ward Neri to marry below his social rank. After Neri falls in
love with his uncle's impoverished dependent, Ermellina, the
youth enlists the aid of the cobbler Benuccio to pose as his
"straw man" and to request Domenico's permission for marriage with the girl. Forever seeking profit, Domenico plays
Benuccio against the debased Geppo, who has already offered
to provide Ermellina with a dowry of one hundred ducats. In
truth, Geppo is acting in the interest of the well-to-do youth
Messer Gentile, son of Domenico's friend Lamberto Lamber-
teschi, who would also object to a match outside the merchant class. Understanding his uncle's greed, Neri arranges
for Benuccio's broker, Agabito, to counter Geppo's offer with
a promise of three hundred ducats. Since he lacks Gentile's
financial resources, Neri has to turn to still another broker,
the unscrupulous Travaglio, to devise a ruse *(beffa)* to defraud
Domenico of the needed sum and then to pass the money off
as payment of Benuccio's offer.

In the struggle between Neri and Gentile for Ermellina
there occur three disguises. The first charade falls to Travaglio, who represents himself to Domenico as the attendant of
a convent and asks the merchant to transport some valuable
wares on a forthcoming business trip to Bologna. Having
gained the old man's confidence, Travaglio hires a Venetian
confederate to play the part of a German commercial traveler
seeking Domenico's company for the Bolognese journey. After the foreign merchant guarantees a generous reward for
Domenico's assistance, the Florentine businessman pledges
four hundred ducats as a token of good faith and places them

in the same suitcase with the German's funds. But the two rogues switch the suitcase with one full of valueless pieces of metal. Thanks to Travaglio's astuteness, Neri has the means to secure Benuccio's nominal marriage to Ermellina.

As frequently happens in Cecchi's dramas, destiny intervenes to undermine the most brilliant ruses. To Domenico's painful surprise there arrives in Florence the long-lost military adventurer Valentino Renzon da Crema, the man who originally discovered Ermellina as a war orphan and placed her with his brother Antonello. Since Domenico's wife is Antonello's widow, Valentino has a valid claim to half of his brother's estate. Because of these upsetting developments, the old merchant tries in vain to find the German in order to cancel their journey. Made suspicious by his inability to locate the foreigner, Domenico opens the suitcase and learns to his horror of the deception. In the meantime, Gentile, with the aid of Geppo and the maid Agata, has entered the Ciuffagni house in the hope of an assignation with Ermellina, but his two treacherous assistants have led the foolish youth to entrapment in a darkened room with Domenico's widowed daughter Violante, who intends to compromise Gentile into marrying her. To effect his ill-fated entry Gentile has had to disguise himself as a domestic. Not long after the enraged Domenico seizes hold of Gentile and turns him over to Lamberto, Travaglio appears at the merchant's home with the aim of cheating Domenico of still more money with a scheme about depositing funds to purchase a consignment of gold thread. After the old man extracts the truth from Travaglio about Neri's complicity, Domenico confronts his nephew and forces him to confess his guilt.

With the benevolent intercession of Valentino, all conflicts vanish. Lamberto realizes that Ermellina is his daughter, who disappeared years before during the chaotic period following Cosimo's ascension to the control of Florence. Valentino graciously concedes his claims to Antonello's estate by bestowing a dowry on Ermellina. Now that Gentile has discovered that girl to be his sister, he agrees to wed Violante. In his immense relief over recovering his lost money, Domenico responds to Valentino's generosity by both accepting the marriage plans and permitting Travaglio's release from criminal prosecution.

Greed constantly motivates Domenico, who appears as the drama's central character. Cecchi provides this character with a depth of biographical detail and psychological development rare in his plays. Born to poverty, Domenico laboriously applied himself to building lines of trade between Bologna, Milan, and Florence. After amassing a respectable amount of capital, this enterprising figure married a wealthy widow and used her fortune to acquire more shops and goods until he became a major man of affairs. Although Domenico's avarice has led critics to compare him to the grasping pimps in ancient Latin comedies,[8] his compulsive need to acquire and to hold onto money reveals a pathological instability rather than a tendency to exploit others for power over them. Money has become an intrinsic part of his being. Neri calls his uncle a miser who values nothing except money, a wretch whose greed increases with the passing of time, even to the extent that he injures his own health by carrying out wearisome tasks instead of paying someone to do the work for him.

Domenico's importance to this play appears evident in a solioquy in act 1, scene 2, where the old man rejoices in his obsessive-compulsive manner over his imminent success in negotiating with Benuccio's broker for three hundred ducats. The verb that the merchant uses here and elsewhere in the play is *"cogliere,"* to acquire, to collect, to gather—the idea of acquisition. Domenico dreams of the investments he will make with Benuccio's money, imagining that the suitor might die and leave all the cash to him without any obligations. In another soliloquy in act 3, scene 8, this entrepreneur allows the audience to glimpse his dishonesty as he contemplates robbing the German on the way to Bologna. Domenico also longs for the foreigner's death since the lack of a receipt will prevent the German's distant heirs from making any claims to the money supposedly placed in the suitcase. The need to call off the business trip and return the cash deposit arouses this agonized outburst from Domenico:

> Oh God!
> Oh my five hundred ducats! Mine!
> Mine! Because the money has been here in my family
> And in my house, I had directed my love
> To it as something that is mine . . .
> (act 4, scene 12)

The impassioned repetition of the possessive *mia* (my, mine) stresses the sensual bond between the merchant and the money even though some of the funds are not rightfully his own. This man lives in a fantasy world where he can annihilate other persons in order to appropriate their fortunes. The shocking realization in act 5 that Travaglio has defrauded him of his money nearly drives Domenico to suicide, for his only reason to live is to accumulate money, the one thing that he can address with the language of love. Travaglio understood how easily he could dupe the merchant by playing on his thirst for gain.

In the character of Domenico the playwright wished to demonstrate how a basically dishonest attitude toward others would eventually lead the merchant to lose what he valued above all other persons and things. But in the comic spirit of renewed hope Domenico retrieves his funds and sees his nephew married to financial advantage. In his closing remarks the now enlightened entrepreneur forgives Travaglio and thanks the rogue for teaching him in his old age how to live.[9]

Although Travalgio's perceptiveness about Domenico's acquisitive character led to the success of the *beffa*, the rogue failed to assist Neri and the girl because his own greed brought him to entrapment at the merchant's home. Once again, superior intelligence meets its limitations in a world where Fortune and the flaws of human character determine the outcome of events. Even when Neri observes in Machiavellian sentiment (act 5, scene 2) how Fortune befriends the bold, frustration all too often rewards brave endeavors. As the play in act 3, scene 4, puns on Travaglio's name, there has to be "travail," which will result in defeat. In contrast with the conventional servants of comedy who always give loyal service to young lovers, Travaglio works in his own interest alone as an unscrupulous opportunist who survives by cheating others. Neri's friend Filippo correctly describes Travaglio (act 5, scene 10) as fit for the galleys. This confidence man with his recourse to disguises represents the fringe element of the professional class in Florence that preys parasitically on tensely divided bourgeois households.

While Domenico has strictly limited an allowance for Neri, the old man's friend Lamberto has indulged Gentile with generosity. This vainglorious youth exhibits traits of the braggart warrior combined with the romantic exploits of the university student, since he is both a graduate of the University of Pisa and an experienced soldier. Gentile admits that he never seriously applied himself to his legal studies, as his one intention was merely to boast about having attended a university. His name expresses his refinement as he delicately plays the gallant around women with his handsomeness, quick wit, skill at dancing, and singing along with all the other social graces. As Gentile's treatment of Violante illustrates, this pretentious fop will practice deception to forward a possible affair with Ermellina. Instead of impressing others, all this dandy succeeds in doing is making himself ridiculous to the servant boy Giannicco, who has to brush the dust off his master's shoes; to the straw man, Geppo, and the maid Agata, whose greed propels them to betray their fatuous benefactor; to Violante, who plans to punish his duplicity and trick him into marriage. Because of the humiliating disguise he has assumed to enter Domenico's house, the young pretender has to hear disparaging remarks that Giannicco makes about him in ignorance of Gentile's presence onstage. Vain folly finally causes Gentile to be labeled a thief after Domenico discovers him and denounces him to Lamberto. What Cecchi was seeking to create with this bourgeois braggart warrior was the portrait of a conceited pretender to the glories of arms and letters who in reality merits derision.

An intermezzo and a madrigal precede each act in this play in an elaborate allegory of the soul's salvation, which reveals the affinity between the author's secular comedies and his religious dramas in their focus on moral issues. In each of the intermezzi the audience could view the soul's progress from infantile innocence to adult sinfulness and eventual liberation through rational guidance. Purity personified proclaims in the opening *intermedio* how Memory, Intellect, Will, and Genius will accompany the soul that appears as a simple little baby in need of spiritual direction. These allegorical figures sing a madrigal exhorting the soul to follow virtue. After the expository first act has presented the various attempts by the love-frenzied Neri to secure Ermellina for himself, the second intermezzo introduces the self-confident deity Love, who boasts how he has displaced Purity from control over the soul and cites the examples of Solomon, Hercules, Achilles, and Aristotle as wise or heroic figures who had to succumb to Love's might. In their madrigal, those four historical and mythic characters declare that no one can resist Love's flames. After the infancy of Purity and early youth under Love, there comes in the third interlude the maturity of Ambition that has ruled the aspiring hearts of Semiramis, Cyrus, Alexander the Great, and Julius Caesar, who all confess in a madrigal to the ardent desire to be remembered for their glorious deeds. The seasons of the soul occupy the fourth intermezzo with a Springtime of Purity, a Summer of Love, an Autumn of mature Ambition, and a Winter of Greed, which holds obsessive sway over humans and drives them on perilous sea voyages to amass fortunes in gold and jewels.

This interlude on the power of greed to direct all of life's energies serves as a moral commentary on the play's central character, Domenico, and the unifying theme in the compulsion to build fortunes no matter what the risks might be or who might be hurt. Legend and history provide the examples of Midas; King Polymestor of Thrace, who murdered a Trojan prince to gain the royal treasure; Crassus, who met death because of his desire for Parthian gold; and Eriphyle, who betrayed her husband for a golden necklace. That enslavement to a god of covetousness forces the greedy quartet to sing a madrigal for the soul's peace from the all-absorbing desire for material gain.

Finally in the fifth interlude happiness releases the soul from bondage through the victorious intercession of Reason that overcomes the appetite for earthly satisfactions of lust and greed. Reason cites various cases in which humans refused to yield to appetite: Joseph of Egypt affirming chastity before temptation; the Spartan Lycurgus declining a kingdom; Fabricius in early Roman history rejecting the bribes of Pyrrhus; and the Emperor Titus, who attempted to rule in justice and gentleness. The closing madrigal announces the peace that ends every worldly desire in the contemplation of God. All these intermezzi function to juxtapose the particular comedy of middle-class Florence in ducal Medicean times against an eternal drama of the soul's triumphant movement toward redemption.

In *Il Servigiale,* it is Domenico who glimpses a redeeming vision of his life as he reflects on the ruse Travaglio has perpetrated by manipulating his greedy nature. As the intermezzi suggest, this comedy has an almost didactic purpose in pointing out the moral danger of avarice. In Cecchi's drama, individual assertion of will against destiny must give way to a view of reality that stresses shortcomings of intelligence and weaknesses of character. The *beffa* of the switched suitcase does nothing to advance Neri's open marriage to Ermellina, and only the surprising appearance of Valentino brings about the desired comic goal. That stranger from the past acts as a divine agent of fate to demolish the purely external obstacles to the marital union by revealing the girl's socially acceptable identity. Neri acknowledges the solider's nearly sacred function with this observation: "That Valentino is not a man; he is / an Angel descended from Heaven for me" (act 5, scene 14). In the urban world dominated by greed, Valentino's generosity seems angelic. While neither entrepreneurial initiative nor criminal cunning succeeds in prevailing over the abuses and the pressures of mercantile society, a spontaneous gesture of charity toward a young couple renews hope in the future.[10]

Empty Promises: Le Cedole

Cecchi's late comedy entitled *Le Cedole,* composed between 1574 and 1579, represents how nobility of long-standing lineage proves valueless without integrity of character and personal wealth. In the prologue to this verse drama, the author comments on the difficulties he encountered in writing the play by referring to the Platonic theory of divine poetic inspiration as a fury that cannot be commanded or commissioned but must arise spontaneously. Numerous efforts in the summertime leisure of his villa produced nothing until suddenly his imagination awakened, and he completed this comedy in a few days. During the period when he wrote the drama, Cecchi's main literary interests were devoted to composing religious plays rather than secular comedies. Although the playwright states in the prologue that he denies himself the title of poet, as the creator of some "rather bad comedies" *(commediacce)* he has heeded poetic fancy to fashion his dramas of social customs and class divisions. In *Le Cedole* Ser Giovan Maria exposed the emptiness of noble titles before prodigality and moral corruption.

A multitude of impersonations accompanies this comedy of intrigue and deception to advance the designs of the Florentine youth Emilio de' Giuochi on the orphaned maiden Angelica. During university studies in Bologna, Emilio fell in love with the girl, but he has failed to consummate an affair with her because of strict supervision by her guardian Veronica. The young man has won some influence over Veronica's second husband, Ramaglia, a vitiated descendant of an ancient Florentine family now reduced to taking manual work as a wool carder or to offering his services as a marriage broker. In order to provide the penniless couple with financial aid, Emilio has assumed a loan by signing a promissory note for one hundred ducats and by turning over his university textbooks as collateral to the Bolognese usurer Eustachio Gambale. As the son of a highly successful merchant, Emilio cannot marry beneath his social station for fear his father, Tegghiaio, will disinherit him. Even after the youth has returned to Florence and has lodged Angelica and her guardians in a house near his home, his situation continues to deteriorate as the time for the loan's payment draws near and Ramaglia falls deeply into debt.

In desperation, Emilio seeks the assistance of his resourceful servant Monello, who immediately improvises a series of actions to obtain funds for the young man and to enable him to have Angelica married to a "straw" husband as a cover. Monello's first assault against Tegghiaio's greed and caution meets defeat when the old man adamantly refuses to pay for the loan even at the risk of litigation. Undaunted in spirit, the servant enlists the talents of the versatile coachman Ghianda to undertake two disguises. Since Angelica is a war orphan of noble Piedmontese background, Ghianda must impersonate the girl's brother, Astolfo di Messer Landolfo d'Andal d'Asti, and lure her away from Veronica into the false wedding with Emilio's front man, Fantassino. Ghianda must also take on a second disguise as Eustachio Gambale in order to confront Tegghiaio and to secure the money that Emilio needs to silence Ramaglia's creditors. Once again the wily merchant outsmarts his adversary by agreeing to pay for the loan through the intermediary of a Bolognese friend, who will hand over the cash only in return for Emilio's textbooks. Ghianda's disguise as Angelica's brother also comes to nothing after a neighborhood woman, Mona Brigida, recognizes him and reveals his identity to an outraged Veronica. Monello's imaginative ruses and Ghianda's criminally histrionic skills absolutely fail to assist Emilio.

Fate alone reverses events after the authentic Eustachio arrives in Florence to present Tegghiaio with the promissory note and to demand payment. Naturally the elderly merchant believes the usurer is an impostor, and the two exchange blows. Taking advantage of Eustachio's fear of being arrested for attacking a Florentine citizen, Monello readily persuades the non-Tuscan usurer to pose as Angelica's father and to seek refuge at Ramaglia's home. In learning the details of the girl's family history, Gambale discloses that he is indeed Angelica's uncle. Since the young woman is heiress to a large fortune, every obstacle to marriage with Emilio vanishes. In the meantime, the young couple have already become lovers because Veronica had placed Angelica in safekeeping with Emilio's mother, Nannina, while the two older women were plotting a stratagem to punish Tegghiaio for his lustful desire for the girl. As a peace offering to honor their family alliance, Eustachio surrenders the promissory note to Tegghiaio. Gambale also pays all of Ramaglia's debts and rewards Ghianda for his efforts on the lovers' behalf. With the wedding of Emilio and Angelica, a solid bond between the Tuscan bourgeoisie and the Piedmontese aristocracy is formed, and impersonations give way to the enriched identity of economic and marital alliance.

Both Emilio and his father trust Monello as the ideal agent to achieve their amorous intentions. Events demonstrate, however, that while their trust is well placed in a loyal servant fully deserving an intimate rapport with his masters, Monello lacks the quality of quiet and slow deliberation before taking any bold action. This hasty servant never pauses to analyze a situation before initiating a scheme. Monello should have known that parental concern alone would never have sufficed to cause the forever calculating Tegghiaio to part with forty ducats as partial payment on his son's loan.

As shown in other comedies of Cecchi, deception succeeds best when a rogue takes into account the psychology of a potential victim. None of Monello's *beffe* accomplish their desired goal since the servant does not take the time to consider circumstances, and, consequently, he never once becomes master of events. Perhaps the defect in character that undermines this skillful assistant is overconfidence in his ability to surmount all obstacles before him.

Excessive reliance on his talents proves to be only one of the reasons for Monello's frustration; pure chance also intervenes to upset his plans. Brigida's unmasking of Ghianda as an impostor comes about solely by accident because she just happens to enter when Veronica is receiving Angelica's supposedly long-lost brother. Similarly, the discovery that Eustachio is a close relative of Angelica occurs as the result of absolutely fortuitous events without any conscious design. Emilio's opportunity to consummate his love for Angelica equally presents itself by a series of happenings that arise independently of the scheming by the youth and his henchman, Monello. In all these occurrences Fortune has determined the outcome for or against the protagonists. If one recalls that during the period of this play's composition Cecchi was mainly engaged in religious writings, it is obvious that the author could not attribute to human intelligence and bold initiative but to casual destiny the credit for resolving the outcome of all endeavors.[11] Since Monello has labored in good faith, notwithstanding his hastiness and Fortune's intrusions, this loyal servant does receive the reward of a purse from Tegghiaio at the play's end and assumes the honor of delivering the envoi.

In exposing the mercenary values of Florentine society Cecchi creates in this play a tense atmosphere like that of contending parties involved in litigation. With his expert knowledge of legal procedure and terminology the playwright describes how the characters have caught themselves in entangled promises and agreements that they are not prepared to honor. By act 1, scene 2, Veronica informs Emilio that the local commercial tribunal has issued a summons against Ramaglia for nonpayment of debts and that two bailiffs *(toccatori)* have "touched" him and warned him of arrest in twenty-four hours unless he clears his accounts with creditors. Ramaglia's one recourse, while expecting financial relief from Emilio, is to take refuge with common criminals in the asylum offered by churches. As Monello remarks sarcastically, debts are responsible for Ramaglia's sudden devoutness.

When Monello first attempts to terrify Tegghiaio into honoring a false promissory note, the servant mentions the dread Eight of Justice and the expensive *"condannagioni"* (legal difficulties, act 3, scene 2) that might develop without prompt settlement of the outstanding loan. Tegghiaio, however, as he will fight for his money, is not easily intimidated. But Monello succeeds in manipulating Eustachio's terror of being a foreigner at the mercy of Florentine courts and police; the scamp intensifies the usurer's concern by claiming that Tegghiaio is a magistrate. In addition to the secular tribunals that can render arbitrary sentences, attention is directed in the drama to the ecclesiastical courts when Emilio proposes to Ghianda that he should deceive Tegghiaio over the fate of the youth's textbooks by saying the Holy Inquisition confiscated them as being suspect of heretical content. The litigious environment that this play presents is one of menace, with summonses to appear at tribunals, the constant fear of arrest, and the prospect of paying exorbitant fines and court costs.

In the playworld of Cecchi's drama, everything and everyone (especially women) are reduced to commodities of legal contention and commercial exchange. One of the verbs that recurs with great frequency is *"consumare,"* meaning to cost, to cause to spend. Parasitic characters like Ramaglia are great consumers of others' money, food, and wine. Conspicuous consumption also appears in the references to the gala fashions of women in upper bourgeois society who would conceal their ugliness with rich apparel. Ghianda, in visiting Angelica in disguise as her brother, astutely wishes to give her a new dress as a gift. But girls of marriageable age are, in Monello's evaluation in act 2, scene 2, just bad merchandise that bring harm to whoever has charge of them. Veronica also has to admit to Nannina's maid, Crezia, that assets of beauty and goodness of character cannot help a girl find a husband because money alone in the form of a dowry substitutes for virtue and loveliness (act 5, scene 1). In this mercenary social setting, young women, textbooks, fine clothes are always being placed on an imaginary scale to reckon their monetary value for the interested consumer.

What values exist other than those that can be measured in their financial effectiveness? A sense of family history and tradition obsesses the most corrupt character in the drama: Ramaglia, a descendant of the Ramaglianti, one of the families of Florence's "first circle" of city walls at its earliest period of urban development. Despite coming from old family stock, Ramaglia appears to be of inferior "metal," just as his name signifies poor copper *(rame)* of unregistered value. Sensual appetite has consumed this vainglorious and impoverished nobleman in his decline to the status at the play's start when he is on the verge of being placed in debtors' prison. Prepared even to prostitute his ward so as to pay his debts and to resume his prodigal ways, Ramaglia forever greets Emilio and Monello with a refrain of the ducats they owe him to purchase his complicity. Whereas to a servant like Monello, with his exposure to bourgeois standards, nobility without wealth has no substance whatsoever, Ramaglia asserts a pride of nobility of blood in a household that once attracted learned scholars and knights. However, there is a painful disparity between Ramaglia's aristocratic rhetoric and his actual meretricious debasement. At the opening of the fourth act Ghianda draws an analogy that accurately describes Ramaglia's deterioration: just as wine in a cask retains its flavor so long as the cask is full or even half full but loses its quality as it sinks to the bottom in the same way, Ramaglia is at the very bottom of the barrel like spoiled wine. Despite pretensions to the noble splendor of the past, Ramaglia remains at the dregs of Florentine society.

In contrast to Ramaglia's representing the decadence of the nobility, Tegghiaio demonstrates the vigorous realism of the entrepreneurial class that has displaced the aristocrats. A youthful mental alertness characterizes the old man, who continually thinks in terms of expenditures and profit while endeavoring to avoid loss. No one, not even Monello, succeeds in outwitting Tegghiaio in financial matters. His one failure is the inability to take Angelica as a mistress, an action that would prove unseemly for a man of his age. In this drama Cecchi does not create a conscious rivalry between father and son for the same young woman, since Tegghiaio and Emilio act independently of each other in their pursuit of Angelica, whose name recalls the enchanting heroine of Boiardo's *Orlando Innamorato* and Ariosto's *Orlando Furioso* that fascinated Europe's greatest warrior knights. Even though Emilio does dissociate his choice of a love partner from financial gain, the youth never openly defies his father's authority and relies without success on stealth to win the girl for himself. Tegghiaio's infatuation with the girl constitutes not so much a deviation from the normal prudence of a masterful businessman as much as another illustration of his acquisitive nature that equates seducing Angelica with a commercial triumph. But his miserly unwillingness to compensate Brigida adequately for her efforts to win Veronica over to the merchant's side eventually leads to his defeat.

Unlike other older men in Cecchi's plays who succumb to an erotic preoccupation with a young woman, Tegghiaio never allows his passion to dominate him to the extent that he might appear ridiculous or menace the stability of his household. Even when he tries to deny that he is seventy and cites the typically inaccurate family record book listing him as fifty-eight, Tegghiaio does not display the domestically destructive amorous frenzy of a character like the aged father Nicomaco in Machiavelli's *Clizia*. In this drama by Cecchi Fortune favors the cautiously proceeding merchant, who escapes the mockery of being locked in Ramaglia's cellar as punishment by Nannina and Veronica for his indecent designs on Angelica. Instead of suffering humiliation, Tegghiaio emerges as a victor with his dignity intact as events beyond his control resolve the economically and socially advantageous marriage between Emilio and the newly recognized Piedmontese noblewoman.

This play also examines the extremely restricted sphere of action for women in a male-dominated world. Monello expresses an attitude bordering on contempt when, in act 2, scene 5, he reminds Ramaglia that in Florence men carry out all the important tasks such as deciding their daughters' marital partners, often without the mothers' approval. Almost the only influence women exert is that of pleading with their

husbands, scolding them for the foolishness that might damage the family's reputation. Older women have to uphold the
standards of social propriety. In act 1, scene 4, Nannina assails
Tegghiaio with verbal fury for his parsimony toward Emilio
and his indecorous desire for Angelica. Respectable women
also have to contend with traitors in their midst like the go-
between Mona Brigida, who appears in the drama as an inept
and vacillating variation of the procuress figure best realized
in *L'Assiuolo's* Verdiana. While Nannina enjoys her position
in a well-to-do bourgeois home, Veronica has to endure the
poverty caused by Ramaglia's irresponsibility. Never once
does the economically harassed Veronica yield to the temptation to compromise the future of her ward either by con-
senting to a lower-class wedding for Angelica with Fantassino
or by agreeing to a financially beneficial liaison with Tegghiaio. Veronica fights for an ideal of honor that redeems her
household from the shame brought by her corrupt husband.
As to be expected in one of Cecchi's plays, only older women
appear on the scene as Veronica keeps Angelica in isolation
with the ironical outcome of the girl's eventual intimacy in
Emilio's house. Cecchi's drama illustrates how honorable
older women struggle to overcome the social and economic
limitations imposed by dominant males in order to defend
the reputation, well-being, and happiness of their families.

Human endeavor in *Le Cedole* by both men and women
encounters definite bounds that the most imaginatively deceitful minds cannot cross. Ruses supported by actual physical disguise do not succeed against miserly distrust or
capricious Fortune. All of Monello's schemes result as futile
intrigues in the attempt to obtain the funds to bring the
young lovers together. The play makes fundamental statements about debts and empty promises for repayment: Ramaglia's vain reliance on a feudal noble past as his credit,
Emilio's willingness to sign promissory notes, and Tegghiaio's failure to reward Brigida as the agent of his passion.
Cecchi points out that there comes a moment of reckoning
when people must acknowledge that the ability to determine
the outcome of events has eluded them. In the play's concluding scene, Monello addresses Tegghiaio and Eustachio with
an appeal for the two wealthy older men to recognize here on

earth what Heaven has already established: the union of the lovers. Guile, economic power, and social rank will give way to a divinely directed destiny.

Carnival Season Deceptions: Le Maschere

With the verse play *Le Maschere*, 1585, Giovan Maria Cecchi realized that his career as a secular dramatist was drawing to a close. The author confesses in the prologue to his advanced age and poor health, but he entreats the audience's grace to accept still another comedy of his. While also disclosing that he wrote the play within six wintry days of isolation at his home, Cecchi defends himself by stating that it has always been his practice to complete a stage work in ten days or less. In the dramatist's opinion, no theatrical piece ever suffered because of the brief time required for its composition. In addition, the author admits that he has abandoned the writing of secular plays for some time, yet not to his artistic detriment, since none of the great arbiters of the comic art like Aristotle or Horace would have been able to find fault with this latest composition. Once again the setting is Florence, for the fourteenth time in eighteen comedies, as Cecchi proudly observes in the prologue. Toward the end of a lengthy experience in the theater, the elderly writer reaffirmed with this play his artistic mastery in recapturing the comic insecurity of life in his beloved native city.

Forged letters and carnival disguises figure as the plot devices in *Le Maschere* that continually undermine the seemingly firm reality of bourgeois existence in the Tuscan capital. As soon as one major character believes he has gained control over events, sudden developments or unexpected reports reverse the dramatic situation and briefly shift advantage to an antagonist who in turn will suffer an unforeseen setback. Over a year before the play opens, Fabrizio Dal Boschetto fled Florence in frustration at the obstacles placed by his father, the physician Manente, to marriage with a maiden of respectable but economically modest background. After learning of Fabrizio's supposed death in Orvieto, both his father and his maternal uncle Baldo Dell'Arca became rivals for the young man's former fiancée, Livia. Unknown to the two old men, the youth Vettorio Ormanni also intends to win Livia's affections. At the drama's start, the members of this amorous triangle of suitors receive the upsetting news that Fabrizio is alive and has recently disembarked at Genoa with a fortune acquired in West Indian trade.

A fierce struggle among the contenders ensues as each tries to negotiate a marriage contract before Fabrizio's return to Florence. Because the girl's mother, Madonna Clemenza, is away in Pisa on family business, the marital candidates exert pressure on Livia's temporary guardian, Aunt Adriana, to resolve the issue in favor of one of them. To achieve their devious ends, the three enlist the assistance of some cunningly deceitful allies: Manente with his servant Catacchio; Vettorio with his retainer Imbroglio; and Baldo with the broker Chima. Fabrizio's one advocate at home is his friend Attilio, who naively confides in Vettorio. The play takes on the appearance of a contest or, as Imbroglia describes it, a war with soldiers and spies fighting for Livia as their prize. The marital strategy of the combatants rests on a series of authentic and false letters dispatched with the intention of subverting each other's cause and securing the desired victory. A genuine letter from Fabrizio to Attilio is rejected by Manente as a trick to convince him to withdraw his suit for the girl. Clemenza's corrupt maid Crezia hands over to Vettorio a letter from Adriana to Livia's mother, and Imbroglia destroys the original letter and substitutes it with one pleading his master's case to the aunt. Manente gains possession of this letter and engages the treacherous Chima to fabricate correspondence from Clemenza to her sister ordering her to arrange immediately Livia's wedding with the physician.

Since the events in this drama are occurring during carnival season, Vettorio hopes to outwit Manente by disguising himself with a mask in order to abduct Livia and to carry her off to Lucca. The youth counts on the collaboration of Crezia, who would never permit the girl to be sacrificed as the bride of an old man. By chance, Fabrizio, who has arrived in town, learns of Vettorio's scheme and determines to take his place in the masquerade. Cecchi introduces here a variant on the plot device of disguise with Fabrizio's substitution of himself for his rival.

Just as the masked lover and Attilio are escaping with

Livia, they encounter Vettorio; and their altercation attracts the police, who arrest the entire group. On hearing of his son's incarceration, Manente finally relents and agrees to a wedding between Fabrizio and Livia, especially since the young man's mercantile successes in the New World have eliminated the need for a large dowry. In the spirit of contradiction that pervades the play, the new society that appears to be forming never becomes a reality after Clemenza comes back to Florence and announces to everyone's astonishment that Livia is not her child but Manente's daughter Porzia, whom gypsies kidnapped as an infant. Manente, Baldo, and Fabrizio have all narrowly avoided committing incest with Livia-Porzia. Now a new tripart marital union emerges wherein Vettorio will wed Porzia, Baldo will marry his former fiancée Adriana, and Manente will take Clemenza as his bride. Because of all his recently gained wealth, Fabrizio will become the most eligible and sought-after bachelor in Florence. Through its rapid succession of forever changing situations and altered family relationships, this comedy as it is carried along by false letters and masked disguises shows how surprisingly insecure life is within bourgeois society, where young and old alike struggle against a precarious reality.

In its general comic design and language, *Le Maschere* recalls the spirited playfulness of Cecchi's early secular dramas written during the years before his conversion. This comedy abounds with double entendres about male genitalia and risqué phrases asserting the virility of elderly characters like Baldo and Manente in their fear of being ridiculed for trying to marry a young woman. The salacious language, however, serves to express the forced sensuality of individuals who doubt their sexual prowess, and there is no lewdness merely to provoke laughter from the audience. It is the never-seen Livia whose youthful beauty arouses the ardent desires of young and old, for this maiden is the drama's center of contention. Because the plot structure revolves around the efforts to secure marriage with the girl, its scenic design aims at a graphic representation of that ongoing warfare of allied parties across the theatrical space. Characters generally enter onstage in groups of two, as either friends (Fabrizio and Attilio), master and servant, or adversaries like Baldo and Manente. Fabrizio's arrival in the city occurs in act 3, scene 3, exactly at the play's midpoint, although his presence has been felt since the drama's start. One of the comedy's most dramatically intense moments takes place at the end of act 3, scene 4, when Fabrizio sees Manente coming onstage, and instead of rushing forward to greet his father after their long separation the youth retreats, seeing in the physician neither an obstructing parent nor a loving paternal figure but his rival for Livia's hand.

By the close of that same third act, Manente does seem to be in ascendancy because of his success in controlling the circulation of letters. Advantage passes to Fabrizio in the fourth act to suggest that Fortune is rewarding his constant love. But the abortive offstage elopement during the last act, effected from an unseen back garden gate, places all the young characters in immediate peril. Even Manente's late attempt at reconciliation proves to be futile on account of Clemenza's startling disclosure about Livia's parentage. Within a period of several hours a surprising turn of events has resulted in continual comic dislocations of a fragile reality that is documented only by forged letters and defensive denials. To a greater degree than in many of his other plays, the author provides cues in *Le Maschere* for the passing of the tumultuous hours on that anxious day to make the audience sense the onset of evening and the coming of night when the multiple weddings will celebrate the end of hostilities. Cecchi's comic vision consists in his portrayal of a world caught in time with its instability, unforeseen developments, and varying sets of realities.

Of all the contending parties, Manente most displays an attitude of boldness that almost carries him to triumph against his other rivals. Even though this miserly physician is the play's most self-deluding character, with his unfatherly refusal to accept the news that his son is alive, Manente's forceful activism will not allow him to surrender to his opponents. At the height of apparent victory, in asking Chima to arrange a wedding banquet, Manente remains true to his greed by ordering inexpensive and not very delectable crows. After he learns that Livia is his child, the physician still haggles with Vettorio's father, Bindo, over the amount of the dowry until Attilio pledges payment for Fabrizio on his sister's behalf. With this consistency in character, it is easy to appreciate Manente's stubborn determination to marry Livia even if he has to alienate his son. This man's selfishness is expressed in a statement to Baldo that a person's closest relative is oneself. The physician's vanity will not allow him to admit defeat, as when he fears that if Vettorio has abducted Livia, she will never be satisfied with an old husband after experiencing the intense erotic joy of love with a young man.[12] Manente's conflicting emotions are passion that makes him blind to family bonds and the dread of ridicule at appearing like a stupid Calandrino from out of the pages of the *Decameron*. Fate safeguards this vain physician from the ignominy of an incestuous marriage, reunites him with both his children, and even spares him the cost of a dowry. In marrying Madonna Clemenza this elderly lover will assure for himself the respect that comes with an honorable and wise choice.

Baldo Dell'Arca resembles Manente in greed and in the self-deceiving excuse that he was justified in breaking off his engagement to Adriana on the pretext of marrying young Livia to produce an heir. A competitive spirit motivates this hunter and sportsman in his contest with Manente for the girl, but news of Fabrizio's being alive is welcome to Baldo, who, unlike the physician, would be willing to abandon pursuit of Livia in his nephew's favor. Baldo's inner conflict arises between competitiveness and greed. Eventually his slowness to pay any fees costs him the support of his broker Chima, who defects to Manente as the less tightfisted of the two misers. In desperation over the physician's apparent victory Baldo falls prey to a swindling scheme by Imbroglia, who persuades the old hunter to write two bills of credit in Vettorio's name, supposedly to convince Adriana to void the marital agreement with Manente. By reprimanding Baldo for the greed that caused Chima's desertion, Imbroglia overcomes the old man's resistance and obtains the money that will actually finance the young couple's elopement. Cecchi portrays Baldo as defeated by his own competitive and greed-dominated obsessions. With the play's comic resolution, however, this outdoorsman will not only regain his money but will also see his dignity restored through marriage to his original fiancée.

Forgery for the unscrupulous Chima seems to be a matter of professional honor, as he takes pride in preparing false documents. Like Ramaglia in *Le Cedole,* this broker claims to be of noble descent despite his present impoverishment. Always seeking his advantage, Chima turns out to be one of the play's most exploited characters when Baldo rewards him with empty promises and Manente compensates him with niggardly honoraria and meager fare. The broker and the physician are generous to each other only with the insults that each casts (act 3, scene 8) about the other's profession. Chima's general debasement reflects the underhanded tasks that the gentlemen-merchants of Florence hire parasitic individuals like this broker to execute for them. As represented in Cecchi's dramas, brokers enjoy in social status a rank far inferior to that of servants, who are officially part of their master's families and who frequently enjoy the protection of their household's livery. A character like Chima becomes reduced to a much scorned instrument of intrigue.

With the opposition that the young characters must face from the older generation, Fabrizio and Vettorio have to resort to subterfuge and force to win their way. Fabrizio, sustained by the memory of their affectionate relationship during exile in Spain and the West Indies, has to return from the "dead" to assert his original claim to Livia's love. Taking advantage of Fabrizio's vulnerability in regard to the girl's feelings, Imbroglia tries to discourage his suit by describing how Livia now despises him for abandoning her and for running off to Rome a year before. This false news compels the youth to utter a long Petrarchistic lament over adverse fact and the loss of love. However, Fabrizio is too much of a self-affirming Florentine entrepreneur to dwell for an extended period in lyrical outbursts; once he becomes reassured of Livia's continuing devotion, he resolutely decides on the masquerade abduction.

The revelation of Livia-Porzia's family relationship to her faithful lover illustrates how fate does act independently of human endeavor and constancy to make Fabrizio a plaything of destiny, which enriches him only to separate him from the one he adores. That same fate also makes Vettorio realize the promise of his name: the "victorious" one, not on account of his boldness in participating in Imbroglia's defrauding scheme and the masked disguise but simply because he alone of the suitors will not commit incest by wedding Livia. Spontaneously generous in rewarding Crezia for her allegiance,

Vettorio does recognize his duplicity in tricking Attilio to confide news to him about Fabrizio's return and then in deceiving Livia about her lover's not being alive; but the impetus of passionate attraction overwhelms his moral reluctance. Even though both young men display an initiative that merits success, circumstances beyond their efforts determine the outcome of amorous combat.

While male characters have to struggle against an arbitrary Fortune, their influence and power far exceed the limitations on action that society imposes on women. When Imbroglia attempts to dupe Baldo, the old man's remark that Adriana has already signed a marriage contract with Manente provokes the servant's derisive comment that before Florentine magistrates a woman's signature has almost no validity. In the intrigues of forged letters, the female characters are the ones who might suffer the most damaging deception, since some of them, like Clemenza, are illiterates who would easily fall prey to criminally inclined individuals like Chima. Clemenza's failure to disclose Livia's true parentage also demonstrates the plight of women before the law: in dying, her husband Fazio left two family farms to Livia but transferred their lifetime use to his widow solely on condition that she keep the secret to herself. Gnawed by conscience and counseled by her father confessor, Clemenza went to Pisa to persuade Fazio's relatives to release her from the promise while granting her control over the farms. Economic bondage accounts for the powerlessness of women, who also lack educational skills provided for men. One of the few assets that women have is reputation, and when Crezia demands that Vettorio must bring a ring to hold a clandestine marriage ceremony, the maid is following a tradition to protect a girl's honor. The conventional playworld in *Le Maschere* clearly defines the future role for enchantingly beautiful maidens like Livia who excite romantic aspirations in old and young men alike but who must one day become submissive wives.

In the prologue Cecchi acknowledges that comedies form part of carnival ritual with the aim of momentarily freeing citizens from the restrictions of routine existence. Carnival season festivities, conducted with the disguise of masks, have a cathartic function:

... the madnesses of the carnival are
the remedy and the antidote ordered
to purge minds ...
(verses 8–10).

Yet, with all the liberties enjoyed within the play's timespan,
characters like Vettorio realize that Florence's ruler tolerates
only certain clearly defined diversions; police agents quickly
apprehend the masked combatants after the feigned abduction. The author knew that orderly social life must go on after
the carnival, and the celebration of triple marriages both
crowns the carnival and marks the resumption of a life bound
by traditions and rules of proper relationships. The time has
arrived for all masks and disguises to be discarded as the
supreme disguise of this play—Livia's identity—is finally
abandoned with resulting pain to her devoted lover and
brother Fabrizio. To the general license of the carnival there
succeeds the fragilely controlled life of bourgeois customs
and tenuous realities.

Conclusion: The Sense of a Comic Moment

Cecchi's dramas display a remarkable sense of the very moment of their performance and their impact on spectators.
Numerous comments in the prologues to the actual holiday
season when the plays were presented create a vivid impression of the immediacy of the events enacted before the audience. The often repeated assertion that the author modeled
his plots on recent incidents in Florence or a nearby Tuscan
town intensified the public's involvement in the playworld.
Through use of interludes in a work like *Lo Spirito*, Cecchi
fashioned a comedy of engagement to draw the attention of
his audiences to the similarities between their lives and the
fictional existence of stage characters. Cecchi stressed the
social importance of his plays to arouse jovial debate and
interchange of viewpoints after the public beheld the mirror
reflection of their laughable obsessions. While leading his
spectators to an experience of their own ridiculous shortcomings, the dramatist adhered to a conception of comedy as a
form of entertainment that could provide enlightening in-
sights to individual and societal failings.

Because the world of the five comedies examined in this chapter is that of the bourgeoisie, the prominent character-types presented by the playwright are a venal lawyer, a hypo-critically pious but greedy go-between, a charlatan astrologer, and traitorous brokers. Cecchi's deep understanding of greed as a powerful motivating force in the psyche transformed mi-sers like Domenico of *Il Servigiale* and Tegghiaio of *Le Cedole* from caricatures to portraits of entrepreneurs acting out of distorted monetary preoccupations. In play after play there prevail terms of cash exchange such as *"pagare," "cogliere,"* and *"consumare,"* so that eros becomes reduced to a transac-tion between commercial partners. Women, deemed as infe-rior wares and treated as possessions, suffer economic and legal subjugation by male characters who regard them as in-struments of their own pleasure. Cecchi also represented the prejudices of class that, in comedies like *Lo Spirito, Il Servi-giale,* and *Le Cedole,* drive young lovers to acts of deception with false letters and disguise in carnival masks so as to over-come obstacles to marriage placed by socially ambitious par-ents. Love's eventual triumph does not come about through daring inventiveness but through Fortune's intervention to reveal the actual identities of major characters and to pro-mote advantageous marital alliances. Whereas in *Lo Spirito* and *Le Maschere* (plays composed at vastly distant times in the author's theatrical career) Cecchi optimistically looked to the future made secure by multiple marriages of young and old couples, in *L'Assiuolo* the dramatist constructed a Man-neristic tour-de-force of criss-crossing adulterous and licen-tious liaisons both derived from the novellistic tradition and expressing a carnival spirit of immediate sensual gratifica-tion. In his secular comedies Giovan Maria Cecchi studied two orders of contemporary experience, one that tried to rec-oncile mercantile values with romantic dreams through ma-trimony and another that advocated the rights of lovers to defy social institutions. The unity of this playwright's vision of life arose in awareness of a comic moment that exposed the vain pursuits of his entrepreneurial society. In his reli-gious dramas Cecchi sought evidence of possible redemption from the moral errors of everyday existence in a world that valued wealth over bonds of affection and family.

4

DRAMAS OF
SPIRITUAL INSPIRATION

The Florentine Tradition of Religious Drama

Spiritual drama served as an integral element of the civic religion that characterized social life in Renaissance Florence. An awareness of the miraculous permeated Florentine society and inspired the invocation of the power in holy relics and images to effect miracles so as to promote individual, family, and communal projects. Performance of sacred dramas formed part of the urban ritual behavior of the Florentines to request the favorable intercession of saints, angels, and the Virgin or to express gratitude for divine assistance already granted. Life in Renaissance Florence, scheduled according to a calendar of saints' days, might be viewed as a continual series of festive celebrations to commemorate or to obtain good fortune through the mediation of a holy agent. Citizens would show their reverence by participating in festive events honoring saints or other holy figures. The groups of young men who made up the confraternities would perform religious plays in meeting halls, private homes, outdoors during good weather, and frequently churches and chapels holding the relics of a saint whose favor was being sought. By the second half of the fifteenth century these sacred plays became known as *sacre rappresentazioni* and were composed in hendecasyllabic octaves with a rhyme scheme in a b a b a b c c.[1]

Staging of *sacre rappresentazioni* by the confraternities demonstrated a continuity of religious ritual that reflected bourgeois Florentine confidence in the miraculous intervention of the divine into human affairs. The various confraternities, or companies of instruction, intended their performances for the edification of the young, who would

127

learn to look beyond the often attractive appearance of vice to the moral danger threatened by sinful behavior. Youthful spectators were to gain useful lessons to recognize and to respect the authority of both Heaven and this world, whether in the clergy, government, or family. This concern for virtuous conduct in family life appears evident in the first known Florentine *sacra rappresentazione:* Feo Belcari's *Abramo e Isacco*, 1449, with its emphasis on the immediate acceptance of authority and faith in divine justice. Even Lorenzo de' Medici produced *Sacra Rappresentazione di San Giovanni e Paolo* for a psychological portrayal of the emperors Constantine and Julian the Apostate on the theme of the good and the evil uses of power. By the final decade of the fifteenth century, when the political harmony of the Laurentian Age was disintegrating, Castellano Castellani questioned in his *La Rappresentazione della Conversione di S. Maria Maddalena* the self-indulgent morality of il Magnifico's era in Florence. To a public who, during Lorenzo's reign, gave itself to adoration of the beautiful and the pleasurable, Castellani, by combining episodes from all the Gospels, delivered a warning on the transcience of earthly delights and the necessity to find stability in Christian faith and renunciation. Whether derived from events in Christ's life, from episodes of the Old and New Testaments, or from the lives of saints, the *sacre rappresentazioni* constitute a drama of heroic religious experience in which the divine was intended to manifest itself on this earth through the miraculous to awaken humankind to eternal destiny.

By the beginning of the sixteenth century, however, the composition of sacred dramas reflected a spiritual crisis. Plays degenerated into sentimental novellistic romances of adventure with plots about princesses in distress, and the only pretext for calling these dramas religious in nature would be a mechanical recourse to the miraculous intervention of the Virgin to rescue the troubled heroines. The miraculous indeed was giving way to the marvelous when religious faith no longer inspired the representation of wondrous events. By the time of the Catholic Reformation ecclesiastical authorities throughout Italy were attempting to prohibit performance of sacred plays. Pope Sixtus V forbade actresses from appearing in any kind of drama in Rome after 1558.

Later, in 1574, Gregory XIII condemned plays as morally licentious and corrupting when he denied private citizens the right to put on dramas in their own homes.[2] In Florence, Archbishop Alessandro de' Medici grew increasingly suspicious of the activities of the lay confraternities in staging sacred plays, and he eventually compelled the members of those associations to perform religious dramas away from the oratories where masses and other rituals were held. As the *sacre rappresentazioni* were losing contact with a vital source of inspiration in the family and the state, performance of those plays seemed an offense to faith rather than its affirmation.

During the second half of the sixteenth century there was an attempt to renew the spirit of sacred plays in Italy so that the public would once again be able to view morally edifying enactments of religious and civic ideals. The endeavor that had the longest lasting effects during the Catholic Reformation was the sacred theater of the Jesuits, who demonstrated that Baroque love of spectacle in arousing powerful feelings of religious ardor and exaltation. Nuns and friars also turned to the frequently reprinted *sacre rappresentazioni* of the fifteenth century to stage modest revivals in their convents and monasteries.

Cecchi participated in the effort to renew sacred drama, and he wrote his religious plays at the express and often insistent request of the members of those ecclesiastical communities. In addition to his spiritual dramas, moral plays, and farces on religious subjects, he also wrote one-act dramas *(atti recitabili)*, like his *Duello Della Vita Attiva E Contemplativa* and the *Disprezzo Dell'Amore e Beltà Terrena*, with allegorical characters that constituted morality plays. Throughout the period when the *sacra rappresentazione* was at its artistic and spiritual peak during the second half of the fifteenth century, Italian authors generally had avoided the abstract characterization of personified vices and virtues such as prevailed in the French *moralités*. Very few of the Italian sacred plays of the Quattrocento contain allegorical figures like Mercy, Truth, Justice, and Peace, since the authors of *sacre rappresentazioni* preferred to show virtue and vice as working in the lives and personalities of seemingly real characters. But it has been suggested that after Protestant dramatists began to employ the morality play as a vehicle to promote reformist doctrines, Italian playwrights took up the form of the morality play with allegorical characters to defend the Roman Catholic faith.[3]

In his play debating the benefits of the contemplative and active lives, Cecchi introduced abstract characters such as Conversion, Contrition, Peace, Pride, Vain Glory, Obstinacy, Virginity, and Marital State along with angels and St. Mary Magdalene. Penitence and Earthly Beauty argue in his drama of contempt for terrestrial satisfaction over the relative merits of faith and delight in sensual attractions. Whether in these morality plays or in his other dramas of spiritual inspiration, Cecchi was seeking to renew the tradition of religious drama in his native Florence. In this chapter I shall study that attempt at renewal in the examples of a sacred drama, two moral plays, and two farces of a spiritual nature. Throughout the period of self-examination and contrition that marked the Catholic Reformation, religious plays like those by Cecchi reflected an ardent longing to recapture the pure and intense spirituality of that earlier era when the *sacra rappresentazione* flourished.

The Fatal Deviation: *La Morte Del Re Acab*

Desire for renewal in a modern spirit is the message of the dialogue prologue to *La Morte Del Re Acab*. Dividing the prologue into two parts, the author examines the way to revive sacred drama in a form acceptable to the expectations of contemporary audiences. In the opening section of this verse prologue a member of Florence's foremost confraternity, the Vangelista (St. John the Evangelist), explains to a stranger who has wandered onstage that after a long period of inactivity the religious association has resumed production of sacred plays with this piece by an author known for his comedies. At the intruder's inquiry whether the present play is an "old-fashioned mystery" *(misterio/Da zazzeroni)*, the actor replies that the dramatist has considered the tastes of an intelligent audience by preparing a modern reworking of an ancient sacred tale. Among the playwright's innovations are the substitution of blank verse hendecasyllable lines for the traditional octaves of the *sacra rappresentazione* and the addition of intermezzi. While blank verse creates a naturalness of dialogue pleasing to the public, the intermezzi with their allegorical spectacle illustrate the moral lesson that the dramatist especially directs to the young people in the audience. From the drama of the violent fate that befell King Ahab and Queen Jezebel for their offense to Jehovah the audience will see how the Lord punishes disbelievers.

First performed in 1559, this play reflects the aspirations of the Tridentine era to bring about a total reform of religious spirit by pointing out the peril that can engulf an entire nation for deviating from orthodox belief and practice. In the author's efforts to present a dramatic form that would be appropriate to this reformistic purpose, he developed a stage work intermediate to comedy and to tragedy. Just as comedy represents events in the lives of private citizens and requires performance generally in the closed space of an interior stage with casts usually no more numerous than four persons to a single scene, modern sacred drama needs the spaciousness of outdoor staging in good weather for a large cast accustomed to elaborate costuming, scenery, and fast-paced action. Although the number of actors in sacred plays exceeds that of comedies, Cecchi remarked that dramatists should not attempt to compose tragedies since that genre employs an unworkable multitude of characters and observes unwieldy rules from ancient Rome and Athens.

For a playwright like Cecchi who modeled comedy after comedy on the regular stageworks of Plautus and Terence, the difficulty of creating a modern tragic form serves as an opportunity to define a sacred theatrical genre unto itself. Ironically, this Florentine author did one day attempt to write a tragedy on the theme of rebelliousness and ambition in the play *Datan e Abiron*, composed after 1580. But in *La Morte Del Re Acab* as well as in other plays like *La Coronazione Di Saul*, 1565, the dramatist took a middle course between the intimacy of comedy and the grandiosity of tragedy. Here Cecchi followed the long-time tradition of confraternities to stage sacred plays in open-air performances that permitted a panoramic presentation of a crucial moment in sacred history. Writing for a public partly made up of students from convent

and monastic schools,[4] the playwright demonstrated his didactic intention to call his audience to the spiritual danger of
sin and the need to return to pious devoutness.

Since the author expressly did not wish to compose a tragedy that according to Renaissance theory should deal with
the fall of socially exalted characters, in *La Morte Del Re
Acab* the sudden destruction of the royal house of Ahab is
represented from the viewpoints of several characters across
various classes, professions, and age groups. In the second half
of the prologue the actor explaining the drama's background
and the playwright's intentions speaks of a "decorum of the
role" wherein each character carries out what is fitting for his
individual part. Whereas lower-class characters are compara-
tively free to pronounce their opinions, having little to lose
and less to hope for, nobles and courtiers must speak with
caution and frequently in secret because they have a great
deal to fear and much to lose by imprudence. Rather than
composing a tragedy focusing on Ahab's fatal mistake of
abandoning the cult of Jehovah, the playwright purposely did
not introduce the Israelite ruler and his ally, King Jehosaphat
of Judah, until the drama's midpoint at act 3, scene 3. The
play opens with a scene between the nobles Eleazaro and Josef
discussing the impending war between Israel and Syria and
then passes in the second scene to a conversation between
the royal servant Siba and Zatto, chief cook to the Baalite
high priest Sedecchia, on the possibility of their being called
to arms.

The author's emphasis falls on the common destiny affect-
ing the entire Israelite nation because of Ahab's yielding to
the demands of Queen Jezebel for him to establish the cult of
Baal as the official religion in his land. Drawing characters
and events from biblical sources in 1 Kings 20–22, 2 Kings 1–
9, and 2 Chronicles 18, Cecchi compressed some of the scrip-
tural episodes while adding new characters of his own in order to show that the follies of monarchs involve all their
subjects. Many of the scenes present two characters commenting on the progress of hostilities between Ahab and the
Syrian ruler Benhadad: as in act 3, scene 1, with the royal
captains Amon and Joab on military preparations for combat
or in the delightfully adolescent argument between the boys
Isac and Levi in act 3, scene 6, over whether children should

join the army. Because the author is seeking to indicate the moral consequences of a nation following the mistaken judgment of a vainglorious and greedy sovereign, this play deliberately lacks a tragic perspective. Instead of being a tragedy, this work is a drama of collective religious morality.

Cecchi's previous experience as an author of regular comedies makes itself felt in his presentation of the identical character-types as in the secular plays, like the parasite, the miser, the braggart, the impudent scamp, and corrupt priests. As a novel variation the author places the parasite Sparecchia within the vicious atmosphere of courtly and sacerdotal circles, where this unscrupulous glutton connives to gain influence and to indulge his insatiable appetite. Through Sparecchia the audience can behold the opportunism, deceit, venality, and hypocrisy prevailing in courts. This parasitic courtier holds no loyalty to any sect or party but considers his stomach his one commitment. Since the Baalite priesthood invites him to the sumptuous banquets that form part of their ritualistic celebration of fertility, Sparecchia inclines toward Sedecchia's faction against the often austere adherents of Jehovah. The downfall of Baal's priests after the death of the king arouses no sorrow in Sparecchia, who arranges a festive dinner so that he can forget about religion and politics.

Exploiting the fear of the miser Zorobabel Ginepri of being drafted into the armed forces, the parasite actually succeeds in defrauding the elderly man with a false scheme to hire a substitute for military service. Like many of the misers in Cecchi's comedies, this old Israelite first engaged Sparecchia's questionable assistance as a go-between in a love affair until the onset of war caused Zorobabel to seek the parasite's friends at court to release him from the threat of conscription. Zorobabel's attempt to compensate Sparecchia with a pair of old boots recalls a similar futile effort by Ambrogio in *L'Assiuolo* with M. Verdiana. However, the parasite warns this old coward that only bribes obtain favors at court. Ironically, his advanced age would have exempted Zorobabel from induction, but, at the start of the final act, the old man enters on scene in full armor blustering like a great warrior and expecting his young ward, Levi, to take his place in the military when all of a sudden in the confusion following the Hebrew defeat any man seen bearing weapons is immediately pressed into combat duty. The miser's fate as a reluctant soldier illustrates that building hopes on the promises of courtiers usually results in costly losses.

This play presents the professional braggart warrior in a Hebrew captain simply designated as "Bravo." On his first stage appearance in act 2, scene 6, Bravo at once brings to mind the rich soldiers in the comedies of Menander, Plautus, and Terence with his mercenary desire to acquire booty through conquest. The word uppermost on Bravo's lips is *"guadagnare,"* "to gain" without risk of injury. This soldier boldly declares he will slay one thousand Syrians on the battlefield. The dreadful contrast between braggadoccio and the horror of warfare becomes evident in the fifth scene of the last act when a dazed Bravo stumbles onstage with a report about Ahab's death and the Hebrew rout. From comic pretensions the braggart passes to the misery of military defeat. Cecchi's artistry in this sacred drama consists in his ability to juxtapose comic self-delusions with the stark reality of a nation's subjugation. The intermediate style of sacred plays between comedy and tragedy permitted Cecchi to represent boastful affectations of martial prowess and the bewilderment of being vanquished.

One character who manages to outwit swindling parasites and cowardly misers alike is the scamp Levi. Just a boy with an urgent longing to join the army, Levi will not hesitate to use theft, deceit, and the menace of violence to promote his own interests. Although Levi at first appears to be sympathetic in telling his friend Isac that physical size and courage are not one and the same, his ruthlessness shows itself in act 4, scene 4, during an encounter with Sparecchia. The parasite who generally manipulates others falls victim to this mere child. Needing ready cash to purchase weapons in order to be eligible for military service, Levi demands that Sparecchia turn over the money advanced by Zorobabel as a bribe to the royal enlistment officer. When the parasite resists, the youth strikes him with the flat of his sword and threatens to run him through unless he surrenders the old man's payment. Combining adolescent arrogance with a precocious sense of calculation, Levi correctly judges Sparecchia to be a coward whose greed will yield to physical danger. Because Cecchi was directing his play as a moral lesson to the young students in his audience, the portrait of the unprincipled Levi would serve as a warning of the undesirable ethical qualities that might lead to crime. For the boy's triumph constitutes no more than the victory of one scoundrel over another.

Traditional *sacra rappresentazione* did not observe the unities of time and place, for the time frame of one of those early religious plays could run from the Creation to the Last Judgment. Also, the stage space for the *sacre rappresentazioni* occupied a series of compartments on top of platforms to create multiple and simultaneous settings for a single drama. The second half of the prologue to Cecchi's *La Morte Del Re Acab* stresses the holiness of the space where the confraternity is performing the play and announces that the setting will be the Israelite capital of Samaria. While most of the drama does indeed occur at some undisclosed outdoor public space in Samaria, the opening scenes of act 2 take place on Mt. Garizim, where the prophet Michea (the biblical Michaiah) intones a prayer for divine justice and experiences a vision of heavenly authority. In classical tradition violent events like the disastrous battle between the Hebrew and Syrian armies as well as the slaughter of Jezebel and her family at the order of the rebel Jehu (Geone) near the palace at Jezreel never occur onstage but are the subjects of reports by individuals fleeing the carnage. Indication of the passage of time can be found in act 3, scene 5, when Michea prophesies the deaths of Ahab, Jezebel, and Sedecchia in less than two days. Also in act 4, scene 4, Levi complains that Sparecchia has caused him two days delay in enlisting in the Israelite army. Whereas the playwright introduced character-types from regular comedy into this sacred drama, he followed the freedom of the *sacra rappresentazione* in structuring temporal and spatial dimensions for the play. By not strictly adhering to the classical unities of time and space Cecchi failed to achieve a powerful concentration and density of dramatic effect in representing the catastrophe awaiting a people who obey their monarch in his religious deviation.

In the prologue the playwright remarks that, although he composed this comedy to please a dear friend, he thought only of satisfying himself in writing the intermezzi. The five interludes and their concluding madrigals form a continuous allegory of the historical role of the Holy Church called the

great Synagogue. Cecchi may have had in mind Cantos 29–
33 of Dante's *Purgatory,* where there occurs an elaborately
allegorical procession of the Church Militant. For his stage
realization of the symbolic procession, the dramatist designed
a counterpoint of monologue by the Church and choral song
by historical champions of that majestic Synagogue. Appearing between the two sections of the prologue, the first intermezzo shows how the Church arose shortly after the
Creation and how it became man's faithful guide and com-
forter following the Fall. Hidden by a thousand veils of religious mystery, the great Synagogue awaits the second coming
for the full revealing of its spiritual promise. Onstage with
the character representing the Church in this tableau are allegorical figures of the cardinal virtues Fortitude and Prudence, along with Old Testament Hebrews from Genesis such
as Adam, Abel, Noah, Abraham, Isaac, Melchisedech, Jacob,
and Joseph. Those righteous Hebrews found salvation because they believed Christ would come as the Messiah. Both
Abel's murder and Joseph's being sold into slavery are interpreted as prefigurations of Christ's betrayal by Judas, antici-
pations of that great sacrifice on behalf of all humanity. In an
appeal for God's pity the Church and the early Hebrews perform a madrigal expressing hope for the saving splendor of
divine forgiveness. While the opening interlude traces the
Church's origins, the second *intermedio* progresses to the legalistic period of religious history as figured by all four moral
virtues (Fortitude, Prudence, Temperance, and Justice) in the
company of Moses, Joshua, Caleb, and some of the Judges like
Jephthah, Samson, and Gideon. Through the conquest and
consolidation of the Holy Land, the Judges firmly established
a rule of law to protect the Church. Cecchi projects these
figures from their biblical past by having them gathered together by the banks of the Arno River to sing a madrigal
praising God's law as the force to inspire humans to do what
is right. Those first two intermezzi initiate a symbolic presentation of the Church's redemptive mission across the
centuries.

Ecclesiastical history moves in the third interlude to Kings,
from Saul onward, into the Judean dynasty with the building
of the Temple as the physical symbol of the covenant between
the Lord and His chosen people. The royal throng delivers a

madrigal on the resplendent divine Light that should rescue the world from spiritual darkness. The tableau of the fourth intermezzo presents the travail of the Jews on account of the moral corruption in both kingdoms of Israel and Judah that resulted in their respective conquests by Assyrians and by Babylonians. Here the four cardinal virtues stand with Zerubabel, Ezra, Nehemiah, and the three highest priests of the Hebrews to point out the need for ethical renewal that made possible the reconstruction of the Temple after the Persians freed the Jews from captivity in Babylon and permitted return to Palestine. All sing a madrigal in joyous expectation of the Redeemer's arrival on earth. The allegory for this play takes on a particularly Dantesque pageantry in the final intermezzo, when the Synagogue has become both the Church Militant and Triumphant riding in a chariot with standards of the Cross and the Holy Host in a chalice. Attending the Church are not only the cardinal virtues but also the three theological virtues Faith, Hope, and Charity along with the Prophets, Four Evangelists, Apostles, martyrs of the true religion, and, as prisoners, Satan and Death. This last tableau reveals how the entire universe has become the Church's realm. The seven virtues, Evangelists, and Apostles intone the closing madrigal on the wondrousness of God's love that can take human form to save the world. These five intermezzi offer an interpretation of the hardships that the Holy Church in Cecchi's own times had just suffered through moral decay and schism, and the allegorical tableaux point to the hope for the Church to regain total victory as a spiritual force through the Catholic Reformation.

Cecchi's drama of a royal death represents the consequences of a historical moment characterized by moral weakness. While the king's captains blame their military reverses on capricious Fortune, both Michea's prayer and his ensuing vision in the first two scenes of act 2 demonstrate how God's justice brings about proper retribution for sin. Both in the prophet's prayer and in the play's prologue there is an emphasis on divine punishment for those who persecute believers of the true faith. Any of Cecchi's spectators who might be tempted by Protestantism and its persecution of Catholics could clearly see the message in the play that they would be condemned for heresy. The false prophets of Baal resemble their sixteenth-century Protestant counterparts in attacking the genuine priests. A sacred aura radiating with divine force infuses Michea's vision and constitutes an additional inter- mezzo in which God the Father sits on his throne at an an- gelic court attended by Justice and Mercy. While Justice entreats God's vengeance on the ungrateful who have aban- doned the true faith, Mercy begs for forgiveness toward the Israelite nation so that they might be turned back to authen- tic belief. After God condemns Ahab and Jezebel, He entrusts their destruction to two devils.

The prayer and the vision show how humans can experi- ence communion with the Divine. Cecchi seeks to indicate that a heavenly directed destiny awaits worshipers in judg- ment of their moral and religious errors. In the tradition of *sacre rappresentazioni* the playwright creates his drama of religious conflict by juxtaposing the solemn with the comic to portray the human follies of greed, vanity, gluttony, and braggadoccio that lead individuals and nations to temporal and spiritual downfall. This Florentine religious drama suc- ceeds in realizing the author's stated intention to create a modern work intermediate to comedy and to tragedy with a moral message for the youth. In *La Morte Del Re Acab* the contention between rival faiths closes in the affirmation of a social order recognizing a God of Love, Virtue, and Justice.

The Penitent's Triumph: Il Figliuol Prodigo

With the moral play *Il Figliuol Prodigo*, written in 1569 and performed during the carnival of 1570, Cecchi endeavored to reconcile the Tuscan *sacra rappresentazione* with the aes- thetic form of the erudite comedy. The author had two ante- cedent versions in fifteenth-century Florentine sacred plays also based on the New Testament parable in Luke 15.11–32: dramas similarly entitled *Il Figliuol Prodigo* by Antonia Pulci and Castellano Castellani. Pulci's version displays an allegor- ical tendency that was not especially typical of the Quattro- cento sacred plays, for, in the sequences where the prodigal encounters seven companions, those youths who lead him astray represent the seven deadly sins. Castellani's play is called a *parabola* (parable) and a *storia* (history) that covers the prodigal's entire career beginning with a street brawl between youths arguing about the vice of gambling and continuing through every important event in the wayward youth's life until the final reconciliation with his family. In both fifteenth-century renderings, the scene is constantly shifting; Castellani in particular employs a technique resembling movie cross-cutting, as when the scene changes from the prodigal's visiting a thieving courtesan back again to his father's house, where the anguished parent laments his son's foolish departure. The sequences in Castellani's drama that occur in a hostelry of ill-fame reveal a delight in presenting vignettes of contemporary life with colorful figures like a jolly but deceitful innkeeper, card sharks, and merry companions ready to exploit the prodigal while he still has his inheritance but quick to abandon him when he is in need. Both of the fifteenth-century renderings rely heavily on moralizing speeches to convey the lesson to be learned from the prodigal's mistakes. Cecchi's debt to his predecessors becomes apparent in his keen observation of contemporary character-types and locale.[5]

This sixteenth-century stage reworking of the parable of the prodigal son illustrates how the playwright transports a biblical tale to late Renaissance Florence. The drama's setting is the Tuscan capital during the author's lifetime rather than New Testament Palestine. Even with this play's many ties to earlier religious dramas, Cecchi's *Figliuol Prodigo* possesses a predominantly classical form in both structure and general characteristics. This prose play in five acts features the usual street scene of erudite comedies. Strict observance of the unity of time is evidenced by a remark by the old miser Argifilo Pallanti in the second scene of the last act: "He is the very one who brought me the letter this morning." Cecchi avoids Castellani's historical approach, preferring the tense concentration of true classical drama by starting his play on the day of the prodigal son's return to his family. The action will proceed over the morning, afternoon, down to the festive evening banquet that the father celebrates in honor of his son's return. Throughout this play the environment remains consistently that of the bourgeoisie in Florence under the Medicean restoration.

At times *Il Figliuol Prodigo* seems to be a modern reworking of Plautine and Terentian material in a mercantile setting. The story of the repentant prodigal, Panfilo degli Amieri, becomes submerged by the intrigue of young Polibio Pallanti to obtain funds from his father, Argifilo. Here the traditional sly servant, Carbone, functions to rescue his young master, persuading the parasite Frappa to present a forged letter of credit for one hundred scudi from Argifilo's brother Polidoro in Rome. When the parasite assumes a disguise and delivers the false letter, the crafty merchant declines to accept the document without adequate assurance of its authenticity. Eventually, Frappa in still another disguise frightens Argifilo out of one hundred fifty scudi with a ruse devised by Carbone, who reports that Polibio has been caught stealing silks and satins from Andronico's shop. Although Argifilo guards his money tenaciously as a man who has labored for years in his business enterprises as merchant and financier, Carbone believes his *beffa* will succeed for two reasons: old Pallanti's bourgeois sense of family honor before any possible scandal and the father's genuine, if not always apparent, love for his son.

With this plot Cecchi penetrates the psychology of a rather miserly entrepreneur to disclose how this merchant does hold values other than purely monetary ones. Argifilo's paternal concern for Polibio's welfare has a parallel in a similar situation in Ariosto's *La Lena*, 1528, where the father, Ilario, accepts a false tale about his son being seized in the act of adultery and agrees to pay a bribe for the youth's release. Until the moment when Argifilo shows his affection for Polibio, this play is structured on a contrast between two fathers: the parsimonious Argifilo and the kindly Andronico, whose generosity in granting Panfilo a patrimony in advance brought about the young man's prodigal misadventures.

The symmetrical opposition of the fathers resembles the pair of brothers in Terence's *Adelphoe* and, of course, Cecchi's *I Dissimili*. Andronico's sadness over his son's disappearance and his joy on Panfilo's return also bring to mind another Terentian father: Menedemus in the *Heautontimorumenos*, with the difference being that the father in the ancient Roman comedy drove his son away by being too harsh whereas in Cecchi's drama Panfilo took advantage of Andronico's affectionate nature. The Italian play opens in a mood of

Terentian pathos where in the first scene Andronico's wife, Mona Clemenza, expresses her grief over her son's absence of two years. In his combination of Frappa's double disguise and the tender sentimentalism of family relationships, the Florentine playwright merges Plautine intrigue with Terentian emotionalism. The biblical source nearly fades away in what is a supremely classical-style comedy.

Perhaps Cecchi's originality lies in his developing from a parable of the New Testament a play about middle-class families, their bonds of affection, and their values. The author studies the extended family that includes town-house servants as well as country tenants. To the story of the prodigal son this dramatist has added the figure of a mother, who is the first character to open the play's dialogue as she reprimands her maid Betta for delaying their attending mass. Both the mother and maid appear as conventionally pious women who take advantage of their daily church visitations to exchange gossip with relatives and acquaintances. Like Castellani before him, the playwright fashioned vignettes of everyday existence in the Tuscan capital. Clemenza's anguish over Panfilo's fate as well as her aloofness to her elder son, Vascanio, in act 3, scene 2, clearly indicates upon which child she has lavished her love.[6]

Vascanio's perfectly proper but cool reserve toward his mother, that *"rispetto,"* which Clemenza finds totally lacking in warmth, may well account for the woman's ill ease before this son. Within the limits of a few scenes, Cecchi portrays Vascanio as a many-faceted individual, one far more contradictory than his biblical counterpart. At his stage entrance in act 3, scene 1, Vascanio shows himself to be an open-minded character who rebukes his servant Romolo for having abused and chased away a ragged stranger asking to be admitted into the Amieri home. When Romolo draws attention to a resemblance between the stranger and Panfilo, the young merchant angrily dismisses the idea that his errant brother might still be alive. Cecchi fully understands and represents how sibling rivalry is founded on resentment. Vascanio's tolerance toward a tattered traveler, whose plight he attributes to cruel Fortune, does not extend to women in general, since this misogynistic bachelor criticizes feminine frivolousness, declaring that if he ever were to take a bride, she would have to obey

him in all ways. Obedience indeed is the key factor to comprehend Vascanio's psyche, as this elder son finds coherence
in life through correct, respectful relationships. Although
Vascanio feels that his father has never adequately rewarded
him for his obedience, his need for the stability of family life
convinces him to take part in the final banquet of reconciliation with his brother. Since Cecchi intended his play to serve
as a moral lesson for the youths in his audiences, the prodigal's humble apology to his father and plea for forgiveness
illustrate proper submission to paternal authority.

One of the modern character-types that the author introduced into this play is Lisa, the *balia*, or family nurse, in
Argifilo's household. Frequently in novellas and plays, the
family nurse figures as a go-between in romantic affairs,
greatly resembling professional procuresses like Verdiana. In
some of Cecchi's comedies, like *Il Corredo* and *Il Medico*, the
nurse appears as a mercenary character lacking in loyalty to
the mistress of the household. Lisa, however, displays the
same sweetness and warmth as the nurse in Cecchi's play
L'Ammalata, for both are self-sacrificing characters. The concluding scene of the first act in *Il Figliuol Prodigo* features a
soliloquy by Lisa in which she describes the unhappiness that
entered her life after the death of Argifilo's wife, Laildomine.
Now Lisa must suffer the constant scolding of her greedy
master. Only her devotion to Polibio prevents Lisa from leaving the household. With this portrait of a good nurse, the
playwright created a positive character in striking contrast to
the numerous evil servants of Renaissance novellistic and
dramatic tradition.[7]

Cecchi also pictured the close relationship between urban
mercantile families and their country tenants in certain
scenes (act 2, scenes 3 and 4; act 3, scenes 3 and 4) where
some of Andronico's peasant sharecroppers arrive in town.
Menico has come to Florence in order to report news of Panfilo's possible return to his parents. The conversations between Menico and the maid Betta, in which the two servants
discuss the exact ingredients for salads and favorite dishes,
reveal Cecchi's expert knowledge of peasant language. Another peasant, Bartolo, is visiting town to buy his strapping
eldest son, Tognarino, some new clothes for a family wedding.
Tognarino's marveling at the sights of the city recalls not only

the country bumpkins in Quattrocento religious plays but also the young man in the preliminary tale to the *Decameron's* Fourth Day who stares in wondrous amazement upon his first trip to Florence. The flavor of rustic farce enters into the drama with the comical comparison between the ignorance of the peasants and the sophistication of the urban environment. On beholding some masks in a show window, Tognarino thinks they are flayed faces. Military armor is defined by these country people as "iron petticoats" worn by soldiers. Tognarino even wants to buy some of the naked white giants (actually statues) in the Piazza della Signoria and to take them home. Cecchi also refers to that period's sumptuary laws, which decreed different kinds of dress for various social classes, because Bartolo must take care only to purchase party clothes for Tognarino that peasants are allowed to wear. All these scenes of country characters in a city setting function to create a full world of the family interrelationships connecting the Tuscan capital with the surrounding farmlands.[8]

With its bourgeois realism, Plautine disguises, and Terentian pathos, *Il Figliuol Prodigo* might seem more a secular drama than a religious play. Throughout the work, however, Cecchi inserts religious references, many of which are commonplaces of everyday speech that the author invests with renewed meaning in the context of the drama of a son who was dead to the world and is spiritually reborn on returning to the shelter of his home. In the play's opening conversation between Clemenza and Betta, God's name is invoked out of anguish about the prodigal's whereabouts. Panfilo later states in the first scene of the second act that he has been led home "by the Lord's grace" in the hope of finding pardon. When Frappa first attempts to swindle Argifilo with the counterfeit letter, the doubtful Polibio exclaims (act 2, scene 6), "Oh God, help me!" Clemenza reassures the impatient Vasconio that Heaven will favor them: "May God grant us the blessing." Again and again in the drama phrases like "Let God to it," "God's kindness," "May it please the Lord," "God be thanked" keep recurring to form a significant pattern of statements that affirms faith in divine power to intervene in the world and to relieve human tribulations. Through God's design the prodigal will realize and repent his error. In its religious context the play's structure requires that all the major characters should attend the final feast of ritual celebration, since the point of the original biblical parable is God's greater delight over the repentance of a single sinner than the moral conformity of ninety-nine nonsinners. Heaven's joy derives from the knowledge that a former sinner will find salvation. The Italian dramatist permits his spectators to behold how the religious tale reenacts itself in the mercantile environment of present-day Florence.

In this play's artistic reconciliation of the classical tradition with the Tuscan sacred drama, it is the parasite Frappa who delivers the envoi for Cecchi's parable. To contribute to the spirit of harmony that comes with Panfilo's return, Andronico rewards the conspirators Frappa and Carbone by giving them articles of clothing, repaying Argifilo the money that was extorted from him, and entrusting the hungry parasite to arrange the banquet. The final festive mood brings the aims of scheming human intelligence in accord with Heaven's will. Cecchi's moral drama *Il Figliuol Prodigo* celebrates the triumph of Christian virtue in a modern society whose culture is profoundly classical.

The Domestic Miracle: La Serpe, Ovvero La Mala Nuora

On composing *La Serpe, Ovvero La Mala Nuora* to be performed by a company of youngsters, Giovan Maria Cecchi felt a need to apologize for the modest proportions of this work designated as a "spiritual farce." The author's defensive attitude finds expression through a preliminary scene and the play's actual prologue that serve to anticipate and to answer some of the criticism and invidious comparisons the drama might suffer. Written mostly as a dialogue between one of the youthful actors and a hypercritical member of the audience, the preliminary scene explains the dramatist's intentions with this brief three-act farce. When the spectator Cammillo complains about the small-scale outdoor staging for the present drama, the actor Fabio replies that the members of the company are apprentices trying to learn their craft. Cammillo's disappointment comes about because he was expecting an elaborately mounted sacred drama with lavish costumes and sets as well as choreographed musical intermezzi, like the production five years before of Cecchi's sacred drama *La Coronazione Del Re Saul* in the presence of Grand Duke Cosimo, the Prince Regent, Joanna of Austria, and her visiting brother, Archduke Karl. Since the performance for that distinguished audience took place in 1569, the date for the presentation of this farce would have to be 1574, in the late Spring or early Summer, on account of the warm weather mentioned in the preliminary dialogue, which favored an open-air staging.

Instead of being a grandiose religious spectacle, this short play used its explicitly limited means for a double purpose: to create amusement *(spasso)* and to train children in the theatrical discipline. To Cammillo's derogatory comment that this whole affair seems a childish venture, Fabio candidly answers that the actors are indeed all children. The youthful apologist also makes the assertion repeated in the prologue that this farce was written in a flash, as in a single stroke of the author's pen, to offer a moral lesson to daughters-in-law and their husbands. After another actor clears the stage, the true prologue begins by repeating that the farce was composed without a great deal of thought solely to provide children with a chance to have some practice in stage production. Cecchi's defensive attitude about this work reveals the relatively low status of farce compared to other genres like comedy and sacred drama. The playwright had not yet worked out the theory of farce as intermediate to comedy and tragedy with special freedoms that he later developed in the prologue to *La Romanesca*, 1585. Because farces had a folk origin in performances in the piazza with mountebanks or at country festivals before peasants, Cecchi knew that illustrious audiences would regard this genre as inferior to the regular theatrical forms. The playwright purposely employed the prefatory scene and the prologue, both in hendecasyllable verse, to give this otherwise modest farcical genre the respectability of his erudite comedies.

Set in contemporary Siena, this play shows itself to be an abbreviated moral comedy as it presents a highly realistic picture of middle-class life suddenly transformed by a divine force. Unlike Cecchi's sacred dramas or a later farce such as

La Romanesca, the cast for the play does not include persons
of exalted noble and political status; rather it concentrates on
the members of a single bourgeois family and those individuals who enter their lives, like neighbors, servants, peasants,
and physicians. The drama's central conflict is one that can
occur in almost any family: problems over money and the
struggle for domestic power. To keep peace at home Fulvio
has had to send away his mother, Lucrezia, because his wife,
Lidia, despised the older woman. Although he has pledged to
provide his mother with basic necessities, at the play's start
Fulvio has not seen her for some months and does not realize
that she is in economic desperation. At Lidia's orders the
servants have not delivered her husband's packages of food
along with a small allowance. Fulvio's reprehensible neglect
of his mother is caused in part by his total financial dependence on the wealthy and propertied Lidia but also from ingratitude toward the self-sacrificing widow who had made
possible the advantageous match. Only the charitable assistance of concerned neighbors and some rebellious servants has
saved Lucrezia from starvation.

Act 1 opens with Fulvio's friend Valerio scolding him for
mistreating the innocent elderly lady who neither interfered
in Lidia's management of the household nor did anything to
offend her daughter-in-law except to go on living. Fulvio
never once endeavored to defend Lucrezia from Lidia's un-
founded accusations about her behavior. In the second act a
dreadful accident befalls Fulvio, who is dozing in bed, when
a serpent suddenly coils around his neck and nearly strangles
him. Neither the ministrations of two physicians nor the con-
jurations of a snake charmer succeed in loosening the animal's grip on the young man. When Lucrezia tries to see her
son, Lidia furiously drives the poor woman away. By the third
act the snake has also entwined itself around Lidia's neck,
and the couple are on the verge of expiring when Lucrezia
appears before them, makes the sign of the cross, and touches
the serpent, which at once releases its deathlike hold and
vanishes. Interpreting this event as a Heaven-sent message
about their evil conduct, Fulvio and Lidia repent their error
and beg Lucrezia's forgiveness. For the first time love reigns
in the family as the penitent Lidia invites her mother-in-law
to return as mistress of the household. At the play's end the

truly united family is about to go to church to thank God for the miracle that has touched their lives and has granted them the opportunity to begin anew.

Cecchi intentionally structured his farce so that the spectators could see themselves mirrored in the familiar setting of a bourgeois home experiencing a crisis of authority. The atmosphere of the first act remains absolutely naturalistic like any of the author's regular comedies. Only in act 2, with the emergency caused by the serpent, does realism start to yield to the supernatural as the writer demonstrates how the divine works on daily life. Lidia's obstinate persistence in sin carries the catastrophe over into act 3, where Fulvio and his wife at last comprehend their grave injustice toward the saintly Lucrezia. As in his full-length secular comedies, the playwright observes unities of time and place. While the scene remains a street outside Lidia's townhouse, the drama's time span does not exceed a few tense hours on a fateful morning. In its rigidly classical structure, this play reveals that by 1574 Cecchi had not yet formulated a theory of the farce as a genre independent of the temporal and spatial restrictions of regular comedy and tragedy such as he was to achieve in *La Romanesca*. Classical influence also extends into the use of a prologue and envoi as well as division into acts and scenes, unlike many of the farces composed throughout the sixteenth century.

Although the contention between Lidia and Lucrezia vaguely recalls a similar situation in Terence's *Hecyra*, this is a thoroughly modern work reflecting the conditions of urban life in late-Renaissance Tuscany. The play's tight construction contrasts with the rapid pace of the language, pulsating in the most natural fashion with proverbs, puns, and playful twists in meaning. The free flow of the dialogue serves to relieve the density of structure while creating for the audience an impression of verisimilitude that causes the public to ponder how their lives might incur sins of arrogance and neglect. With its solidly classical form reduced to three acts and with its vivid language, Cecchi's spiritual farce represents a moment of extreme trial within a family that finds salvation through tearful repentance.

Despite this play's brevity, the author successfully introduces wide-ranging characters who become involved in the crisis of the serpent and the ensuing miracle. Within the family at the drama's center, Fulvio proves to be vacillating and passive in regard to his wife. Having grown up on the economic fringe of the middle class and having lost his father during childhood, this irresolute young man never acquired the self-assertiveness to resist the domination of someone who could exercise financial control. Even house servants like the maid Betta respect only Lidia's authority and constantly ask her permission to carry out Fulvio's orders. During the farce's initial scenes this youth wavers between fear of irritating his wife and concern for his reputation in the Sienese community.

Although Fulvio does not suffer from guilt over his failure to appreciate his mother's lifetime of efforts on his behalf, he is capable of being put to shame by Valerio. Only the menace of a mysteriously caused death compels him to acknowledge that guilt and to show the contrition that redeems him from sinfulness. Fulvio's wife does not share his penchant for being shamed by the criticism of others; to the complaints about her cruelty toward Lucrezia this fierce young lady reacts with resentment and vindictiveness. Angered by the neighbors who boldly express their disapproval to her in church, Lidia does not see the hypocrisy of her actions: pretending to be a devout Christian while taking advantage of a penniless victim. Instead of lessening her maliciousness, the daughter-in-law attempts to add humiliation to injury by arranging to send Lucrezia a basketful of stale bread and bad wine. Enjoying an inheritance of a townhouse, three farms, and cash from her brother, Lidia glories in her ability to purchase expensive clothes when her mother-in-law is languishing from malnutrition. Not even the threat of Fulvio's death suffices to awaken Lidia to the injustice she has committed against her husband and especially against her mother-in-law. It takes the shock of the serpent's attack, the arrival of a priest to deliver extreme unction, the presence of gravediggers, and Lucrezia's generous blessing to the aggrieved couple before Lidia understands the enormity of the wrongs she has perpetrated. The clarity of vision that finally comes to Lidia upon being saved permits her to make amends for her cruelties. Cecchi's spiritual farce points optimistically to the promise of redemption and the establishment of domestic harmony.

In Lucrezia the author wished to portray a practitioner of one of the most difficult Christian virtues: patience before disappointment, betrayal, and persecution. Refusing to take her son to court in order to spare him the embarrassment of legal action, Lucrezia would also never think of defying her ungrateful daughter-in-law. Only one member of the nuclear family, her young grandson, Lelio, fully appreciates Lucrezia's loving qualities. Cecchi's has reenacted onstage Christ's comment that "a child shall lead them" through this engaging boy's spontaneous outpouring of affection for his grandmother. Lelio's disarming sweetness contrasts with Lidia's mean-spirited attitude and Fulvio's weak-willed consent to wrongdoing. To an at last jubilant boy comes the pleasure of pronouncing the play's envoi when he sees his family reunited in gentle devotion. The playwright deliberately closes this drama for children with Lelio's animated speech, for the boy represents a future of hope.

Within the extended family of servants and retainers, two characters champion Lucrezia's cause. The maid Tessa shares the hardships of the old woman's undeserved banishment, but, instead of behaving with patience, this combative employee would like to see Fulvio and Lidia called to account before judicial authorities. An intensely caring individual, the maid tries to protect those she loves: displaying righteous indignation at Lucrezia's mistreatment and showering Lelio with tenderness. Poor Tessa falls victim to a prank by the servant boy Grillo, who slaps her in the eye with a back-handed gesture as he describes the serpent's frightening length. Even though this impertinent child has refused to take his responsibilities seriously, he instinctively rushes to Lucrezia's assistance by smuggling food to her. Acting and speaking like a buffoon does not prevent the mischievous lad from recognizing an injustice, which he attempts to undermine. With characters like Lelio, Tessa, and Grillo the dramatist enhances his work with a positive spirit of loving defiance.

Pure satire out of the tradition of *sacra rappresentazione* inspires the portrait of the venal physicians Maestro Antonio and Maestro Pietro along with their accomplice, the snake charmer Ferrando. Characterized as wallet-emptiers, the physicians place monetary profit over the patients' welfare. While clients languish in agony, those two colleagues in deceit fawn over each other with exaggerated ceremoniousness. Masking the superficiality of their medical knowledge with enigmatic Latin phrases, the physicians do not hesitate to enlist the snake charmer's services and therein to prove their affinity with the quacks who perform in public squares. All three abandon Fulvio and Lidia as a lost case after their expensive remedies come to nought. Through this trio of greedy incompetents who confuse medical science with chicanery, Cecchi demonstrates that hope must be directed to a force higher than the flawed skills of human ingenuity.

Those sophisticated quacks meet their match in Lidia's tenant farmer, Menico, who succeeds in tricking the physicians into giving him a free consultation for his ailing wife. In some interpolated scenes at the start of act 3, the author reintroduces the familiar situation of peasants' coming to town, but with the significant difference that, instead of gazing with wonder at the city's sights, the harassed farmers Trilla and Menico communicate their resentment against the urban rich who have exploited them and have reduced them to beasts of burden. Their one defense is in playing simpletons, whether to cheat landowners of a portion of the harvest or to outsmart supercilious city-dwellers like the two physicians. Menico clearly perceives how the contemptuous pair regards his wife's illness as beneath their serious concern, but the wily peasant acts like a country bumpkin just to elicit a medical opinion and proposed treatment from the haughty pair whose greed he cleverly leaves unsatisfied with a vague promise of future payment in foodstuffs. In the religiously optimistic atmosphere of the present comedy, Menico takes hope from news of the serpent's disappearance and looks to Lucrezia as a worker of miracles.[9]

To complete his gallery of character-types Cecchi includes a conscientious Father Confessor whose main concern is to arrange the expected funeral of Fulvio and Lidia, two gravediggers who are eager to collect a pair of corpses, and a crapulous deliveryman who blusters in a dialect intended to pass as Umbrian but sounding like Neapolitan. There exists another version of this verse play, expanded to a full length of five acts and given the designation of *"commedia"* under the title *Serpe Ovvero Suocera E. Nuora.* In 1590, three years after Cecchi's death, the Company of St. Mark performed the lengthened version. It is still debatable as to whether the farce or the five-act comedy was written first.[10] Curiously, the expanded rendering does not feature all the folk elements that enliven the farce, such as the concluding scene of the first act, in which the self-indulgent deliveryman pronounces a soliloquy praising bread, cheese, meat, and wine. The aesthetic attractiveness of this farce consists in its being sufficient unto itself as a bourgeois morality play.

How convincing is the religiosity inspiring this play about a domestic miracle? Shortly before the close of the nineteenth century a prominent scholar-editor judged this spiritual farce to reflect religious superstition in the way characters like Valerio are quick to attribute the serpent's assault to divine chastisement or in the way Lucrezia dismisses the animal by making a sign of the cross and touching it.[11] It is imperative for a reader of later times to consider this play in regard to the moral and theological spirit of the Catholic Reformation as well as to the long-established Florentine belief that Heaven did manifest itself in everyday life by miraculous intervention. While Cecchi poked fun at the credulous acceptance of the incantations cast by a snake charmer, his faith remained that of a Catholic who had undergone a crisis of conscience. His great achievement in this farce was to have created some of his most refreshing and ingratiating characterizations within a typical middle-class environment that all at once is transfigured by divine grace. Expressing the values of Tuscan civic religion, Giovan Maria Cecchi affirmed in his farce that God in His Providence holds all citizens accountable for their moral decisions and actions.

The Defense of Industry: Lo Sviato

Toward the last quarter of the sixteenth century a significant change in attitude took place among the members of the Florentine bourgeoisie. In a class that for centuries had affirmed a business ethic of industriousness, application, resourcefulness, and economic realism tempered by entrepreneurial daring, there developed a feeling of contempt for commerce and manufacturing. As individuals sought to

win positions of importance at the Medici court and to acquire noble titles, they began to scorn the very pursuits that
had made their families wealthy and respected throughout
the city. Names like shopkeeper, merchant, and manufacturer
became associated with shame by persons who thought business affairs were beneath them. Instead of instructing their
sons to assume control of the family firms, many parents
encouraged their children to study gentlemanly arts like
horsemanship and fencing to the exclusion of mastering the
fine details of industry and merchandising. In that permissive
atmosphere gambling soon grew into a fashionable pastime,
and money that should have gone into investments was un-
profitably diverted into that vicious practice.[12] To illustrate
and to combat the erosion of basic bourgeois values, Cecchi
wrote the moral play *Lo Sviato*, composed during the final
period of the author's theatrical activity between 1580 and
1587. Above all, the playwright hoped to show how the abandonment of the business ethic would accompany a decline in
religious devotion among the young, who, instead of emulat-
ing proud family traditions of industriousness, might succumb to the temptations of vice. Through this verse play
with its setting in present-day Florence, Cecchi was attempting to point out the moral dangers for a citizenry to renounce
what once made their community economically and cultur-
ally great.

This drama's prologue reflects one of the emphases of the
Catholic Reformation: the devotional aspect of religion. Good
Christians must attend to the routine of ritualistic practice,
such as going to mass, observing fasts and holy periods, and
carrying out necessary good works. The prologue states that
from infancy children should become accustomed to being
devout. The prologue recommends particularly for the benefit
of youths the cult of the Virgin, who would lead the wayward
back to the path of salvation. Here the author especially expressed that parents and guardians ought to protect children
from evil companions whose influence would be worse than
the devil's because a gesture like making the sign of the cross
might not suffice to drive away corrupting friends. With this
devout drama *("commedia . . . devota")* Cecchi is offering the
public a morally uplifting pastime. As in the prologue and
preliminary dialogue of *La Serpe*, the writer begs spectators

to look with kind understanding at the efforts of the youthful amateur actors who have to be apprentices before they can become masters.

Cecchi's play appears as a study in corruption and in the heavenly intervention that rescues an adolescent from diabolical contact. After losing his father, wealthy young Lamberto dei Lamberti has fallen in with the broker Mico, who plays on the naiveté of the boy's mother, Gostanza, as he progressively leads her son to perdition. In his evil design the broker has enlisted some vitiated allies like the dancing-master, Giansi, and the fencing-instructor, Chima, who wish to fleece the young man as they pretend to train him in their arts. Already at the beginning of the play, the first signs of Lamberto's moral weaknesses are evident in that he has spent the night before the drama's start carousing and gambling, with considerable losses. There is an obvious similarity to the story of the prodigal son except that the parable from the New Testament remains on a purely naturalistic level while this play moves into the supernatural. As a remedy for the self-indulgence that might ruin this seventeen- or eighteen-year-old youth, his elderly guardians, Fazio and Giannozzo, close the third and final scene of the expository first act speculating whether marriage might arouse a sense of responsibility in the lad.

Throughout the following two acts, Lamberto falls more and more under the sway of Mico and his cohorts, who convince the boy to rebel against his mother's authority and to contract some extravagant debts by hiring new servants and by purchasing an expensive horse. As Gostanza and her sister Maria become increasingly alarmed about the deterioration in Lamberto's attitude and behavior, they steadily lose control of the domestic situation because of the young man's refusal to heed the counsel of his guardians. By the fourth act Lamberto appears a completely different person, dressed in the swashbuckling fashion of a rich nobleman. This would-be cavalier does not hesitate to browbeat the diligent family cashier in order to obtain the funds to pay for his lavish expenditures.

The drama reaches the point of crisis in the fifth act, after Mico has used violence against Fazio and has accused the honest family friend of deliberately mismanaging the Lamberti business affairs. At the height of Gostanza's anguish over her son's incipient profligacy, Divine Providence intercedes on the family's behalf when suddenly an elderly man with a long white beard and dressed in dark clothes resembling those of a priest appears and confronts Mico. To the astonished members of the Lamberti household, Mico is unmasked as the Devil, and the old visitor reveals himself as an angel sent by the Virgin to save the boy because he never neglected to attend mass. After an extended debate between Mico and the angel over the conflicting values of a life given to a gentleman's dissipations or dedicated to bourgeois industry, the Devil has to withdraw in defeat. Lamberto begs forgiveness and accepts the angel's counsel for him to marry and to become the father of a family. The youth will proudly carry on the traditions of Florentine shopkeepers and entrepreneurs.

As in *Il Figliuol Prodigo,* this moral drama possesses the classical structure of five acts following unities of time and place. Yet, although action is compressed into the events of a few hours that determine the course of a young man's life, the play's background is eternity, which makes its presence felt in the participation of the angelic visitor. The drama's interpretative schema projects the immediate temporal level into the possible futures that other persons imagine for Lamberto: a life of marital and business responsibilities or a decade of wasting vital energies and his fortune in voluptuous pursuits. In act 4, scene 1, Mico manipulates Lamberto's apprehensions about marrying by vividly describing the premature and depressing old age that results from taking a bride in one's adolescence, becoming a father before twenty, and then becoming a grandfather by thirty-five. All the individuals who surround the youth turn the street scene outside the Lamberti home into a battleground to win his soul for good or for evil.

Beyond the actual stage setting, the dialogue paints a picture of Florence as a city of both temptations of sin and opportunities for salvation. Evenings in the Tuscan capital offer the uplifting experience of a family like the Lambertis holding a musical soiree highlighted by the performance of religious songs; the gatherings of flagellant confraternities to administer mortifying disciplines and to produce sacred dramas; or the meretricious attractions of expensive gaming houses with banquets, choice wines, recitations of the bawdiest tales from the *Decameron* as entertainment. While Mico pretends to Gostanza that her son is frequenting holy confraternities at night, the demonic corruptor is actually introducing the boy to the dissipations of the jolly brotherhoods, through which he will lose his wallet and his soul. The city of Florence assumes the role of a major actor in the testing of a young man's virtue.

Perhaps this play's fundamental structural weakness is its failure throughout four acts to prepare the audience for the intrusion of the supernatural in the final act. Except for a sketchy presentation of the plot in the prologue, spectators would otherwise think they were beholding a conventionally realistic comedy about the problems that afflict a middle-class family after the father's death. It is not until after the second scene of act 5, when Gostanza calls out to God to send an angel, that the drama brusquely moves to the plane of the struggle between Heaven and Hell. Mico's humiliating retreat from the earthly scene is accompanied by a change in the work's basic structuring unit, blank verse, to a sonnet that Lamberto recites in awestruck gratitude to the Virgin. Both the abrupt shift to a divine dimension and the introduction of a different verse form cause an artistic imbalance with the effect of producing a slightly disjointed quality between the realistic first four acts and the transfigured fifth act. The lack of complete stylistic and thematic cohesion gives evidence to Cecchi's difficulty in defining for himself the nature of "devout drama," for in the last lines of the envoi this play is called a "history, mystery, or exemplum." Displaying neither the consistently sustained naturalism of *Il Figliuol Prodigo* nor the convincingly anticipated miraculous intervention of *La Serpe*, the drama of the wayward youth appears as a partially realized attempt to represent the history of an exemplary combat within the framework of classical comedy.[13]

With its central theme of the battle for the salvation of a young man's soul, *Lo Sviato* appears as a play of relationships among characters who array themselves into two contending parties. Among the defenders of Lamberto's virtue, the family maid Lucia at first appears easily corrupted, as she seems in act 1, scene 2, to be lending support to the cheating designs

of the instructors Chima and Giansi, but actually this loyal
servant is as ingenuous as her mistress in believing the two
schemers have no intention except to train the boy in social
arts like fencing and dancing. This maid turns out to be the
first character to recognize Mico's devilish nature when at
the end of act 4 she angrily puns on his name, calling him a
creature of the *"nimico,"* the infernal enemy. By the drama's
close Lucia foresees a stable future for the family as she announces the news that their cat has just given birth to three
kittens, a sure sign of a forthcoming wedding. It is this maid
who delivers the envoi. The unappreciative Lamberto has
protectors of his honor and his fortune in his guardians Fazio
and Giannozzo, along with the conscientious family cashier,
who represent a class of dedicated functionaries that regard
their reputation to be more valuable than any ill-gotten
profit. None of these characters who are devoted to safeguarding the Lamberti family would be able to prevail against the
depredations of Mico's cohorts were it not for the grace that
comes from the Virgin, for the steadfastness characterized by
Fazio and Giannozzo has to confront the evil symbolized by
Mico and the moral weakness that Lamberto has yet to
overcome.

Like a military commander familiar with his troops, Mico
assembles a formidable force of unscrupulous partisans.
Giansi and Chima exhibit the resentment of individuals who
dwell on the fringe of the middle class that hires them to
instruct their young but never admits them to their privileged
number. Taking advantage of the family's love of music,
Giansi won entrée to the Lamberti home, where he hoped to
organize concerts, masquerade balls, and productions of comedies so as to defraud his patrons. Chima procures in act 3 a
ragged scamp named Trappolino to become Lamberto's servant, and within a single act the ragamuffin reappears dressed
in costly livery to be charged to his new master. As Lamberto
notes from the boy's name, this young wag might try to en-
snare his patron in a plot of his own, since "Trappolino"
means "the little trap." Even in his recent service to an impoverished courtier who had to pawn all his possessions,
Trappolino resembles the title character in the anonymous
Spanish tale *Lazarillo de Tormes*, 1554, which includes an
episode in which the starving hero attends a penniless, but

proud, nobleman. In fact, Trappolino is more of a *pícaro*, a rogue, than the protagonist in the Spanish tale because of his readiness to take part in that environment of cheating that forms around Lamberto.

To tend to the young man's new horse, Giansi engages a recently discharged German soldier named Lanz from the military troops of the *"Lanzknechte"* serving to enforce the Spanish domination of Italy. Lanz speaks a comic language mixing German, Italian, and Spanish; mispronouncing Italian words like *"bever"* (to drink) as *"befer."* The besotted condition of this soldier illustrates the third and most advanced state of intoxication, which Mico analyzes for Lamberto in act 2, scene 3, as ranging from cheerful to tipsy and then to soused. Lanz's employment in a bourgeois Florentine household is Mico's manner of insulting the intelligence of Lamberto, whom the demon expects to drag down to the soldier's bestial level.[14] For with all his pretense of avuncular caring, Mico always remains a creature of wickedness whose sole motivation is to abase Lamberto by confounding his protectors and by enlisting unprincipled tutors, picaresque scamps, and besotted soldiers in his insidious scheme.

Part of Mico's success in inserting himself into the affairs of the Lamberti household derives from the insecurity that Gostanza suffers. In Gostanza the author was pointing out an exception to the general rule about the social status of widows. Ordinarily, Florentine widows became the most economically independent women, enjoying the use of the estates left to them by their husbands, but the terms of Massimo Lamberti's will permit Gostanza to live on the income of the family fortune so long as she does not remarry. Since Lamberto is the heir to the estate, Mico plays on Gostanza's precarious situation and encourages the boy to assert the authority that comes to him with his financial superiority over his mother. Gostanza's reluctance to accept the suggestion of Fazio and Giannozzo for her son's marriage also follows from the widow's fear that a well-dowered daughter-in-law might usurp her place in the household. In no way does the dramatist intend Gostanza to appear a manipulative combatant for control over her son and his fortune; instead the playwright portrays an honorable and loving lady caught in a difficult financial situation. Indeed, it is the depth of this mother's tender devotion that causes the rather dangerous permissiveness by Gostanza to accept the influence that Mico establishes over her son, since she believes the broker to be acting in Lamberto's best interests. It is the widow's torment and confusion before the onslaught of Mico's contradictory rhetoric and potentially violent behavior that finally summon the angelic visitor to restore harmony to the family and to expel the satanic enemy. In her fervent love for her son, Gostanza allows the marriage that will introduce Lamberto to the responsibilities of adulthood.[15]

At times speech seems to take control of the play, adding nothing to plot or to characterization but bursting forth like an independent force. The momentum of language sweeps discourse along regardless of logical coherence, as in a conversation in act 2, scene 2, between Giannozzo and Fazio, who digress from talking about Lamberto's need for a wife to praise the healthy air of the countryside as contrasted to polluted cities. This nearly autonomous power of speech also prevails in the proverbs that appear to spring spontaneously from the dialogue: "One hand washes another"; "You still have milk in your mouth"; "Mother-in-law and daughter-in-law go together like rain and hail storms"; "While you have teeth in your mouth, you can never know what concerns you." The proverbs possess a concreteness of expression that impart material reality to abstract ideas. Through use of proverbs speakers can convey their thoughts in striking images of sense experiences, as when the supremacy of crapulence in the Tuscan capital is described in this manner: "Today in Florence gluttony slaughters more than knives do."

Along with this rhetorical abundance, which does not always appear to be under control, Cecchi also displays a conscious mastery of stylistic resources so that generally in this play the dramatic situation dominates the linguistic situation. Lamberto's speech progressively deteriorates, moving from respectful deference to a tone of flippancy and resentment against authority. Metaphorical language also expresses the drama's primary concern about the young man's fate, as in the conspiratorial conversation in act 1, scene 1, between Giansi and Chima, who employ a variety of words signifying the "nets" that will enmesh Lamberto in their swindling schemes. Speech acquires a legendary tone early in act 2 when the maid Lucia describes Gostanza's hesitations about permitting her son to marry in a tale about how the sun once took a bride in India and then produced so many fiery offspring that the world was almost destroyed in flame: the consequences of marriage might be additional problems for a family. A note of expectation prevails in the play's language to anticipate Lamberto's eventual ruination or redemption.

Of all the characters, the one who has greatest command of the Tuscan language to persuade others to his wicked will is Mico. From his lips speech takes on an aphoristic concision, as in act 4, scene 1, when he cautions Lamberto with the truly wise observation that persons who fail to commit foolish acts of fancy in their youth will later do so in old age. To impress the boy with his erudition this corruptor quotes from ancient philosophers and the Psalter. The demon's speech can switch from a mildly bantering tone to a mellifluous insistence or to a paternal concern for Lamberto's future. Gostanza and her counselors cannot prevail against the hypnotic powers of Mico's arguments, but he meets his verbal match in the angelic visitor. Linguistically and dramatically, the play reaches its climax in the lengthy and eloquent *tour-de-force* of the duel with words between the two opponents. The verbal intensity of their argument recalls the medieval theatrical genre of the *contrasto* (a farce in the form of a debate), a confrontation of the allegorical rivals Vice and Virtue in morality plays. The debate almost reaches a draw, until the angel compels Mico to reveal his infernal identity and to confess how envy of the happiness in the Lamberti household motivated him to play the masquerade in order to imprison the lad's soul in Hell.

What Mico ardently advocates in the dispute with the angel is the love of fashion that Cecchi regarded as a sign of the decadence menacing Florentine society. Although the Tuscan middle class traditionally emphasized the importance of displaying the marks of a family's fortune with elegant clothes, large townhouses, and country estates, by the close of the sixteenth century that stress on exterior show often no longer reflected the reality of a household industriously devoting its energies to acquiring wealth through trade. The outward transformation in Lamberto's manner of dress, from a conservative if rather old-fashioned style to a dashing foppishness, indicates how this adolescent abandons the customs of his social group to imitate the attire of the Medicean nobility. Learning an effete style of dancing, bearing arms as though in constant readiness to defend his honor, and engaging a retinue of servants decked out in gaudy livery stand out among the gentlemanly activities that Lamberto adopts in his illusion of one day being elevated to the circle of the granducal court.

This taste for luxuriousness that inspires the practices of an upper-class culture would in the playwright's judgment prove disastrous in influencing the conduct of an impressionable youth lacking the discipline to restrain his desire to be accepted into noble society. In act 2, scene 1, Cecchi extended his critique of conformity to exaggerated fashions to the passion for the grotesque coiffures and elaborately trimmed hats that ladies of economic means showed off at social gatherings. This seductive ostentation reveals the spiritual stagnation of a class substituting vanity for honor that can be won only through labor in commerce, finance, or professions like medicine and law.

In this devout drama Cecchi placed the Florentine business ethic within a Christian context. With the mentality of an accountant the angel asserts in the debate that an entrepreneur who gains his fortune by honest means and then shows charity to the poor receives merit in Heaven. A writer of the Tridentine era like Cecchi would see no conflict between a mercantile career and the demands of Catholic morality so long as a businessman carried out with sincerity the rites of the faith. Even though the playwright did not aesthetically anticipate the divine intervention occurring in the fifth act, contemporary Florentine audiences would easily have accepted a dramatic conclusion whereby praying to the Virgin every morning and evening resulted in a miracle. Lamberto's repentance conforms to the requirements of the Catholic Reformation because in acknowledging his sinfulness the youth admits to that basic human weakness that must turn for strength to the superior grace of the celestial court.

The True Neighbor: *Il Sammaritano*

Christ's parable of the good Samaritan, recounted in Luke 10. 29–37, inspired the playwright to write the farce *Il Sam-*

maritano, circa 1584, in order to illustrate what makes a responsible neighbor. This farce is intended to be serious and pleasurable at the same time. The author declares in the prologue of this verse drama that he wishes to present his Christian audience with matters that are both noble and Christian while offering them entertainment that is morally correct and high minded.[16] Unlike *Il Figliuol Prodigo,* the present dramatization of a Christian parable will not be set in modern times but in Palestine during the era just preceding the birth of Jesus, mainly because Christ narrated the adventure of a wounded commercial traveler in the past tense. As typical with the performances of Cecchi's religious plays, the prologue indicates the extreme youth of the actors ("fanciuletti," quite young boys) who are acquiring the rudiments of dramatic art from the experience of this very presentation.

All events in this three-act farce take place at a country inn set outside Jerico, where the kindly Samaritan has taken a man that he found injured on the highway. Cecchi's focus falls on the period of time not described in the Bible, for instead of representing scenes of the traveler's assault by bandits on the highway and his being passed over by a Levite and a priest before the Samaritan's arrival this play concentrates on the personnel of the inn and their fear that the Samaritan might never return to pay for the injured man's medical expenses and his lodging. As a refrain running throughout the first two acts one hears the groans of the patient, who is in apparently fatal agony. The innkeeper's son-in-law Doech opens the farce by sending his servant-boy Mosca to town to fetch a physician, Dr. Matatia, to return to the patient as soon as possible because his wounds refuse to heal. Knowing his father-in-law's desire for profit at the least cost, Doech in all his spontaneous generosity has determined to continue the Samaritan's charitable work by seeing to increased care for the patient. By the start of the second act Dr. Matatia finally reaches the inn, but because of the Samaritan's absence the physician neglects the wounded traveler while demanding immediate payment for prior medical services. News of the attack on the stranger has also caused business at the inn to fall off by two-thirds. In the meanwhile, two peasants arrive there to tell Dr. Matatia that thieves have stolen all his livestock.

With the return of the Samaritan in the third act the apprehensions of the inn's management are set at rest, while a mysterious young traveling companion of the Samaritan promises to treat the patient with a special unguent. Miraculously, all the injured man's wounds vanish, and he is able to leave his room to thank his benefactors. The enigmatic youth identifies himself as an angel whose mission has been to crown the merciful gestures of the Samaritan with success. For just as that benevolent merchant reacted to the wounded man with love, so does God regard all His creatures without distinctions of race and sect. After the angel disappears in flames, the patient and the Samaritan announce that they will accept the true faith of the Hebrews and decide to live together. The Samaritan has shown everyone how to be a neighbor to his fellowman in distress.

Unlike a sacred drama such as *La Morte Del Re Acab*, this farce is not set at the center of major dynastic reverses. Instead, the author examines the life of a modest inn suffering the pressures of political unrest. Searching between the lines of the Evangelical parable, the playwright introduces the servants, slaves, famished travelers, and preoccupied proprietors whose existences will be illuminated by a miracle. Cecchi intensifies the biblical tale with a supernatural dimension that would satisfy the religious expectations of contemporary Italian audiences. Once again adapting a farce to the structural limitations of regular drama, the writer represents a time period running from morning to late afternoon of a day that begins in anxiety and ends in wondrous jubilation. In the prologue and throughout the play Cecchi displays a highly developed historical sense rare to the Renaissance theater, demonstrating his intimate knowledge of biblical history. The prologue expressly states that the events in this work are supposed to be occurring during the reign of Hyrcanus the Ethnarch and High Priest. From accusations by various characters about marauding Roman highway patrols and the troops of Antipater it is possible to situate the drama during the politically chaotic period between 63 and 40 B.C. when control of Palestine was passing from local rulers to the Roman government. To worried innkeepers and wary travelers the world seems to be falling apart without any guidance or protection from the forces of the state. The playwright convincingly relates the circumstances of the assault and theft of the Canaanite traveler whom the Samaritan rescued to the broad social picture of internal turmoil throughout Judea as that region loses its independence.

This drama's stage space, remaining outside the inn, becomes an almost besieged scene as terrified peasants bring reports of bandit raids on their flocks or as travelers delay their journeys in the hope of assembling caravans to proceed in precarious security. Every once in a while a somewhat incongruous anachronism disrupts the accurately constructed historical portrayal, as in a reference to the savory cuisine of Tuscany; but Cecchi deliberately uses those anachronisms to draw parallels for his public between the turbulence in ancient Palestine and the violent disorder in Florence before Cosimo consolidated the Medicean Restoration. The play offers its spectators the reassurance that even at the moment of greatest political anarchy a superior heavenly force beholds all human deeds and will intervene to deliver deserving individuals from their present afflictions.

Although the Samaritan and the Canaanite appear as name figures who represent respectively the attitude of charity and the situation of victimization, the characters whose lives they touch possess well-defined personalities. Doech alone among the members of the inn's staff shows a saintly patience toward the injured guest. In his conversations with the inn's perpetual guest, the parasite Bomba, this young assistant innkeeper reveals his affinity with the Samaritan originating in the fact that both feel themselves to be outsiders among the Hebrews. Coming from the idolatrous Idumean nation, Doech accepted conversion to the Jewish faith only after his father's death. With the fervor of many converts, Doech considers becoming a scribe or rabbi in order to challenge the powerful but hypocritically greedy Pharisees who dominate the Hebrews' religious life.

In Doech the Christian spectators could recognize the portrait of an individual attracted to faith because of a profound conviction, as he is about to assume a spiritual profession at a time of general crisis in a land not even his own by birth. Doech's father-in-law, Ozia, resembles the comic innkeepers in most Italian sacred dramas such as *Il Figliuol Prodigo*: gracious, affable as long as a guest's money lasts, generous in promises but not in delivery, intent solely on running his establishment to financial advantage. Cecchi adds a facet to Ozia's personality not generally depicted in innkeepers: the apprehensions of a businessman in a country where no one can move in safety. Ozia's inn is neither so small nor so remote that it can stand apart from political and military upheavals.

This particular farce has sometimes been called a satire of physicians because of its trenchant portrait of the venal Dr. Matatia.[17] Overbearing toward patients, servants, and peasant tenants alike, the physician acts as though the whole world is at some enormous obligation to him. Cecchi creates an entire genealogy for this insolent medical practitioner, as disclosed in a conversation at the start of act 3 between Mosca and Matatia's servant, Nibbio, who continually complains how the physician starves the members of his household in contrast to the sumptuous fare that the inn's servants enjoy. Born in Matarea of peasant background, Matatia combines the astuteness of country people with the education of city-dwellers. The physician's air of self-confidence even when his treatments are without effect derives from his charlatan father, an astrologer from the line of Maccabeans who was accustomed to deceiving the gullible. Those who have to depend on Matatia either as their master or as a medical attendant give vent to their fierce resentment through a verbal play between his name and the word "*matto*": a madman whose greedy eccentricity nearly drives others insane.

In order to deal with this difficult character others have to adopt an aggressive or deliberately deceitful approach, as when Mosca lures Matatia back to the inn to reset the Canaanite's bandages by telling a lie that the Samaritan has returned with a large sum of money to settle all debts. To the characterization as pretender must be added the characterization as miser; despite the fortune that this physician has accumulated, he subjects himself to numerous deprivations and inconveniences for which he projects the blame onto his servants. On his trip to the inn Matatia has to alight from the enfeebled mule that he has never fed properly, but the physician reproaches his servant Nibbio for causing him to complete the short journey on foot. Cecchi demonstrates that without the providential assistance of Heaven, the miserliness, rudeness, and arrogance of a Maestro Matatia generally triumph in a world where social injustice prevails.

While the physician's hatefulness alienates others, the parasite Bomba relies on his charm and pleasing wit to win and to hold the good will of his acquaintances. Physically a Falstaffian type, the parasite never leads anyone astray because he does not want to be chastised as a scapegoat figure. Through his infectious cheerfulness Bomba enjoys the fate of being included rather than excluded. The parasite admits that he feeds and dresses himself with words whose gracefulness he has polished to a high art by carefully listening to other people. With aptly cited proverbs, sparkling metaphors, and conceits turned with a Baroque intricacy, Bomba shows himself to be a master raconteur who not only entertains but also counsels with a wisdom that he has perfected on his journeys to the sage philosophers of Greece. This parasite actually appears less of an impostor than Dr. Matatia, since the persons who pay for Bomba's Sybaritic meals never feel exploited. For the inn this parasite acts as an informal but extremely effective public relations representative constantly persuading guests to partake of the establishment's delicious fare. His success in retaining clientele more than pays for his crapulence despite the accusations of servants who call Bomba a wine-imbibing sycophant.

To Doech the parasite assumes the role of confidential advisor forever attempting to relieve the youth's anxieties with distracting anecdotes like the one about a debtor who could not sleep until midnight wracking his mind to find a way to discharge his bills when he decided to let his creditors pass the rest of the night fretting over his account. Language as used by Bomba becomes a form of therapy. Just as Bomba forever endeavors to avoid experiencing pain, he refrains from inflicting it on those around him. When the angel announces how God often permits a minor injury to occur in order to produce a miraculous result, Bomba expresses his hope that Heaven will never put him to the test. In this engaging character the playwright has described an Epicurean who, while fleeing the world's suffering and seeking its gastronomic delights, repays his benefactors with congenially reassuring companionship.[18] Because of his central importance to the life of the inn, Bomba closes the farce by delivering the envoi in which he announces he will see to the evening's dinner while everyone else goes to the Temple to celebrate the miracle.

Perhaps the most realistically drawn characters are the peasants Maciulla and Scorpa, who appear late in the second act with news about the roving bands of thieves preying on herds of cattle. Cecchi presents the speech of these two country figures as distinctly different from that of the other characters, even the inn's servants, with whom the peasants enjoy a warm rapport. Verbal contaminations combining words like *"fisco"* (public treasure) and *"vescovo"* (bishop) to form *"fiscovo"* (tax collector), rustic distortions of words that describe urban practices, and precise terms for the various kinds of salad greens that Scorpa gives to the servant-girl Cleofe all contribute to an exact portrayal of a rural experience as opposed to the experience of city-dwellers, who cannot appreciate the land, livestock, and the problems of defense against brigands.[19] In the confrontation between Maciulla and his landlord, Dr. Matatia, the spectators could see the oppressive exploitation of the peasantry by a member of the professional bourgeoisie whose insensitivity to the dangers of living and working in a poorly protected countryside shows itself in his placing financial responsibility on his tenant to compensate him for any animals that thieves have stolen. Instead of introducing the peasants in this farce as country bumpkins, Cecchi studies how adverse working conditions reduce the farmers to abused instruments for managing the country property of well-to-do citizens.

Like their peasant counterparts, the members of the servant class fare better or worse depending on the relative generosity of their masters. The playwright delights in playing with the names of the servants: Mosca is a fly, Nibbio is a kitebird, and Bomba makes the inn his home base *(bomba)*, with the greatest difference between them being that the parasite succeeds in avoiding work and the two boys do not. Even though Mosca and Nibbio generally match each other in quick intelligence, resourcefulness, and a penchant for harmless mischief, the good fortune of the former to be employed at the inn puts him at an enormous advantage over his underfed friend. Among the young servant-women in the play the author points to distinctions not so much in employers but in their legal status. Cleofe is a free woman who flirts with servant-boys and peasant-lads alike without anyone to reprimand her so long as she restricts her amorous dalliance to her inferior class. Cecchi depicts actual historical conditions in ancient Palestine with the foreign slave Marta, whose abject circumstances at the inn cause her to resent Bomba's privileged situation. When the parasite tries to coax her with promises of jewelry to prepare him delicious meals, the slave-woman contemptuously snatches the gift from him without committing herself. With her imperfect mastery of the language in the land of her captivity, Marta rarely conjugates verbs and uses personal pronouns with the infinitive: "*Tu voler darmelo*" ("You to want to give it to me"). This slave shows a marked preference for the verb "*voler*," as indeed could be the case of all captives, servants, and rustic tenants who spend their lives wanting what their masters enjoy. In Cecchi's plays speech discloses the mentality and social condition of his characters.

Through the sermon that the angel delivers toward the farce's close the playwright allegorically interprets his drama. The Canaanite's visit to the Temple in the holy city of Jerusalem resembles man's original innocent state. After the traveler leaves the sacred precinct and encounters the thieves who strip him of his goods and his clothes, his miserable plight recalls humankind in a postlapsarian state deprived of all natural gifts. Neither the Levite nor the priest as representatives of a religion founded on law and ceremonies could assist the fallen figure, who required a different kind of spiritual support. Just as the Samaritan comes to save the Canaanite, recognizing in the injured man the universal image of God, so will Christ descend from Heaven to redeem humankind with grace that works miracles like the unguent to heal the traveler's wounds. Since the farce takes place during the period ending the pre-Christian era, the angel's sermon serves as a prophecy of the Messiah's advent to remove original sin from the world. This farce's allegorical dimension extends into its four intermezzi with their madrigals performed by symbolic figures to represent various stages of the soul: pristine innocence; descent into sin under the law of nature; the harsh rule of a law inscribed on stone tablets; and redemptive rule under a law of grace.[20]

Cecchi intends his play to awaken Christian imagination to the need to renew religion's spirit in everyday life. The angel asserts that an act of mercy pleases God more than a sacrifice at the temple. Although *Lo Sviato* advocates the importance of observing rituals, the formal celebration of religious services without an accompanying demonstration of good deeds becomes an empty, hypocritical gesture. Of the farce's characters, Doech becomes prominent because of his sincere efforts to make charity a way of life and to introduce reform against self-righteous control of religion by the Pharisees. While the Samaritan's works of mercy offer an inspiring model, this title character remains in the background until the final act. Christ's parable of the good Samaritan illustrates how a spontaneous act of kindness joins individuals as neighbors in God. The farce provides an answer to a question raised in Luke 10.25: how would one gain eternal life? Charity makes religion a living experience. The world in which Cecchi lived was one of clerical abuse not unlike that of ancient Palestine, and satirical remarks in this farce about self-indulgent clergymen who urge others toward abstinence say as much about contemporary Italy as about biblical Judea. Cecchi's brief play elevates the New Testament parable to a supernatural level of encounter between humans and the divine as the angel's visit reveals the coming Incarnation with its mission of everlasting redemption.

Conclusion: Toward an Urban Theater of Religious Nature

In this dramatist's plays of spiritual inspiration, religion and commercial enterprise support each other. The dramas address an ethical message to an urban public composed of merchants, financiers, members of guilds, physicians, lawyers, and clergymen who all participated in the social restoration achieved by Cosimo I. While the dramatist carried on the tradition of *sacre rappresentazioni* to affirm the values of Florentine civic religion founded on family, class, and commune, he also advocated the goals of the Catholic Reformation for a reawakening of Christian conscience. Whether the plays are modest farces, moral dramas in a contemporary setting, or expensively staged religious spectacles, their presentation of a conflict in social, economic, and family relationships usually reaches a moment of crisis that calls forth the divine's merciful intervention. Implicit to this belief in heavenly assistance is an acknowledgment of limited human power to determine the outcome of events. Just as in the secular comedies Fortune overturns ingenious *beffe,* in the sacred plays divine Providence reverses a threat of eternal damnation. A fundamental conviction about the structure of reality governs the world view of Cecchi's religious dramas and gives them coherence: in either a play about the collapse of a dynasty *(La Morte Del Re Acab)* or one about the struggle for dominance in a family *(La Serpe, Ovvero La Mala Nuora)* a protective celestial force intercedes to reestablish harmony. Throughout the plays that constitute Cecchi's urban religious theater, individual and collective errors of greed, impatience, and ambition must yield to a superior Will that banishes agents of evil and brings about a reign of just authority.

For both the sacred dramas and farces the author sought to create an artistic form intermediate to comedy and tragedy. The use of prologues, division into acts and scenes, the close with envois, and the frequent choice of blank verse hendecasyllable lines illustrate the formal similarities between Cecchi's regular comedies and his religious plays. Another line of aesthetic continuity between the writer's secular comedies and his sacred dramas lies in the common character-types that both introduce: braggart captains, parasites, misers, scamps, corrupt priests, wayward students. The parasite may appear as a deceitful courtier like Sparecchia in *La Morte Del Re Acab* or a congenial sage like Bomba in *Il Sammaritano.* Climactic scenes of moral insight like the devil's unmasking in *Lo Sviato* or the remorse of Lidia and Fulvio in *La Serpe* achieve theatrical effectiveness within the classical structure that Cecchi adapted from the models of ancient Roman comedy and folk farce. By emphasizing a "decorum of roles," the playwright hoped to fashion a wide social range of characters such as nobles, shopkeepers, servants, and peasants who were to be distinguished in economic status, privileges, traits of speech, and manners while being deemed equal in the sight of God. Speech especially points out differences in class and in region, urban versus country background, mentalities of bourgeois affluence or servile need, affectations of academic education as opposed to the folk wisdom of proverbs. Eloquence may also take the form of a diabolically false rhetoric that leads youths into temptation or it may effect an enlightening persuasion toward redemption through virtue.

Although Cecchi wrote his religious plays to satisfy the requests of friars in their monasteries and nuns at their convents or to please friends who belonged to lay confraternities, his abiding motivation was to appeal to the youths of his era so that they might combat the rapid erosion of values in late-sixteenth-century society. Even when the playwright apologized in the prologues of *La Serpe, Lo Sviato,* and *Il Sammaritano* for the amateurish performances of young actors by pointing out the profitable training they would receive in histrionic skills, Cecchi's interests went far beyond perfecting the casts' stage technique. The author stressed the moral usefulness of those dramas to enlighten actors and public alike to the responsibilities of faith, the need for love within the family, the opportunity to acquire eternal life, and the effectiveness of prayers. With the presence of children at his plays as both actors and members of the audience the dramatist was able to carry out his didactic intention. The playwright wanted the young to continue the most vital traditions of Florence's commercial society within the context of its heritage of civic religion.

Historically, Cecchi's religious plays stand midway between the *sacre rappresentazioni* of the High Renaissance and the sacred theater of the Baroque era in Italy. Although the confidence in human ability that characterized the Laurentian Age had vanished, Cecchi's dramas of spiritual inspiration optimistically affirmed a union of the temporal and the eternal when divine love would respond to the anguish of troubled worshipers. The religious viewpoints of this Florentine writer differ from those of the Italian Baroque dramatist Federico Della Valle (circa 1560–1628), who felt involvement in political and worldly affairs to be a vain and painful experience while he yearned for the inner peace offered by faith.

Cecchi retained an essentially comic vision of life, so that the playworld of his religious dramas shows a balance between edification and amusement by ridiculing the extravagance of certain character-types and social groups while cautioning the public to see onstage the reflection of their own moral errors. With farces, historical spectacles, and devout dramas whose settings might be ancient Palestine or contemporary Tuscany, this author represented life as inspired by a sacred force that gave meaning to all social, economic, and political undertakings. In Cecchi's religious plays a transfiguring divine presence attends with grace the embattled scene of human life.

5
CONCLUSION: CECCHI'S RECONCILIATION OF THEATRICAL TRADITIONS

Throughout his long career as a dramatist Giovan Maria Cecchi sought to reconcile the major literary traditions of sixteenth-century Italian theatrical practice. For his penetrating study of entangled human relationships in a bourgeois community this playwright joined Plautine devices of disguise and subterfuge to the modern spirit of carnival masquerade. To represent how romance disrupts the routines of the world of commerce, which usually reduces marriage to a business transaction by assigning a dowry, the author resorted to a pathetic Terentian mood of emotionalism. Cecchi's ambivalent art uncovers a comic disparity in society with its conflicts in values between generations, between the contradictory desires of the young, and between antithetical systems of education. This same dramatist, who described the inventiveness of young lovers and loyal servants in overcoming the tyranny of greedy parents, also revealed the tensions within middle-class households where husbands and wives compete for economic control on the decline of their romantic attractions for each other.

In comedies inspired by the *Decameron* and the Italian novellistic tradition Cecchi not only exposed the hypocrisy of elderly husbands who attempt to enslave their young wives while pursuing their own erotic adventures but also portrayed the triumph of adulterous passion that vindicates those women whose sensual longings have been wrongfully repressed. Although this writer upheld the vital importance of entrepreneurial resourcefulness and even justified commercial endeavor in religious terms, he never hesitated to disclose the corrupting effects of venal attitudes that turn love into a not-always-fair exchange of goods and services. With his various types of religious plays Cecchi freed his characters from the imprisonment of present time and compromising circumstances so that they could gain a brief glimpse of the eternal and prepare themselves for a reception into grace. In regular comedies that either take their plots directly from Plautus and Terence or proudly claim to set forth recent events, in historical spectacles that show a nation being put to a trial of faith, in farces and full-length moral dramas that depict a domestic warfare that only Heaven can resolve—in these theatrical traditions the Florentine dramatist employed all the arts of stagecraft and all his linguistic powers to convey a sense of human solidarity rendered vulnerable by comic shortcomings but forever guarded by divine love.

Cecchi's final play, *La Romanesca*, 1585, constitutes a concluding statement about the dramatist's effort to reconcile theatrical traditions and antecedents. This farce has its origins in the *maggio* festivals of rural regions celebrating May's promise of renewal. A mood of fable prevailed in the *maggio* spectacles, whose heroes were not only religious figures but also Grecian lords and feudal knights. Working within the festive tradition of the *maggio*, Cecchi employed the prologue of *La Romanesca* to assert the autonomy and artistic importance of the farce as a dramatic genre:

> Farce is a third new subject
> Between tragedy and comedy: it enjoys
> The breadth of both of them,
> And it flees their narrowness, because
> It takes unto itself great lords and princes,
> Which comedy does not do. It also takes in,
> As if it were either an inn or a hospital,
> The masses, both the low and plebian,
> Which Lady Tragedy never wants to do.
> Its actions are not restricted: it accepts
> Merry events and sad ones, secular and ecclesiastical,
> Urban, rural, dreadful and pleasant.
> It makes no account of place: it forms its stage
> Both inside a church and on a square or anywhere.
> Nor does it take account of time. Therefore if it does
> Not finish in one day, it will take two or three.

The Florentine writer perceived farce as an accommodating peasant-girl in contrast to haughty Lady Tragedy. Although Aristotle never acknowledged farce as a valid dramatic form, Cecchi in a typically humanistic effort to find classical authority for contemporary literary endeavors cited a farce that was performed at Caligula's court to that emperor's displeasure. Liberated from observing unities of time and place, farce had one invariable characteristic for Cecchi: it must be in verse.

In plot, subject matter, and characterization, *La Romanesca* fulfills all the expectations expressed in the author's prologue but does so within the condensation of classical style. Its three acts must be considered a full-length drama comparable in extent to the erudite comedies or the sacred histories. The scene is modern-day Rome with a view of the Colosseum. Like tragedy, this farce presents fictitious characters of exalted social rank such as the much persecuted English crown princess, Isabella; her husband, the king of France; the Roman governor; English and French nobles; diplomats. In the manner of comedy, this play also includes private citizens such as servants, a tailor, beggars, a nurse, and guards. With his usual sensitivity to subtle nuances of language, Cecchi carefully distinguishes the speech of his characters. While the governor of Rome speaks in a solemn style befitting his dignified rank and uses biblical proverbs to illustrate his arguments, the Florentine tailor Parentraccola spices his crude tavern conversation with earthy proverbs. Ambassadors and court officials deliver eloquent, though somewhat overlong addresses to their superiors. Cecchi structures the scenes within each act according to a contrapuntal fashion between those occupied by members of the aristocracy and those taken up by the lower classes, between moments of melancholy reflection and moments of rejoicing. Since events occur during the year of a holy jubilee, Rome appears as a means for royal and humble pilgrims alike to realize their quests.

The farce *La Romanesca* partakes of romance to arouse a sense of wonder about the way Fortune will alter the lives of the lofty French monarch, who has arrived in the Italian holy city seeking his lost bride, and the pilgrim Claudio, who is hoping to find his true friend, Sempronio, for whom he once made a supreme sacrifice in their youth. Three major sources provide the background of marvel for this farce. Boccaccio in *Decameron* 10, 8, relates an idealistic tale in which young Gissippo incurred the vengeful wrath of a powerful clan by allowing his friend Tito to take away the fiancée that was intended for him. The two friends eventually met again in Rome, where Tito attempted to repay his debt to Gissippo by confessing to a murder for which his innocent benefactor was condemned to death. In Cecchi's farce the Roman Sempronio makes an identical confession to rescue the Frenchman Claudio Labretto, who suffered poverty and exile for yielding his marital rights over to his Italian classmate at the University of Paris. Cecchi takes his Boccaccian source and plays upon its pathetic overtones. While the author of the *Decameron* stresses the psychological states of his main characters, the Renaissance dramatist focuses on the cruel reverses of Fortune.

The source for Cecchi's story of the flight of Princess Isabella from the incestuous desires of her father, King Adovardo of England, lies in numerous folktales about princesses who sometimes mutilated themselves by cutting off their hands to deter their fathers' illicit demands. Before Cecchi the tale of the persecuted princesses became the subject of various *sacre rappresentazioni* like the fifteenth-century *Rappresentazione di Stella* and the early-sixteenth-century *Rappresentazione di Santa Uliva*. A second fairytale motif for this farce is that of the pitiless mother-in-law who takes advantage of her son's absence to order the murder of her defenseless daughter-in-law and grandchild, a fate from which Isabella and her son escaped only through the compassion of the Duke of Nemours, who disobeyed the commands of the French queen-mother. Preceding Cecchi's attempt to dramatize those folk sources about persecuted princesses is a Latin play by an anonymous Italian Dominican friar: *Comoedia Sine Nomine*, written between 1450 and 1460. Cecchi surpasses all of his predecessors by harmoniously fusing his diverse sources into a concentrated drama. The artistry of the Florentine playwright consists in his ability to reconcile a multitude of literary antecedents into a unified work without discord, wherein the modern world of Rome becomes the scene of

romantic quests that bring to a happy end the long separation of two friends and the relentless persecution of a
princess.

Aesthetic unity in the Italian farce comes through the
theme of Fortune, which serves as the play's dominating
force. It was Fortune that had separated Claudio and Sempronio and had prevented their reunion at the drama's start.
Unlike many Renaissance writers who usually differentiated
between Fortune and Destiny, Cecchi tended in this farce to
equate the two as he structured his complicated plot on a
series of coincidences that prove to be the workings of that
inscrutable Fortune or Destiny. Even the stratification of society depends on the whims of Fortune, for as a servant-boy
observes in act 2, scene 1, that insensitive force fashioned the
lowly class of domestics from the dregs of primeval humanity. Poetically, the drama's climax arrives in the fourth scene
of act 3, when the servant Roncola describes a painting that
is an emblematic representation of Fortune as a lady sitting
atop a tree whose boughs are laden with precious items such
as jewels and crowns as well as valueless objects like brooms
while an infinite number of men and beasts wait below for
the lady to shower her gifts on them. This picture of a passive
humanity at the mercy of Fortune is the product of an artist
expressing a lack of confidence in individual initiative that
characterized the pessimism of the Catholic Reformation. In
contrast to Dante, who regarded Fortune as an impartial
power necessary to bring about change in the world, Cecchi
depicted it as a capricious agent and made it the moving force
of his drama.

In order to illustrate the swift and entirely unpredictable
might of the sometimes cruel and other times generous Fortune, the author compressed *La Romanesca* by observing the
unities of time and space. Within a single day Fortune elevates Lady Isabella from the humble status of imperial Roman nurse to her legitimate rank as queen of France and
England. The private misfortunes of the friends Claudio and
Sempronio end with their exoneration from the charge of
murder and the reinstatement of Claudio's noble titles and
estates by the French monarch. Cecchi created in this farce a
secular morality about the rewards of private virtues such as
the constant love between Isabella and her royal husband

despite years of separation and the devotion of two friends who value their relationship above life itself. Without directly introducing allegorical characters, the author represented Fortune as the play's inspiring presence. Cecchi integrated the varied elements of his romantic farce within the unifying theme of that arbitrary Fortune that reigns supreme over life.

Comedy served for Giovan Maria Cecchi as the means to represent the *"imago veritatis"* (image of truth) that permitted his audiences to glimpse a redeeming vision of themselves in their moral strengths and weaknesses. Hoping to entertain while instructing, the Florentine writer adapted the ancient Roman comedy of manners to the needs and the conditions of his own times. With literary resources such as Plautine and Terentian plays, the Italian novellistic tradition, biblical parables, sacred history, and romantic folktales, Cecchi created a diverse comic theater that expressed the aspirations of late Italian Renaissance society to reconcile the wit and spontaneity of pagan culture with the Christian view of human existence. The plays of this dramatist offered his public the consolation that, despite the reverses of Fortune or the intrigues of Satan, the anguished cries of a devout Christian would call forth the miraculous intervention of Heaven. In Cecchi's secular comedies there prevails a carnival spirit of revelry and masquerade that precedes the Christian season of sacrifice, while his moral plays point to the promise of restoration and salvation.

Two directions Italian theatrical activity took after Cecchi's time were the improvised theater of the Commedia dell'Arte and the pure sound and marvelous decor of melodrama in opera. Cecchi's learned comedies point to the masked stock characters and involved amorous intrigues of the professionally acted Commedia dell'Arte, while his grandiose sacred dramas with their colorfully represented intermezzi about scenes from biblical history anticipate the staged marvels of Baroque opera and Jesuit religious theater. The theatrical works of Giovan Maria Cecchi document the evolution of aesthetical sensibility in sixteenth-century Florence that later culminated in the establishment of traveling Commedia dell'Arte troupes and the birth of opera with the Camerata de' Bardi.

NOTES

Notes to Chapter 1: Introduction

1. J. R. Hale, *Florence and the Medici: The Pattern of Control,* 136–143, describes absolutist government under Cosimo I.

2. Riguccio Galluzzi, *Istoria del granducato di Toscana sotto il governo della Casa Medici,* I, Bk. 1, Ch. 8, discusses repressive rule in Florence.

3. Eric Cochrane, *Florence in the Forgotten Centuries 1527–1800,* 53–56, analyzes the efforts of the Medicean government to revive Tuscan commerce and industry.

4. The exploitation of peasants by city-dwelling land investors is investigated by P. J. Jones, "From Manor to Mezzadria: A Tuscan Case-Study in the Medieval Origins of Modern Agrarian Society," 193–241.

5. See Cochrane, *Florence,* 78, concerning the cultural unity in Florence.

6. A date of 11 February 1541, for the change in name is assigned by Richard Samuels, "Benedetto Varchi, the *Academia degli Infiammati,* and the Origins of the Italian Academic Movement," 627; but Armand De Gaetano, "The Florentine Academy and the Advancement of Learning through the Vernacular," 33, assigns a date of 25 March 1541. De Gaetano interprets Cosimo's motives in encouraging the Florentine Academy as being extremely political in nature while Samuels speaks of the duke's multifaceted cultural program to enhance the reputation of Florence.

7. Cochrane, *Florence,* 90–91, describes the city's renovation.

8. Eric Cochrane, "The End of the Renaissance in Florence," 7–29, here tries to determine the historical moment when vigorous inquiry and experimentation in Florence gave way to complacency.

9. Altoviti's career and the opposition he met from Cosimo, who even confiscated the prelate's personal property, are examined by Arnaldo D'Addario, *Aspetti Della Controriforma a Firenze,* 121–23, 338–39, 364, 504–505. D'Addario provides an excellent history of Cosimo's ecclesiastical reforms and the currents of the Catholic Reformation in Florence, including a large selection of documents from the period.

10. Ibid., 420–21.

11. There is some debate as to whether Cecchi was born on 14 or 15 March 1518. Fortunato Rizzi, *Le Commedie Osservate di Giovan Maria Cecchi e La Commedia Classica del Secolo XVI,* 7, holds to the fourteenth while Raffaello Rocchi, *Drammi Spirituali Inediti Di Giovanmaria Cecchi,* I, vii, suggests the fifteenth. A full genealogy with charts of the Cecchi family can be found in the appendix to Ugo Scoti-Bertinelli, *Sullo Stile Delle Commedie In Prose Di Giovan Maria Cecchi,* 163–73.

12. Rocchi, *Drammi Spirituali Inediti,* I, ix, mentions the plea to the city's magistrates for justice.

13. For information about the criminal activities of members of the Cecchi clan see Bruno G. R. Ferraro, "Giovanni Maria Cecchi, the *Commedie Osservate* and the *Commedia Erudita* in Sixteenth-century Italy," 25. The Ferraro dissertation is a superb source of information on Cecchi's life and his secular

comedies, offering extensive discussion on the comic theater of the period. Recently, the Canadian researcher Konrad Eisenbichler, working from Florentine archival records, has suggested that Matteo, Prudenza, and Piero may have belonged to a Cecchi family not at all related to Ser Giovan Maria.

14. For the decline in the wool trade at the time of Cecchi's entry into the partnership see Jacqueline Brunet, "Le Paysan et son Langage dans L'Oeuvre Théâtrale de Giovanmaria Cecchi."

15. Baccio's *Ricordo* can be found in Luigi Fiacchi, ed., *Commedie di Giovan Maria Cecchi*, I, 6–9.

16. For an edition of the *Dichiarazione Di Molti Proverbi* consult the one prepared by L. Fiacchi entitled *Dei Proverbi Toscani* (Milan, 1838).

17. Cochrane, *Florence*, 134, describes popular piety in Florence.

18. An edition of the *Cicalamento* is in G. Romagnoli, *Scelta Di Curiosità Letterarie Inedite O Rare Dal Secolo XIII Al XIX*. Cecchi's intense joy in relating anecdotes here in the *Cicalamento* as well as in his comedies, with a marked Boccaccian taste for caricature, is explored by Aldo Vallone, "La Vocazione Al Racconto Del Cecchi," 303–313.

19. Rizzi, *Commedie Osservate*, 16, draws attention to the characterization of German Catholics by Cecchi.

20. D'Addario, *Aspetti*, 402–405, gives an extract from the *Sommario*, which he intends to publish later in a complete edition.

21. Information on Cecchi's success as a dramatist has been provided to me by Konrad Eisenbichler in "The Religious Drama of Giovan Maria Cecchi," 26–27. Also cf. Rizzi, *Commedie Osservate*, 8–9.

22. Bernard Weinberg, *A History of Literary Criticism in the Italian Renaissance*, I: 203, 237–38, 586–88; II: 666–67; examines theories on comic genre by Pino da Cagli, Riccoboni, Rossi, and Ceruti. The interaction between theatrical practice and dramatic theory concerns Jackson I. Cope in his chapter, "Critics and *Commediografi* in Sixteenth-century Florence," *The Theater and the Dream: From Metaphor to Form in Renaissance Drama*, 77–97. Cope asserts the powerfully continuing tradition of Ficinian Neoplatonic thought that influenced literary theorists like Francesco Buonamici in his *Discorsi poetici*, 1587, which acknowledged the duality of reality and illusion in stage performances. For Cope the perennial argument of comedy is "return, regeneration, a restoration" (p. 87), as he sees evidenced in Anton Francesco Grazzini's multidimensional play *La Strega*.

23. I disagree with Wylie Sypher, who in following Freud in "The Meanings of Comedy," 37, speaks of the spirit of comedy and carnival as an unmasking. Carnival especially allows people to replace the *personas* of daily existence with comic masks of buffoonery. Mikhail Bakhtin, *L'oeuvre de François Rabelais et la culture populaire au Moyen Age et sous la Renaissance*, trans. Andrée Robel, 198–276, analyzes carnival spirit in its pagan rejoicing in bodily pleasures.

24. Samuels, "Benedetto Varchi," 607, describes the involvement of academicians in play productions.

25. For a study of Tuscan stagecraft consult A. M. Nagler, *Theatre Festivals of the Medici, 1539–1637*, trans. G. Hickenlooper, 2–3.

26. Cf. this observation by Susanne Langer, "The Comic Rhythm," 124, "Comedy is an art form that arises naturally wherever people are gathered to celebrate life, in spring festivals, triumphs, birthdays, weddings or initiations."

27. Fiacchi, *Commedie di Giovan Maria Cecchi*, I, 19, n. 2, mentions the Archduke's visit. Details on other state performances can be found in Nagler, *Theatre Festivals*.

28. An example of the attention now being paid to the drama is a confer-

ence sponsored by Harvard and Columbia Universities in November 1978 on
the theme "Renaissance Theater in Northern Italy: The Court and the City
(1400–1600)," and published as *Il teatro italiano del Rinascimento*, ed. Maristella Lorch.

29. Cochrane, "The End of the Renaissance," 10, speaks of Italian urban
orientation to the street.

30. A recent example of the painstaking work required to establish the
numerous variants in versions for a single play has been beautifully worked
out by Jacqueline Brunet, "*L'Acqua Vino:* une (deux, trois?) farce(s) de G. M.
Cecchi," 139–74.

31. Three scholars who are presently engaged in researching all the variant
versions of individual Cecchi plays are Jacqueline Brunet of the Centre national de la Recherche scientifique in France; Bruno G. R. Ferraro of the
University of New England in Australia; and Konrad Eisenbichler at the
University of Toronto. Professor Ferraro has recently visited libraries in Italy
containing manuscripts of Cecchi's plays, and he is preparing a critical edition of *I Contrassegni.* The first English translation of any Cecchi play, *L'Assiuolo,* has appeared in print in a version by Konrad Eisenbichler as *The
Horned Owl.*

32. This chronology has been elaborated by Ferraro, "Giovanni Maria Cecchi," in the tables following p. 34.

33. Following indications in Baccio's *Ricordo,* Rizzi, *Le Commedie Osservate di Giovan Maria Cecchi e La Commedia Classica de Secolo XVI,* 17,
uses those categories. Cecchi also wrote some one-act plays, often of an
allegorical nature, generally called *atti recitabili* (scenic acts).

Notes to Chapter 2: Comedies of Ancient Inspiration

1. Arnaldo D'Addario, *Aspetti Della Controriforma A Firenze,* 113–14,
analyzes the role of the "Monte delle Doti."

2. George Duckworth, *The Nature of Roman Comedy,* 145, speaks of the
conflict between Lesbonicus and Lysiteles.

3. For studies on the function of the prologue in erudite comedies consult
the following two essays by Emilio Goggio: "The Prologue in the *Commedie
Erudite* of the Sixteenth Century," 124–32; and "Dramatic Theory in the
Prologues to the *Commedie Erudite* of the Sixteenth Century," 322–36. A
significant lecture that studied the prologues of Cecchi's secular and religious plays was given on 10 April 1980, at the Toronto Renaissance and
Reformation Colloquium by Konrad Eisenbichler on the occasion of receiving first prize in the Young Scholars' Competition for the study entitled
"Dramatic Genre in the Prologues of Giovan Maria Cecchi."

4. For technical names of character-types see Northrop Frye, *Anatomy of
Criticism,* 172–73. For the notion of literary ambivalence I wish to thank my
colleague at Kent State University, Lyliane Kerns, who is currently writing a
monograph on the technique of ambivalence in Fénelon's *Le Télémaque.*

5. Ferraro, "Giovanni Maria Cecchi," 225, n. 2, compares Moro to Friar
Cipolla.

6. The diminished role of *beffe* is analyzed by Guy Lebatteux, "La Crise de
la 'Beffa,' " 179–201.

7. Filippo Ravignani recalls the father, Filogono, in Ariosto's second comedy, *I Suppositi,* 1508.

8. Bruno G. R. Ferraro, "Giovanni Maria Cecchi, the *Commedie Osservate*

and the *Commedia Erudita* in Sixteenth-century Italy," 226–27, cites deleted passages.

9. In analyzing this play I am following the original prose versions as printed by the Giolito De Ferrari Press in Venice, 1550. There is also a verse recasting published by the Giunti Press in Venice, 1585. The verse revision shows no significant changes in plot or characterization although the fast-paced dialogue of the prose original loses much of its effectiveness in the expansive metric reworking.

10. Fortunato Rizzi, *Le Commedie Osservate di Giovan Maria Cecchi,* 190, draws attention to the use of colorful names as playful puns in the dialogue of this play.

11. Ferraro, "Giovanni Maria Cecchi," 256–57, discusses misogyny in the drama.

12. Rizzi, *Commedie Osservate,* 66–67, comments on the anachronism of the slave-girl, asserting there was no slavery in Renaissance Italy. But David Wilkins, "The Black and Oriental in Italian Renaissance Art," points out that there was a large subclass of domestic slave-girls of Tartar extraction working in the major Italian urban centers.

13. Adelfia and her beloved Alfonso belong in Frye's class of the *eiron* figures, the heroine and hero; see Frye, *Anatomy of Criticism,* 173. Filippo is an *alazon*.

14. Ferraro, "Giovanni Maria Cecchi," 312–13, speaks of the word *"fanciulla"* as a leitmotif in the comedy.

15. Ibid., 335, mentions the economy of words Cecchi uses to set a character like Meino in his background.

16. Ibid., 308–310, analyses how in their argument Alfonso leaps on Ippolito's last words. Ferraro's discussion of verbal devices in this comedy is very penetrating.

17. E. J. H. Greene, *Menander to Marivaux,* 7, speaks of bourgeois tensions and their reflection in comedy.

18. Gilbert Norwood, *The Art of Terence,* 106–130, asserts that the collision between Micio and Demea creates and sustains dramatic interest in *Adelphoe.*

19. Daniel Boughner, *The Braggart in Renaissance Comedy,* discusses the literary and historical background of the braggart warrior.

20. Ibid., 54, includes comparison to Dantesque names. To gain an appreciation of the social prominence of fencing, consult Allan Gilbert, "The Duel in Cinquecento Drama and its Relation to Tragicomedy," 7–14.

21. Rizzi, *Commedie Osservate,* 165–167, examines how Cecchi directly translates verses from the *Asinaria* that describe the activities and moral character of the courtesan and her maid. But he also comments on the great difference between Angelica, who suppresses her liking for Fabio at the urging of her affluent suitor, Lanfranco, and the young Philenium in the *Asinaria,* who reciprocates the affections of Argyrippus. To gain a picture of a thoroughly mercenary courtesan and her cynical maid Cecchi looked respectively to Phronesium and Astaphium in the *Truculentus.*

22. Vincenzo De Amicis, *L'Imitazione Latina Nella Commedia Italiana Del XVI Secolo,* 142–43, discusses the role and function of the parasite in ancient society and Renaissance comedy. Ferraro, "Giovanni Maria Cecchi," 178, translates the meaning of Sparecchia's name.

23. Jacqueline Brunet, "Le Paysan et son Langage dans L'Oeuvre Théâtrale de Giovanmaria Cecchi," 195–96, describes the originality of Tognon di Bartolo.

24. Salvatore Di Maria, "The *Beffa* as Metaphor in the Italian Renaissance,"

209–211, 213–14, explores the inadequacy of the ruse and the failure of the *beffatore* (the player of the ruse) along with the danger of desecrating the marriage between Fabio and Selvaggia. Di Maria stresses that the purely casual discovery of Selvaggia's identity is in accord with the desire of Divine Providence for the chaste celebration of a wedding.

Notes to Chapter 3: Comedies of Modern Inspiration

1. Robert Melzi, "From Lelia to Viola," 67–81, analyses the psychological forces at work in the transvestite figure.

2. Bruno G. R. Ferraro, "Giovanni Maria Cecchi, the *Commedie Osservate* and the *Commedia Erudita* in Sixteenth-century Italy," 449, mentions the parallel between money and sex in the play. Michael Ruggerio, *The Evolution of the Go-between in Spanish Literature Through the Sixteenth Century*, traces the social background and the literary development of the go-between by Spanish writers.

3. See Ferraro, "Giovanni Maria Cecchi," 423, again for discussion of the cash nexus.

4. Ireneo Sanesi, *La Commedia*, Vol. I, 780–81, cites the use of chests in novellas.

5. Ferraro, "Giovanni Maria Cecchi," 455, as a conscientious critic feels that Cecchi does not succeed in clarifying the heavily muddled material whose failure is aggravated by a mediocre display of wit and humor.

6. Gene Brucker, "Sorcery in Early Renaissance Florence," 7–24, comments on the pragmatic approach of Italian sorcerers.

7. Stage space in this play is one of confrontation and contention, as in act 3, scenes 7 and 8, when police agents accost Laura to force her to pay her deceased husband's debts. Also compare act 5, scene 3, in which Neri, Guido, and Aristone gather outside the door of Anselmo's house, and the merchant appears at an upper-story window. As with the chests, this is a drama of invasions and penetrations of shut-off enclosures.

8. See Fortunato Rizzi, *Le Commedie Osservate di Giovan Maria Cecchi e La Commedia Classica de Secolo XVI*, 143.

9. Salvatore Di Maria, "The *Beffa* as Metaphor in the Italian Renaissance," 223–24, studies Domenico's character.

10. Rizzi, *Commedie Osservate*, 12, n. 1, suggests that *Il Servigiale* might have served as a source for Lope de Rueda's play *Armellina*.

11. Di Maria, "*Beffa* as Metaphor," 206–207, emphasizes the capriciousness of *caso* in determining events in this play.

12. Consult Ferraro, "Giovanni Maria Cecchi," 550–53, for an analysis of Manente's vanity.

Notes to Chapter 4: Dramas of Spiritual Inspiration

1. An exciting discussion of religious festivals, sacredness of place, time, and objects in Florence is provided by Richard C. Trexler, "Ritual Behavior in Renaissance Florence: The Setting," 125–44.

2. Louise George Clubb, *Giambattista Della Porta Dramatist*, 72–73, studies the ecclesiastical attempts to suppress theatrical activity and the counter

endeavor to bring sacred dramas into conformity with the reformistic
program.

3. Ferdinando Neri, "Studi sul teatro italiano antico," 21, n. 1, speaks of
the late beginnings of morality plays in Italy arising as a reaction to Protestant plays. Bernard Spivack, *Shakespeare and the Allegory of Evil*, 262–66,
examines a Protestant fideistic portrait of *The Life and Repentance of Mary
Magdalene* (1566) by the English dramatist Lewis Wager.

4. Konrad Eisenbichler, "Dramatic Genre in the Prologues of Giovan Maria
Cecchi," 12–13, observes that with this early religious drama the audience
starts to play a role in the type of spectacle it beholds and that locale (a
convent school) can dictate subject matter. The edition of *La Morte Del Re
Acab* by Gaetano Milanesi, *Commedie di Giovanmaria Cecchi*, Vol. I, 604–
605, includes the fragment of a prologue for the use of the nuns of the
convent of Holy Spirit.

5. Background on the two fifteenth-century plays is in Giovanni Ponte,
*Attorno Al Savonarola: Castellano Castellani E La Sacra Rappresentazione
in Firenze Tra '400 e '500*, 101–103, 121–25. The text of Castellani's *Il Figliuol Prodigo* is in *Sacre Rappresentazioni Del Quattrocento*, ed. Luigi Banfi,
265–323. Marvin Herrick, *Italian Comedy in the Renaissance*, 4–5, provides
further information on the Castellani version.

6. Apollo Lumini, *Le Sacre Rappresentazioni Italiane Dei Secoli XIV, XV e
XVI*, 284, points out the novel introduction of the prodigal's mother.

7. Bruno G. R. Ferraro, "Giovanni Maria Cecchi, the *Commedie Osservate*
and the *Commedia Erudita* in Sixteenth-century Italy," 138–39, discusses
the figure of the *balia* in Cecchi's comedies.

8. Jacqueline Brunet, "Le Paysan et son Langage dans L'Oeuvre Théâtrale
de Giovanmaria Cecchi," 122–200, 211, n. 177, 246–47, 261, examines the
peasants in this play and their deformation of language.

9. Ibid., 242–44, 261, looks at Trilla and Meino as well as the encounter
with the physicians.

10. Both F. Pintor, in a review of Rocchi's edition of Cecchi's *Drammi
Spirituali Inediti*, published in *Rassegna Bibliografica Della Letteratura Italiana*, 53–57, and Giovanni Grazzini, "Giovan Maria Cecchi," 299–303, uphold the priority of the farce over comedy. But Fortunato Rizzi, *Delle farse e
commedie morali di G. M. Cecchi*, 7, argues that the writing of this comedy
precedes the farce's composition.

11. See Rocchi, *Drammi Spirituali Inediti*, I, lxxxvi–lxxxvii.

12. Eric Cochrane, *Florence in the Forgotten Centuries 1527–1800*, 113–
15, discusses the general Florentine distaste for business in the late sixteenth
century.

13. Ireneo Sanesi, *La Commedia*, Vol. I, 384, points out the incongruity
between the first four acts and the final act.

14. Alberto Agresti, *Studii sulla commedia italiana del secolo XVI*, 116–
20, dwells on the Italian patriotism inspiring this anti-German portrait. Lanz
is described as fit to live best in a stable, a person with such bestial manners
that he is indeed well qualified to tend to animals.

15. Vicenzo De Amicis, *L'Imitazione Latina Nella Commedia Italiana Del
XVI Secolo*, 39, speaks of the love that blinds Gostanza to the discipline that
her son needs.

16. Giovanni Grazzini, "Giovan Maria Cecchi," 302, claims that this farce
appears in both verse and prose renderings. Brunet, "Le Paysan," 254, n. 416,
argues very convincingly that there is only a verse rendering but that the
transcription gives the appearance of prose. Brunet, 259, also mentions a
manuscript of the *Figliuol Prodigo* in the Communal Library of Siena that is
in terza rima and that differs in plot development and cast of characters from

the 1569 version. Eisenbichler expresses doubt that the terza rima version is actually the work of Cecchi because of the many stylistic differences from the author's other writings.

17. Rocchi, *Drammi Spirituali Inediti*, Vol. I, lxviii, and Rizzi, *Delle farse*, 146, n. 3, both characterize the farce in this manner seeing the physician as a central figure.

18. Rizzi, *Delle farse*, 235–36, discusses Bomba's role as a country inn sage.

19. Brunet, "Le Paysan," 227–33, examines the speech of the peasants in this farce and other plays.

20. Rizzi, *Delle farse*, 42, n. 1, describes the intermezzi, and in the prologue Cecchi comments on the allegory in the entr'actes. Unfortunately, Luigi Fiacchi, *Commedie di Giovan Maria Cecchi*, Vol. 1, does not include the intermezzi in his edition of the farce.

BIBLIOGRAPHY

Primary Sources

Commedie in versi. Venice: B. Giunti, 1585.

Commedie di Giovan Maria Cecchi, edited by Luigi Fiacchi. Milan: Silvestri, 1850.

Commedie di Giovanmaria Cecchi, edited by Gaetano Milanesi. Florence: Le Monnier, 1899.

Drammi Spirituali Inediti Di Giovanmaria Cecchi, edited by Raffaello Rocchi. Florence: Le Monnier, 1895.

La Romanesca, edited by Diomede Buonamici. Florence: Cenniniana, 1874.

L'Assiuolo. In Vol. I of *Commedie Del Cinquecento,* edited by Nino Borsellino. Milan: Feltrinelli, 1962.

Dei Proverbi Toscani, edited by Luigi Fiacchi. Milan: Silvestri, 1838.

Lezione O Vero Ciclamento Di Maestro Bartolino Dal Canto De' Bischeri. In *Scelta Di Curiosità Letterarie Inedite O Rare Dal Secolo XIII Al XIX.* Bologna: G. Romagnoli, 1868.

Secondary Sources

Agresti, Alberto. *Studii sulla commedia italiana del secolo XVI.* Naples: Royal University, 1871.

Bakhtin, Mikhail. *L'oeuvre de François Rabelais et la culture populaire au Moyen Age et sous la Renaissance,* trans. Andrée Robel. Poitier: Gallimard, 1970.

Banfi, Luigi, ed. *Sacre Rappresentazioni Del Quattrocento.* Turin: UTET, 1963.

Boughner, Daniel. *The Braggart in Renaissance Comedy.* Minneapolis: University of Minnesota Press, 1954.

Brucker, Gene. "Sorcery in Early Renaissance Florence." *Studies in the Renaissance,* 10 (1963): 7–24.

Brunet, Jacqueline. "Le Paysan et son Langage dans L'Oeuvre Théâtrale de Giovanmaria Cecchi," *Ville et Campagne dans La Littérature Italienne de la Renaissance,* edited by Anna Fontes-Baratto et al. Paris: Sorbonne, 1976.

———. "L'Acqua-Vino: une (deux, trois?) farce(s) de G. M. Cecchi,"

Culture et Religion en Espagne et en Italie aux XVᵉ et XVIᵉ Siè-cles, edited by M. Ballestero et al. Abbeville, France: Centre national de la Recherche scientifique, 1980.

Clubb, Louise George. *Giambattista Della Porta Dramatist.* Princeton: Princeton University Press, 1965.

Cochrane, Eric. *Florence in the Forgotten Centuries 1527–1800.* Chicago: University of Chicago Press, 1973.

———. "The End of the Renaissance in Florence." *Bibliothèque d'Humanisme et Renaissance,* 27 (1965): 7–29. Studies the decline of creative vitality in late sixteenth-century Florence.

Cope, Jackson I. *The Theater and the Dream: From Metaphor to Form in Renaissance Drama.* Baltimore: Johns Hopkins University Press, 1973.

Corrigan, Robert W., ed. *Comedy: Meaning and Form.* San Francisco: Chandler, 1965.

D'Ancona, Alessandro. Review of Rocchi's edition of Cecchi's *Drammi Spirituali Inediti.* In *Rassegna Bibliografica Della Letteratura Italiana,* 4 (1896): 31–32.

D'Addario, Arnaldo. *Aspetti Della Controriforma A Firenze.* Rome: Publications of State Archives, 1972.

De Amicis, Vincenzo. *L'Imitazione Latina Nella Commedia Italiana Del XVI Secolo.* Florence: Sansoni, 1897.

De Gaetano, Armand. "The Florentine Academy and the Advancement of Learning Through the Vernacular." *Bibliothèque d'Humanisme et Renaissance,* 30 (1968), 19–52.

Di Maria, Salvatore. "The *Beffa* as Metaphor in the Italian Renaissance." Diss. University of Wisconsin 1978.

Duckworth, George. *The Nature of Roman Comedy.* Princeton: Princeton University Press, 1952.

Eisenbichler, Konrad. "Dramatic Genre in the Prologues of Giovan Maria Cecchi." Unpub. lecture, 10 April 1980. Toronto Renaissance and Reformation Colloquium.

———. "The Religious Drama of Giovan Maria Cecchi." Diss., University of Toronto, 1981.

———. *The Horned Owl.* Waterloo, Ont.: Wilfrid Laurier University Press, 1981. (Translation of Cecchi's *L'Assiuolo.*)

Ferraro, Bruno G. R. "Giovanni Maria Cecchi, the *Commedie Osservate* and the *Commedia Erudita* in Sixteenth-century Italy." Diss., Flinders University of South Australia, 1974.

Frye, Northrop. *Anatomy of Criticism.* New York: Atheneum, 1970.

Galluzzi, Riguccio. *Istoria del granducato di Toscana sotto il governo della Casa Medici.* Florence: Marchini, 1822. Originally published in 1781.

Goggio, Emilio. "The Prologue in the *Commedie Erudite* of the Sixteenth Century." *Italica,* 18, 3 (1941): 124–32.

_____. "Dramatic Theory in the Prologues to the *Commedie Erudite* of the Sixteenth Century." *PMLA*, 68 (1943): 322–36.

Grazzini, Giovanni. "Giovan Maria Cecchi." *Enciclopedia Dello Spettacolo*, III, 299–303. Rome: Le Maschere, 1956.

Gilbert, Allan. "The Duel in Cinquecento Drama and its Relation to Tragicomedy." *Italica*, 26 (1949): 7–14.

Greene, E. J. H. *Menander to Marivaux.* Edmondton: University of Alberta Press, 1977.

Hale, J. R. *Florence and the Medici. The Pattern of Control.* London: Thames and Hudson, 1977.

Herrick, Marvin. *Comic Theory in the Sixteenth Century.* Urbana, Ill.: University of Illinois Press, 1950.

_____. *Italian Comedy in the Renaissance.* Urbana: University of Illinois Press, 1960.

Jones, P. J. "From Manor to Mezzadria: A Tuscan Case-Study in the Medieval Origins of Modern Agrarian Society." In *Politics and Society in Renaissance Florence,* edited by Nicolai Rubinstein, 193–241. Evanston, Ill.: Northwestern University Press, 1968.

Langer, Susanne. "The Comic Rhythm." In *Comedy: Meaning and Form,* edited by Robert W. Corrigan. San Francisco: Chandler, 1965.

Lebatteux, Guy. "La Crise de la 'Beffa.'" In *Formes et Signifcance de la "Beffa" dans la Littérature italienne de la Renaissance,* edited by A. Rochon, 179–201. Paris: Sorbonne, 1972.

Lorch, Maristella, ed. *Il teatro italiano del Rinascimento.* Milan: Comunità, 1980.

Lumini, Apollo. *Le Sacre Rappresentazioni Italiane Dei Secoli XIV, XV e XVI.* Palermo and Naples: LaCava and Steeger, 1877.

Melzi, Robert. "From Lelia to Viola." *Renaissance Drama,* 9 (1966): 67–81.

Nagler, A. M. *Theatre Festivals of the Medici, 1539–1637.* Translated by G. Hickenlooper. New Haven, Conn.: Yale University Press, 1964.

Neri, Ferdinando. "Studi sul teatro italiano antico." *Giornale Storico Della Letteratura Italiana,* 65 (1915): 9–27.

Norwood, Gilbert. *The Art of Terence.* New York: Russell and Russell, 1965.

Paratore, Ettore, et al. eds. *Il Teatro Classico Italiano Nel '500.* Rome: Accademia Nazionale Dei Lincei, 1971.

Patrides, C. A. "The Bloody and Cruelle Turks: The Background of a Renaissance Commonplace." *Studies in the Renaissance,* 10 (1963): 126–35.

Pintor, F. Review of Rocchi's edition of Cecchi's *Drammi Spirituali Inediti.* In *Rassegna Bibliografica Della Letteratura Italiana,* 10, 3 (1902): 53–57.

Plaisance, Michel. "Espace et Politique dans les Comédies Florentines des Années 1539–1551." In *Espace, Idéologie et Société au
XVIᵉ Siècle,* edited by J. Hernandez, et al., 59–119. Grenoble: University Press of Grenoble, 1975.

Ponte, Giovanni. *Attorno Al Savonarola: Castellano Castellani E
La Sacra Rappresentazione In Firenze Tra '400 E '500.* Genoa:
Pagano, 1969.

Pullini, Giorgio. "Teatralità di alcune commedie del '500." *Lettere
Italiane,* 7, 1 (1955): 68–97.

Radcliff-Umstead, Douglas. *The Birth of Modern Comedy in Renaissance Italy.* Chicago: University of Chicago Press, 1969.

———. "Cecchi and the Reconciliation of Theatrical Traditions.
Comparative Drama, 9, 2 (1975): 156–75.

Rizzi, Fortunato. *Le Commedie Osservate di Giovan Maria Cecchi
e La Commedia Classica del Secolo XVI.* Rocca S. Casciano: Cappelli, 1904.

———. *Delle farse e commedie morali di G. M. Cecchi.* Rocca S.
Casciano: Cappelli, 1907.

Rodini, Robert. *Antonfrancesco Grazzini: Poet, Dramatist, and
Novelliere.* Madison: University of Wisconsin Press, 1970.

Ruggerio, Michael. *The Evolution of the Go-between in Spanish
Literature Through the Sixteenth Century.* Berkeley: University
of California Press, 1966.

Samuels, Richard. "Benedetto Varchi, the *Accademia degli Infiammati,* and the Origins of the Italian Academic Movement." *Renaissance Quarterly,* 29, 4 (Winter 1976): 599–633.

Sanesi, Ireneo. *La Commedia.* Vol. I. Milan: Vallardi, 1954.

Scoti-Bertinelli, Ugo. *Sullo Stile Delle Commedie In Prosa Di
Giovan Maria Cecchi.* Città del Castello: Lapi, 1906.

Spivack, Bernard. *Shakespeare and the Allegory of Evil.* New York:
Columbia University Press, 1958.

Sypher, Wylie. "The Meanings of Comedy." In *Comedy: Meaning
and Form,* edited by Robert W. Corrigan. San Francisco: Chandler,
1965.

Trexler, Richard C. "Ritual Behavior in Renaissance Florence: The
Setting." *Medievalia et Humanistica,* 4 (1973): 125–44.

Vallone, Aldo. "La Vocazione Al Racconto Del Cecchi." *Humanitas,*
5 (1950): 303–313.

Weinberg, Bernard. *A History of Literary Criticism in the Italian
Renaissance.* Chicago: University of Chicago Press, 1961.

Wilkins, David. "The Black and Oriental in Italian Renaissance Art."
Unpublished Lecture, 6 October 1971. University of Pittsburgh
Center for Medieval and Renaissance Studies.

INDEX

Adimari, Marco Antonio, 19
Altoviti, Antonio, 13, 15
Ammannati, Bartolomeo, 10
Aretino, Pietro, 28
Ariosto, Ludovico, 28, 30, 31, 53, 60, 78, 98, 100, 116, 140
Aristotle, 10, 25, 30–31, 118, 174

Baldesi, Giovan Francesco, 19
Belcari, Feo, 128
Bembo, Pietro, 8
Beolco, Angelo (Ruzante), 19, 79
Berni, Francesco, 23
Bibbiena, Bernardo, 98, 100
Boiardo, Matteo Maria, 78, 116
Boccaccio, Giovanni, 4, 8, 21, 34, 41, 44, 55, 59, 71, 82, 84–85, 86, 87–88, 94–95, 175. See also Decameron
Bruno, Giordano, 28, 31

Caligula, 174
Castellani, Castellano, 128, 138–39, 141
Castiglione, Baldesar, 8, 100. See also Libro del Cortegiano
Cecchi, Baccio, 18, 20, 24, 23, 34
Cecchi family, 16–18
Cecchi, Giovan Maria: life, 16–25; L'Ammalata, 33, 142; L'Assiuolo, 32, 85–96, 117, 126, 133; Le Cedole, 33, 34, 110–18, 123, 126; Compendio di più ritratti, 23–24; I Contrassegni, 32–33; La Coronazione di Saul, 28, 145; Il Corredo, 33, 142; Il Debito, 32, 33; La dichiarazione di molti proverbi, 21, 22; I Dissimili, 32, 64–73, 83; Il Donzello, 33; La Dote, 32, 33, 36– 48, 82; L'Esaltazione della croce, 28, 35; Il figliuol prodigo, 35, 138–44, 155, 161, 163; Gli Incantesimi, 32; Lezione o vero cicalamento di Maestro Bartolino, 23; La Maiana, 33, 81; Il martello, 33, 36, 73–81, 83; Le maschere, 33, 34, 118–25, 126; Il medico, 33, 142; La moglie, 32, 33, 48–57, 82; La morte del Re Acab, 130–38, 162, 169; Le pellegrine, 33; Ragionamenti Spirituali, 22; I rivali, 33, 81; La romanesca, 34, 145–47, 173–77; Il sammaritano, 160–70; Gli sciamiti, 33; La serpe, ovvero la mala nuora, 144–51, 169–70; Il servigiale, 32, 33, 103–10, 126; Il sommario de' magistrati di Firenze, 24; Lo spirito, 33, 96–103, 125, 126; La stiava, 32, 33, 44, 57–64, 83; Lo sviato, 151–60, 169–70
Cellini, Benvenuto, 7, 28
Ceruti, Frederico, 26
Charles V, 1, 4
Cicero, 30
Cini, Giovambattista, 28
Commedia dell'Arte, 177
Crusca, Accademia della, 22

D'Ambra, Francesco, 28
Dante, 8, 10, 76, 136–37. See also Divine Comedy
Decameron, 23, 34, 41, 44, 55, 59, 71, 84–85, 87–89, 95, 98, 122, 143, 155, 172, 175. See also Boccaccio, Giovanni
Della Porta, Giambattista, 31
Della Valle, Federico, 170
Dialogo intorno alla nostra lin-

gua, 8. *See also* Machiavelli,
  Niccolò
Divine Comedy, 10, 76–77, 100,
  136. *See also* Dante
Doni, Anton Francesco, 25

Eleonora (of Toledo), 2, 28

Frye, Northrop, 35

Gelli, Giovan Battista, 8, 28
Giannotti, Donato, 28, 57, 59,
  61
Giovio, Paolo, 7
Giraldi Cintio, Giambattista,
  30, 35, 40, 42
Grazzini, Anton Francesco, il
  Lasca, 24, 30–31

Horace, 25, 31, 96, 118

Joanna (of Austria), 6, 28, 145

Landi, Antonio, 28
Langer, Susanne, 35
Lazarillo de Tormes, 156
Libro del Cortegiano, Il, 8. *See
  also* Castiglione, Baldesar

Machiavelli, Niccolò, 4, 8, 11,
  28, 30, 31, 61, 81, 89, 91–92,
  94–95, 107, 116
Medici, Alessandro de' (Duke),
  1, 17
Medici, Alessandro de' (Pope
  Leo XI), 15, 27, 129
Medici, Cosimo I, de', 1–13, 17,
  19, 26, 28, 53, 65, 105, 145,
  163, 168
Medici, Ferdinando de', 28
Medici, Francesco de', 6, 20, 28,
  145
Medici, Lorenzino de', 28
Medici, Lorenzo (il Magnifico),
  1, 128
Menander, 76, 134
Molière (Jean Baptiste Poque-
  lin), 62

Naldini, Battista, 25

Paul III, 13
Petrarch, Francesco, 8, 76, 123
Pino da Cagli, Bernardo, 25
Pius IV, 13
Pius V, 6, 13–14
Plautus, Titus Maccius, 29, 34,
  71, 82, 85, 131, 134, 140–41,
  143, 172–73; *Asinaria*, 75–79;
  Casina, 81; *Menaechmi*, 49–
  56; *Mercator*, 57–64; *Miles
  Gloriosus*, 75; *Mostellaria*,
  40; *Trinummus*, 36–46; *Tru-
  culentus*, 75, 77
Poccianti, Michele, 25
Poliziano, Angelo, 100
Prince, The, 11, 100. *See also*
  Machiavelli, Niccolò
Prose della volgar lingua, 8
Pulci, Antonia, 138

Quintilian, 99

Raphael, 28
Riccoboni, Antonio, 25
Rossi, Nicolò, 25–26

Santagostino, Tommaso, 55
Savonarola, Girolamo, 2, 14
Shakespeare, William, 49–53;
  The Comedy of Errors, 57; *A
  Midsummer Night's Dream*,
  57
Segni, Mariotto, 19
Sypher, Wylie, 35

Tasso, Torquato, 46
Terence (Publius Terentius
  Afer), 29, 34, 45–46, 82, 85,
  131, 140, 141, 143, 172–73;
  Adelphoe, 65–73; *Andria*, 49,
  50, 52, 54; *Eunuchus*, 75, 77;
  Heautontimorumenos, 81,
  140; *Hecyra*, 147
Trissino, Gian Giorgio, 23

Umidi, Accademia degli (Accademia Fiorentina), 8–10, 22

Varchi, Benedetto, 7, 99
Vasari, Giorgio, 7, 10, 28